GLOBALIZED QUEERNESS

Library of Gender and Popular Culture

From Mad Men to gaming culture, performance art to steampunk fashion, the presentation and representation of gender continues to saturate popular media. This series seeks to explore the intersection of gender and popular culture, engaging with a variety of texts – drawn primarily from Art, Fashion, TV, Cinema, Cultural Studies and Media Studies – as a way of considering various models for understanding the complementary relationship between 'gender identities' and 'popular culture'. By considering race, ethnicity, class and sexual identities across a range of cultural forms, each book in the series adopts a critical stance towards issues surrounding the development of gender identities and popular and mass cultural 'products'.

For further information or enquiries, please contact the library series editors:
Claire Nally: claire.nally@northumbria.ac.uk
Angela Smith: angela.smith@sunderland.ac.uk

Advisory Board:
Dr Kate Ames, Central Queensland University, Australia
Dr Michael Higgins, University of Strathclyde, UK
Prof Å sa Kroon, Ö rebro University, Sweden
Dr Andrea McDonnell, Emmanuel College, USA
Dr Niall Richardson, University of Sussex, UK
Dr Jacki Willson, University of Leeds, UK

Published and forthcoming titles:
The Aesthetics of Camp: Post-Queer Gender and Popular Culture
by Anna Malinowska

Ageing Femininity on Screen: The Older Woman in Contemporary Cinema by Niall Richardson
All-American TV Crime Drama: Feminism and Identity Politics in Law and Order: Special Victims Unit by Sujata Moorti and Lisa Cuklanz
Are You Not Entertained?: Mapping the Gladiator across Visual Media by Lindsay Steenberg
Bad Girls, Dirty Bodies: Sex, Performance and Safe Femininity by Gemma Commane
Conflicting Masculinities: Men in Television Period Drama by Katherine Byrne, Julie Anne Taddeo and James Leggott (Eds)
Fat on Film: Gender, Race and Body Size in Contemporary Hollywood Cinema by Barbara Plotz
Fathers on Film: Paternity and Masculinity in 1990s Hollywood by Katie Barnett
Film Bodies: Queer Feminist Encounters with Gender and Sexuality in Cinema by Katharina Lindner
From the Margins to the Mainstream: Women On and Off Screen in Television and Film by Marianne Kac-Vergne and Julie Assouly (Eds)
Gay Pornography: Representations of Sexuality and Masculinity by John Mercer
Gender and Austerity in Popular Culture: Femininity, Masculinity and Recession in Film and Television by Helen Davies and Claire O'Callaghan (Eds)
Gender and Early Television: Mapping Women's Role in Emerging US and British Media, 1850–1950 by Sarah Arnold
The Gendered Motorcycle: Representations in Society, Media and Popular Culture by Esperanza Miyake
Gendering History on Screen: Women Filmmakers and Historical Films by Julia Erhart
Girls Like This, Boys Like That: The Reproduction of Gender in Contemporary Youth Cultures by Victoria Cann
'Guilty Pleasures': European Audiences and Contemporary Hollywood Romantic Comedy by Alice Guilluy

The Gypsy Woman: Representations in Literature and Visual Culture by Jodie Matthews
Male and Female Violence in Popular Media by Elisa Giomi and Sveva Magaraggia
Masculinity in Contemporary Science Fiction Cinema: Cyborgs, Troopers and Other Men of the Future by Marianne Kac-Vergne
Positive Images: Gay Men and HIV/AIDS in the Culture of 'Post-Crisis' by Dion Kagan
Postfeminism and Contemporary Vampire Romance by Lea Gerhards
Queer Horror Film and Television: Sexuality and Masculinity at the Margins by Darren Elliott-Smith
Queer Sexualities in Early Film: Cinema and Male-Male Intimacy by Shane Brown
Screening Queer Memory: LGBTQ Pasts in Contemporary Film and Television by Anamarija Horvat
Steampunk: Gender and the NeoVictorian by Claire Nally
Television Comedy and Femininity: Queering Gender by Rosie White
Tweenhood: Femininity and Celebrity in Tween Popular Culture by Melanie Kennedy
Women Who Kill: Gender and Sexuality in Film and Series of the PostFeminist Era by David Roche and Cristelle Maury (Eds)
Wonder Woman: Feminism, Culture and the Body by Joan Ormrod
Young Women, Girls and Postfeminism in Contemporary British Film by Sarah Hill

GLOBALIZED QUEERNESS

Identities and Commodities in Queer Popular Culture

Helton Levy

BLOOMSBURY ACADEMIC
LONDON • NEW YORK • OXFORD • NEW DELHI • SYDNEY

BLOOMSBURY ACADEMIC
Bloomsbury Publishing Plc, 50 Bedford Square, London, WC1B 3DP, UK
Bloomsbury Publishing Inc, 1385 Broadway, New York, NY 10018, USA
Bloomsbury Publishing Ireland, 29 Earlsfort Terrace, Dublin 2, D02 AY28, Ireland

BLOOMSBURY, BLOOMSBURY ACADEMIC and the Diana logo are
trademarks of Bloomsbury Publishing Plc

First published in Great Britain 2024
Paperback edition published 2025

Copyright © Helton Levy, 2024

Helton Levy has asserted his right under the Copyright, Designs and
Patents Act, 1988, to be identified as Author of this work.

For legal purposes the Acknowledgements on p. viii constitute an
extension of this copyright page.

Cover design: Ben Anslow
Cover images (Clockwise): Christine and the Queens, Global Citizen Live
concert, Paris, September 25, 2021 (© Bertrand Guay / AFP / Getty Images);
Mahmood, Eurovision Song Contest, Tel Aviv Fairgrounds, May 17, 2019, Tel
Aviv, Israel (© Michael Campanella / Getty Images); Pabllo Vittar, Carnival
(© Alexandre Paes Leme / Dreamstime); Matt Lucas as Dafydd Thomas,
'Little Britain' live stage show, the Guildhall, Portsmouth, October 24, 2005
(Photo © Yui Mok / PA / Alamy).

All rights reserved. No part of this publication may be: i) reproduced
or transmitted in any form, electronic or mechanical, including photocopying,
recording or by means of any information storage or retrieval system without
prior permission in writing from the publishers; or ii) used or reproduced in any
way for the training, development or operation of artificial intelligence (AI)
technologies, including generative AI technologies. The rights holders expressly
reserve this publication from the text and data mining exception as per
Article 4(3) of the Digital Single Market Directive (EU) 2019/790.

Bloomsbury Publishing Plc does not have any control over, or responsibility
for, any third-party websites referred to or in this book. All internet addresses
given in this book were correct at the time of going to press. The author and
publisher regret any inconvenience caused if addresses have changed or sites
have ceased to exist, but can accept no responsibility for any such changes.

A catalogue record for this book is available from the British Library.

ISBN: HB: 978-1-3502-9278-9
PB: 978-1-3502-9282-6
ePDF: 978-1-3502-9280-2
eBook: 978-1-3502-9279-6

Series: Library of Gender and Popular Culture

Typeset by RefineCatch Limited, Bungay, Suffolk

For product safety related questions contact productsafety@bloomsbury.com.

To find out more about our authors and books visit www.bloomsbury.com
and sign up for our newsletters.

CONTENTS

List of Illustrations and Tables	viii
Acknowledgements	x
Series Editors' Introduction	xi
INTRODUCTION: GLOBALLY QUEER? A TALE OF TWO WORLDS	1
Chapter 1 COMMODIFYING QUEER CULTURE	37
Chapter 2 QUEER NEWS	67
Chapter 3 QUEER ARTISTS	91
Chapter 4 TRANS CONTENT CREATORS	133
Chapter 5 GLOBAL PLATFORMS, LOCAL CHARACTERS	161
CONCLUSION: FROM GLOBALIZED QUEERNESS TO POSSIBLE HOMECOMINGS	195
Index	217

ILLUSTRATIONS AND TABLES

Figures

1. Doris Day in a scene of *Calamity Jane* (1953), directed by David Butler. © Warner Bros Pictures. All rights reserved. 1953. Image Courtesy of Alamy Stock Photo. — 2
2. The casting of *My So-Called Life*. Wilson Cruz is the first from the left. © ABC Television. 1994. Image Courtesy of Alamy Stock Photo. — 18
3. RuPaul in *Wofoo To Wong Foo, Thanks for Everything! Julie Newmar*. © Universal Pictures. 1995. Image Courtesy of Alamy Stock Photo. — 21
4. Count of sections that hosted the news about queer popular culture (including the US). — 80
5. Countries cited in news reports about queer culture – except the US (n). — 83
6. Citation and cross-citation of countries in queer news topics – including the US. — 84
7. Clodovil Hernandes arrives at the Brazilian Congress in 2009. Photo: Jose Cruz, Agencia Brasil. — 101
8. Word cloud with the most repeated terms in all trans-YouTube videos sampled. — 142
9. Word cloud with the most repeated terms in trans YouTube in English. — 143
10. The relationship between topics and coherence, uniform distribution, and corpus distribution. — 148
11. The most repeated terms according to corpus distribution (>0). — 149
12. Trans YouTube topic as per exclusivity index (<1). — 151

Tables

1. Countries with the highest number of topical references to queer popular culture and mentions to queer artists in news media articles. 76
2. Topic description. 78
3. Topic names according to keywords found in LDA analysis. 147

ACKNOWLEDGEMENTS

Finishing this book has been such an enormous challenge to me, not least because of the impact of Covid-19, but also hectic teaching schedules and other well-known challenges of modern academia. Writing and publishing is nevertheless a gratifying effort, the end of a long process of thinking and maturing ideas that are too alive to rest. To me, this book has signified revisiting distant memories and living again many stages of my experience both as an insider and an outsider in queer culture, often the latter. This book would not have been possible without the trust I received from this series' editors, Claire Nally and Angela Smith, who viewed this project in such a germinal state. And yet, they believed in me and the potential of what was to come. At Bloomsbury, Anna Coatman and Veidehi Hans have provided me with a generous schedule and precious advice. Thanks to them, all demands could be balanced for what turned out to be an ambitious project. I would like to say thank you to the book's reviewers for their invaluable contribution and generosity in recognizing the book's values despite initial flaws. I want to recognize and appreciate the work done by my research assistant Lorenzo Polverari, who has helped with the completion of the interviews. I am grateful to Stephen Maddison, Giuseppe from Corato, and Hongwei Bao for lovely ideas. I am especially appreciative to my family and friends for understanding the enormous job demands faced and my frequent absences. I dedicate this book to all local queer performers and popular artists that have silently thrived for decades and eased the lives of many living outside the mainstream.

SERIES EDITORS' INTRODUCTION

Globalized Queerness: Identities and Commodities in Queer Popular Culture by Helton Levy is a welcome addition to the Bloomsbury Library of Gender and Popular Culture, offering one of the first accounts of the impact of globalizing queer identities. The book establishes an initial discussion of how local queerness has been represented historically as small, prejudiced village life, which is abandoned in favour of more tolerant and urban society. As a corrective, *Globalized Queerness* reflects upon how far the Global South and other marginalized indigenous communities are excluded from this dominant narrative. As such, Levy emphasizes the need to offer an analysis of queer practice beyond Anglocentric perceptions, instead addressing the idea of the *glocal, mestizaje* and transculturation.

The book maintains that the construction of queer identities as 'global' events has shaped how we evaluate artists and performers and has impacted on queer authenticity. One key example of formulaic and homogenized queerness is *RuPaul's Drag Race*, which as Levy maintains, has commodified drag aesthetics, whilst erasing local nuances such as language or visual cues, for consumption by a global audience. The case studies presented here highlight alternative modes of queerness and are drawn from TV shows, visual arts, dance, and both online and offline queer communities, such as fandoms, trans YouTubers, modelling and celebrity. The author argues that the use of the word 'queer' throughout this book is a strategic alternative to a co-opted form of homosexuality, represented by a commercial, whitewashed, and normative representation of gayness. Queer encompasses a broad range of identities, including but not limited to gay, lesbian, transgender, non-binary, and many others.

The book also provides a framework to *genealogize* queer media productions, and therefore, whilst offering a rich and distinctive contribution to queer studies, it is also a useful companion volume to several other books in the Library, such as Anamarija Horvat's *Screening Queer Memory: LGBTQ Pasts in Contemporary Film and Television* (2021). More broadly, several other books from the series provide a dialogue with this volume, including Darren Elliott-Smith's *Queer Horror Film and Television: Sexuality and Masculinity at the Margins* (2016), Katherine Lindner's *Queer Feminist Encounters with Gender and Sexuality in Cinema* (2017) and Shane Brown's *Queer Sexualities in Early Film: Cinema and Male-Male Intimacy* (2016).

INTRODUCTION

GLOBALLY QUEER? A TALE OF TWO WORLDS

Take me back to the Black Hills / The Black Hills of Dakota / To the beautiful Indian country / That I love
— *Calamity Jane*, 1953

This is Doris Day singing at the head carriage alongside Lt Gilmartin (Philip Carey) and Katie (Allyn Ann McLerie) as they cut across a vast range of mountains in the idyllic American Midwest. *Calamity Jane* (1953), the Hollywood film, evokes feelings of nativism and love for one's place of birth. The film has echoed the quintessential American scouting and portrayed Calamity Jane with charisma, friendliness, and femininity. This image opposed the historical Martha Jane Cannary (1852–1903), who embodied nativism, masculinity, and struggle. Day's angelical presence has captivated the audience for decades. The legendary production has encapsulated many ambiguities that involved queer media appearances in the 20th century: suggestive relationships and its diva aspects (Pheasant-Kelly, 2013) while fitting heteronormative expectations. The film displayed the usual guns and violence, but it primarily spared itself from what it should have been: a tale about a queer woman who lived in 19th-century Missouri.

The fact that early Hollywood avoided any possibility of queerness is no news, with a few exceptions over decades (Mann, 2001). In *Calamity Jane*, the enduring myth of the 'heroine of the plains' has sported macho boots and a rigid pose, but also silly gestures and erratic behaviour. Calamity Jane was transported to the screens, theatre, and cartoons exactly like that: with her queerness having always been denied until very recently. What is Calamity Jane if not her queer affection for the land and her origins? To what extent is her nativism part of her queerness? Doris Day's character, a sketch of both hetero and homosexual behaviour, also tells us about the uneasy queer belonging in the media. Whether one can be queer and remain a local character in the media starts a conversation on how contemporary queerness is global. Queerness has become an acceptable way of life, as long as it is aligned with cosmopolitanism and received media standards.

While Jane, the woman, has suffered a 'gendered makeover' over time, that is, adjustments to conceal or reveal masculine or feminine qualities (McDonald, 2007), there is something inheritably folk American that localizes Calamity Jane and seals her importance in the public imagination. Like many other characters, she had her queer traits erased or relativized (Pheasant-Kelly, 2013). The problem here stems from the constant linking between stereotypical aspects of localness, whether her toughness or accent, with her detachment from the feminine. It is as though both queerness and Midwest persona were walking side-by-side, with their gun tied to the hips. This coupling of queer identity, later assumed to be a global feature, with her local credential is not irrelevant at all. Like Jane, many queer characters in mainstream media also deserve a renaissance in the terms and circumstances they were brought up in this world. More than biographical justice, one needs to diversify sources of knowledge and creativity.

This book's chief argument dwells on the recurrent but underexplored connection between globalizing queerness, making it cosmopolitan and rootless, and the position of queer cultures that, in turn, go underground in media and popular culture. The problem with debunking genuineness in a concept that is essentially hacked off and blurry lies in cementing

Figure 1 Doris Day in a scene of *Calamity Jane* (1953) directed by David Butler. © Warner Bros Pictures. All rights reserved. 1953. Image Courtesy of Alamy Stock Photo.

queer identities as just one. However, one should remember that queerness is not necessarily the same as being queer. Queerness can be invented, colonized, and homogenized. It can base on true or false stories. It can be predicated on lucrative industries. On the other end, local queerness has been portrayed with fear, persecution of queers and through tales of unpunished homophobia. In received wisdom, the small village is where queers leave behind primarily because of oppressive local realities. Like the American Jane, queerness has been negotiated on such simplistic terms that it can be easily exploited by mainstream culture. Somehow, it has depleted itself of language or ethnical backgrounds, historical proximities, or radical forms of pride.

Globalized Queerness surveys artists and media producers who self-identify as LGBTQ or whom the public know as gay, lesbian, trans, or queer (henceforth, queer). The book's chief idea is to focus on how the construction of queerness as a global event has shaped the appearance and reading of artists and personalities over time. To that purpose, it was necessary to leverage queerness as one phenomenon, as seen in the multiplication of media products, platforms, and discourses. *Globalized queerness* can thus spread from the press, the visual arts, and the Internet. Essentially, I defend that globalized queerness has transformed queer culture to result in the deprecation or invalidation of local queer knowledges. It is also argued that queer authenticity and sincerity can help prioritize archives and personal histories as replacements for queer commodities. Queerness, in turn, trivializes what could be the time for recognizing people in the LGBTQ spectrum.

Growing up in the 1980s Global South, queer viewers like myself experienced first-hand the wealth of local and global references imported into my media environment. Local performers dubbed Gloria Gaynor's 'I Will Survive' in broken English. Queer artists usually spoke the local language when defending themselves from street attacks, but English was their language of self-projection and Saturday nights. Gay slang was imported into the script of Latin American *telenovelas*, as *local* queer characters appeared briefly or without receiving any credit. In the early 2000s, in isolated northeast Brazil, in the only gay bar of a small conservative town, everyone heard Madonna's *Frozen*. Her show-to-no-one performance was played aloud in a public square under the 40-degree Celsius heat (100 F). Scenes like this made me always imagine the large degree of American queerness fulfilling the lives of the local listeners I was brought up with. To make sense of whatever queerness was to me and others, a journey that included American thrash culture and, very rarely, acts of resistance against the homophobic realities that awaited us on the streets (Nicholus, 2020).

As Sara Ahmed argued in her book *Queer Phenomenology* (Ahmed, 2006), the sense of orientation or disorientation one develops regarding queer objects is, at times, random and follows unscripted rules. The fact that I, like many other queer viewers in the 1980s, were *oriented* by the prominence of American queer products, their celebrities, and the AIDS crisis did not stop us from *learning* from these things. Fast forward thirty years and the massive growth of queer repertoire increases the *disorientation* that homogenizes rather than liberates. As multiple queer populations acquire the chance to *learn* about all things queer in real-time, should they also have the choice of unlearning about whatever culture, trait, or reference they do not need to live their lives?

As we shall see, globalized queerness promotes the *orientation* of actors and objects towards target behaviour or languages, but, in the long run, it falls short of queering things up. There are not only cultural boundaries that are erased in the name of the queer markets but also clear racial or postcolonial undertones that need problematization. The extent to which globalized queerness erases the right to be a member of a local queer audience or a participant in an app or platform remains the crux of being queer in the digital age. The book seeks to understand the acquisition of global queer repertoires as much as the forgetfulness that encompasses every *new* name that appears on the screen.

This investigation took five years to select the most appropriate historical and theoretical frameworks that allow for a sustainable critique of media-based queer movements. It is possible to see problems in current forms of escape from normativity voiced by artists and producers without condemning such hard-won efforts for visibility. To unearth local queer knowledge is to return queerness to its marginal source of resilience and power. The following sections reassess queer media and culture by criticizing inherited perceptions that silently prioritize American realities at the expense of others. Eventually, categories such as globalized and localized became necessary to shed light on normative interests disguised as products. Later, questions arise: do queer artists or media producers acquiesce to forms of knowledge and circulation that limit one's autonomy? To what extent can global audiences bring queer media closer or farther from local oppressions and languages? Can we, the queer public, evade globalized queerness at all?

The global and the local in queer media and culture

The recent popularization of programmes and queer media in the last two decades (2000–2020), even if stereotypically, has propelled a constellation of writers, directors, and characters. The GLAAD, Gay and Lesbian Alliance Against Defamation, has reported 773 characters scheduled to appear on television during the 2021 season (GLAAD, 2022). The *Where We Are on TV* report 2021 edition saw 118 recurring characters on primetime cable TV, including leading series such as the *L Word, Generation Q, Euphoria,* and *Killing Eve* (GLAAD, 2022B). One learns that the three major streaming platforms, Hulu, Amazon Prime, and Netflix, featured 29 regular and transgender characters in their productions. These include 15 trans women, 12 trans men, and two non-binary trans characters. Taking *RuPaul's Drag Race*, for example. Since the show's debut in 2009, it has reached over 21 countries in franchised or local versions. RuPaul has not only re-shaped drag presence as a regular fixture in mass media, but it has done so by using a single logo, an aesthetic, a language, or a story that accommodates them with a larger paying audience.

This expansion of queer media includes other formats and products worldwide, as much as styles, tastes, and languages. From bareback porn (Mercer, 2017; Florêncio, 2020) to reality TV (Lovelock, 2019); from queer bodies (Lindner, 2017) to ideas of promiscuity (Payne, 2014) and individual entrepreneurship and dissent (Maddison, 2000). Globalizing responds to the aim of queering everything, including heterosexual scripts into gay and lesbian productions (Burgett & Hendler, 2020:203). In a field where semantics work as a groundbreaker, could queering up things function as a semiotic hallmark for global inclusion and coalition (Zebracki & Milani, 2017)? Beyond the disputed issue of where queer identity really lies (Milani, 2013), does this scenario mean the takeover of smaller markets and cultural landscapes?

Writing in the 1990s, Alexander Doty (Doty, 1993) argued that popular culture empowers queerness as such a phenomenon. It elicits queer responses to queer and non-queer media productions, which are all levelled up as queer media. In search of a 'queer reading' of media texts as opposite to heteronormative intakes, he writes:

> My use of the terms 'queer readings,' 'queer discourses,' and 'queer positions,' then, are attempts to account for the existence and expression of a wide range of positions within culture that are 'queer' or non-, anti-, or contra-straight. I am using the term 'queer' to mark

a flexible space for the expression of all aspects of non- (anti-, contra-) straight cultural production and reception. As such, this cultural 'queer space' recognizes the possibility that various and fluctuating queer positions might be occupied whenever anyone produces or responds to culture.

Doty, 1993:24

To that point, one could argue that thirty years later, queer media is hardly this space for 'fluctuating' positions. Instead, it works as a label that will inevitably deliver one thing. Whether a set of behaviours, slang, and opinions from various performers, whether a trademark, a new business, or a funny little thing. Whenever regional media partners acquire the latest *RuPaul's Drag Race* season, they know what to expect from the final product. They may dub participants' voices to the local language or change a drag's name to fit a national term. By doing so, their globalizing stance erases all other possible positions, except the one initially thought for the American market. The English language, the lifestyle, the signs, the hashtags, the device holding, the design or apps, the advertisers – all these ingredients will undoubtedly corroborate this version of *queerness*.

To a large extent, shedding light on this process of globalization of queer media means investing in first capturing one possible meaning for this word. As Rantanen (2005) explains, defining and conceptualizing globalization has primarily meant determining several consequences of globalization versus seeing globalization only as the domination of some territories over others. Giddens (1990), for example, has seen these as distinct parts worth separate reflections. Boyd-Barrett (1998) and others are sceptics of globalization, except if it comes through as a confluence of private media spheres, preferring *imperialism*. Accounts such as Fraser's (2007) saw transnational public spheres functioning according to the interests of the few, whereby a sharper focus on social justice would be viable and desirable. Likewise, for Flew (2018), the Internet impact levelled media access as a kind of post-globalization. Even though these ideas are not focused on queer or gender studies, they help settle this book's interest in *globalizing* or *globalized*, as a continuous, complex, specific dynamic between two or more media actors, as opposed to *globalization*, seemingly a faceless, over-institutionalized power relationship. Here, the use of *global* corresponds to its geographical dimension, as far as *globalized* is used on critical grounds to mention the ultimate capitalist and unidirectional side of a queer language or event.

The close knitting between media publicity and LGBTQ+ current events, centred mainly on the United States and Europe, leads to many assumptions about market decisions that apply to other publics. Altman (1997) mentioned the *global gaze* and *global gays* about mingling identities between LGBTQ markets in the Australasia region. Still, in the Asia Pacific region, several festivals attempted to regionalize the visibility of queer media production (e.g., Tan, 2019). There have been many other initiatives to revamp queer scenes regionally. One can criticize the lack of rupture from varying attachments to Western cultural industries. In this book, my approach prioritizes the enormous distribution cycles through multiple languages, cultures, national borders, and platforms of products from the same industries. This limitation to further media and cultural interactions across multiple regions characterizes the *globalized* queer culture as a set of simplified queerness yet shareable or ultra-commercialized exchanges coming from the West. Nonetheless, I am aware that all mentions of things *global* cannot result in a rigorous geographic or culturally diverse perspective, as many other queer communities fail to appear in this work.

As a result, I focused on queer media or cultures that can be traded or accessible both in Western and non-Western settings as chief characteristics of *global* queer media. Its opposite, the local, appears as the queer culture with less impact outside its geographic borders or media affordances. This sharpening was necessary to promote an analysis that privileged the commercial and cultural influence *across* queer cultures instead of only within a single community. On the other side, there have been conscious exclusions of what one could see as queer culture. For instance, parodic displays of homosexuality deemed as harmful or indirectly leading to homophobia (Adams, 1998) were not considered as part of the queer culture spectrum if satisfying a heterosexual point of view only. In the same way, pornographic content belongs in a separate conversation.

In sum, the book takes on *local* or *global* as terms that broadly function as markers for cultural production and distribution as well as gay liberation struggles. By using *global*, I look at the lucrative queer culture represented in TV series, parlance, or digital records from prominent and wealthy industrial centres (namely, primarily headquartered in Western Europe and the United States). By using *local*, I mean the exact opposite. It means traces from smaller towns, villages or cities that do not belong to or are the object of attention for European or American cultural industries. Although there is no intention to narrow down on the exact cultural industries the study represents, *local* and *global* can also denote ways of exerting broader influence in gathering large audiences. For example, as much as drag race gets various regional productions, it *becomes* global because it frequently refers to the well-exported American *RuPaul's Drag Race*. Otherwise, once cultural productions do not share this common understanding across the border, it tends to be local as it is not borne out with this globetrotter aim. In any case, the globalization of queer media cannot be apprehended only through market flows. As I discuss next, there is an issue of knowledge exchange that pertains to the quality of the queer acts that become global or local and their transversal importance.

Queer mediatization and the issue of knowledge

More than countries and continents, queer life has always been connected to a clear notion of what is on the inside or outside. Sedgwick's (1990:72-73) reflections on the dualities of the closet impart the need to escape historical binaries by exchanging information. As Sedgwick noted: the 'pairings' to which queer people have been submitted, including the 'masculine/feminine, majority/minority, innocence/initiation, natural/artificial', she concluded that 'knowledge/ignorance is not merely another metonymic chain of such binarisms'. The knowledge issue stirs more points about *which pieces of knowledge* are necessary to avoid the one's pigeonholing and homophobia. In other words, what role can the media play in opening queer culture to heterosexual society? The debate on *global* or *local* can also refer to *one* type of queer knowledge over others available regardless of their geographical place. Globalized queerness, ideally, could also represent a renovated world of multiple queer lives and knowledge available.

Knowledge and *sex* have become conceptually inseparable from one another – so that knowledge means, in the first place, sexual knowledge: 'One's preferences and intentions regarding others; ignorance, or lack of information on one's sexual life; and epistemological pressure of any sort seems a force increasingly saturated with sexual impulsion' (Sedgwick, 1990:73). That being the case, more media circulating, more information about what everyone does, including in other societies. Conversely, the way societies across the world have learned about one another's forms of gender and sexuality over time remains uncharted. What we know remains circumscribed to the intense movements that have fought against homophobia over the 20th century. American

LGBT activism has had an edge in carving out its unique channel with the world that remains to this day.

Other experiences of forging positivity about non-normative sexualities have been less interesting for mass culture or remained in obscurity for a long time. Arguably, the thriving *Institute for Sexual Science*, Weimar Germany, founded by Magnus Hirschfeld (1868–1935), was much less known if one compares it with the 1969 storming of Stonewall in New York City. As the liberation movements of the 1970s are more indebted to the latter than the former (Dose, 2014), the liberation project, at least as a media product, has more roots in Greenwich Village, New York City, than anywhere else. In his pioneering vision, Hirschfeld should have been more popular as a global champion of *queerness*. The myriad of homosexuals and transexuals who attended his practice, even though inspected under a medical lens, prompted his interest in China and the world. Moreover, his friendship with Li Shiu Tong (1907–1993) is an overlooked aspect. This transnational and homosexual union has not featured in activists' voices for the next generations.

As the birthplace of modern queer globalization, New York City also has its alternative history of mediatizing queerness before the liberation movements of the 1970s. In his study of the formation of this 'gay world' in the early 20th century, Chauncey (2019) saw several myths and paradigms involving exchanging knowledge between homosexuals in the city. If the Gay Liberation movements argued that maximum visibility would overcome oppression, including homophobic police, restrictive laws, and societal concerns, the pre-Liberation world had created its codes and ways. As the author explains:

> Gay men had to take precautions, but, like other marginalized peoples, they were able to construct spheres of relative cultural autonomy in the interstices of a city governed by hostile powers. They forged an immense gay world of overlapping social networks in the city's streets, private apartments, bathhouses, cafeterias, and saloons, and they celebrated that world's existence at a regularly held communal event such as the massive drag (or transvestite) balls that attracted thousands of participants and spectators in the 1920s.
> Chauncey, 2019:2

The fact that gay men in early New York City could orbit around their spheres of influence without counting on any public communication channels offers another reading of the issue of knowledge. In short, if media production would prove vital for the following Liberation waves, whether in pamphlets or small newspapers, earlier homosexual circles could if not thrive, exchange news about themselves in key gathering places. Secondly, unlike Berlin 1933, a thriving gay community not existing with scientific purposes would produce genuine knowledge that would lie outside the long treaties of medicine.

Another example of queer knowledge through the media goes back to the AIDS crisis. With the US being one of the epicentres for discoveries and investigations during the early epidemic phase, raising awareness about AIDS was also a way to inform the gay community worldwide. To inform on the virus was also to spread knowledge about gay social life, its meanders, as well as to contribute to the widespread surveillance of gay sexual habits. Up to this day, the *Aids.gov* website reserves a whole section for the media treatment of the issue. Dozens of covers in *Newsweek*, and *Time* magazine have undoubtedly led to the mirroring of similar coverage in other parts of the world, but from an American perspective. In Brazil, for example, a popular singer, *Cazuza*, was featured on the cover of the leading *Veja* magazine in April 1989 with the headline: 'An Aids victim agonizes in public.' This cover shocked the country due to its crude depiction of a frail, thin, and seemingly dying man's face (Grangeia, 2015). Arguably, such coverage was elicited by American publications that, at that point, had been covering the issue for a few years.

If American media has eased essential information about AIDS in critical times, it has also blazed the trail for more coverage at other levels. Today we know that only a few times it has elucidated men's sexual preferences and clarified the right to dignity in mainstream society (Kinsella, 1989:251). On the other hand, it has sensationalized the very dramas it exposed. It took decades to ease the burden of AIDS in a frame that fit homosexuals on screen, leave alone according to their regional circumstances, access to treatment, and resilience in the face of local pressures. The aim to portray would continue in Hollywood as fictional productions thrived, mainly from the United States. Oscar-winning *Philadelphia* (1993) became the epitome of the 'AIDS movie', without which no famous face would have personified the legal and psychological dramas involving patients. The film convincingly 'nationalized the gay body' while representing American values of struggle and overcoming (Corber, 2003). This aesthetic would be heard and reproduced in many other contexts, including Bollywood (Singhal & Vasanti, 2005).

Past these decades, and despite the advances achieved, one may ask whether these media flows have maximized queer visibility in a few hands. More than the received wisdom of being open and proud about LGBTQ+ affairs, one can also ask questions regarding the conditions of queer representation from a few decades ago echoing in the 2020s. *One* type of queerness, *one* face that serves mainstream society, and *one* type of queer knowledge that starts and overflows. The bulwark against homophobia can have other collateral effects, including global profit schemes traded on queer media, new forms of public alienation, or perfecting unsellable realities abroad. The worldwide success of films like *Cabaret* (1972) hinted that the mainstream media could seem to improve less ideal homosexual realities. Despite hitting the box office of many countries, it arguably portrayed a deceptive portrait of the original queer Weimar context (Pullen, 2016:77). Eventually, it hit Broadway, ultimately becoming another projection of the American media complex. Snippets of this excessive reading into the American reality inspired Vito Rossi (1981) to catalogue in *The Celluloid Closet* as it happened with similar soundbites of gay life in other films.

This book continues the conversation on opening new perceptions about queerness as more than the continuation of this epistemological universe mentioned above. Beyond this legacy of Western-rooted, US-centred enterprises, one needs to see new foundations so that a reappraisal of queerness as organically interwoven in the fabric of many other countries and cultures can receive the same kind of treatment. Much more is happening that helps us to, for the first time, see queer knowledge in the media in other colours and languages. The trans scene, for example, has never seen so much content produced about itself. Trans YouTube has quickly become an exciting space of contention, disagreements, and battles for meaning and resilience, whereby trans folks can tell things in their languages. Despite all the issues involving modern social media, the Internet has proved better than any previous experience on trans knowledge, and it should be part of this whole revamp of queer knowledge, for example. Next, I contend that understanding globalized queerness also involves rejecting false positives of LGBT liberation in exchange for global truths that are harder to harmonize and often unavailable at first glance.

Globalization as reproduction and rejection

After all, are these decades of American-centric queer self-knowledge alleviating contexts of oppression and homophobia elsewhere? Frederic Martel (2018) argued in *Global Gay: How Gay Culture is Changing the*

World that American-led gay culture has also helped to stabilize homophobia in distinct countries, including those in North Africa. The author dwells on the case of a few non-Western countries where changing terminologies allegedly demonstrate an overall improvement in homophobic traditions. Whether in clans, tribes, and societies, the fact that the notion of being *gay* has become popular conducts to another epistemic relationship with homosexuality, as he points out:

> Today, the term *mithly* is a sign of hope. Like *tongzhi* in Asia and gay anywhere else in the world, it is a positive word that is spreading in the Arab world. It attests to the fact that things are changing. *Mithly* in Arabic means 'homosexual' or 'gay' but also 'identical' or 'like me.' And, unlike much more derogatory words (such as *heth* or *neqch* in North Africa or *khawal* and *shaadh* in Egypt or yet *louter, tobjeh cheezzz,* and *byintek* in other Arab countries), *mithly* is neutral and without negative connotations. Nowadays, it is the word used on progressive Arab channels – for example, on Al Jazeera.
>
> Martel, 2018:99

Martel's arguments generalize a lot of the queer experience as being anchored in words. By over-crediting symbols such as the rainbow flags, pride parades, and celebrity come-outs, epistemological change nearly equates these events to an institutional change. By briefly touring a little fringe of dense realities across the globe, Martel leverages these bits of queer media globalization to an understanding that other places have reached – or are close to – Western standards of homosexual tolerance. Martel imagines mini-Wests as the ultimate archetype for gay recognition and, therefore, peace. Over-optimistically, gay acceptance is a process that continues the thread of films like *Philadelphia*. By sharing stories of queer success, one will conquer solid queer positions while skipping more intense questions regarding family, religion, and political affairs. It is not only too little what Martel visualizes as a queer future, as it does not cut deep into existing belief systems that characterize the present. Is stopping being refused to mean that queers are finally accepted?

To the credit of Martel's argument, this kind of perception of queer acceptance as semiotic penetration in society is increasing thanks to the globalization of queer media. It sells nuggets of visibility under acceptable terms as if queer liberation was a matter of politeness. As we shall see, the media often purports to carry a message of liberation that fails to go beyond commodity or commodity takers. As Susan Sontag famously pointed out in *Notes on Camp* about 'homosexuals', who, according to her, are 'aristocrats of taste' (1964). Masters of self-design, *they* are consequently too unreliable sources who do not live up to their constructed persona. This assumption is consonant with what Leo Bersani (1995:12) wrote about the 'gay presence' in Western culture: 'The more we tell about ourselves, the more we are congratulated for being ourselves.' Martel's portrait of the 'global gay' refers to this sort of globalization as an end. The so-called queer culture is a laboratory for self-congratulation. It overshadows the local queer person without further ambitions, leading to the compulsory episteme.

Doty acknowledges (1993:2–3) that the word *gay* was already not holding it in the middle of the 1990s, insofar as *queer* could work as an efficient aggregator which did not imprison LGBTQ individuals. What should one say about the 2020s? One could argue that *queerness* continues as this fluid amalgamator but carries more contradictions than ever (Heinz et al., 2002; Lubitow & Davis, 2011). The whole spectrum of 'queer readings' or 'queer positions' connects to a series of queer media products that *cover* minoritized audiences more than *come* from them. For example, the overarching assumption of covering them as representing them has left significant populations behind. Brilliant filmmakers such as Barbara Hammer, Su Friedrich, and Jan Oxenberg, were on the sidelines when all that mattered was the AIDS crisis and Hollywood readings of *queer* gay affairs. The same could be said about the Global South (Santos, 2014).

In this sense, *Globalized Queerness* argues for localizing queer media studies as creating a critical space of its own. The book does not purpose to repair historical absences based on geographical realities. The study reviews them as a pathway to engage with a globalized reality of many other exclusions. Looking at the academic sphere, Hongwei Bao's (Bao, 2021), Queer Media in China, for example, illuminated this adjacent place of current queer media in a country that has dealt with homosexuality with such a unique blend of oppression and adaptation. In such cases, queerness may still prevail within an effort of liberation, but flows of massification and marketization bite back against fresh efforts to diversify. In this case, recognizing the amalgam that *used* to represent queerness globally as obsolete can disentangle some of the knots regarding the identities and commodities that can influence being queer today with or without global queerness.

As I discuss next, to localize queerness today is to address these issues beyond semantic popularity or pink-washed interfaces. Focusing on queer popular culture and media hints at a critical approach toward its globalized interface. To understand the *globalized* nature of its names and acts, one must go back to the national beginnings, and transnational relationships often obscured or unnamed (Browne et al., 2017). It is urgent to re-establish ethnical matrixes and spheres of affective belonging, naming the *local* as that congregation of forces that have uniquely formed queer folks across time.

Localizing queerness and its culture

To assign any *local* label to queerness is initially problematic. Still, the fabric of queer culture has knowingly stemmed from several moments made from peripheral communities, Black, Asian, and Latino folks, the impoverished, the diasporic, the unsettled, and so on. Globalized queerness exists at their expense. However, the *locale* does not exist on its own. It becomes an epistemic value in opposition to the bulk of queer references manufactured every day. As Sedgwick (1990:11) warns, one always having to decide between homo and heterosexual only serves the 'self-corrosive efficacy of the contradiction inherent to these definitional binarisms' in which she suggests 'to profit, in some way, from the operations of such an incoherence of definition.' The inner aspect of this profiting from queer culture lies in constructing the queer as a mechanism that finally satisfies societal expectations.

Localizing queerness in this book follows this effort of escaping *globalized queerness* by raising questions about other realities. As Annamarie Jagose (1996) summed up a long time ago:

> An initial response to the successful consolidation of gay and lesbian identities in the ethnic model was a demand for equal recognition of non-normative categories of identities. In certain cases, this developed into dissatisfaction with categories of identification themselves and a questioning of their efficacy in political intervention.

More recently, a few scholars have noticed that queer theory is founded on the writings of White, European-descended, West-based scholars (e.g., Barnard, 1999; Hames-García, 2011). As Amin (2020) summarizes concerning its normative weight over the rest of the world:

> The result was that queer theory became at once a sophisticated critique of identarian knowledges emphatically not defined by the study of gays and lesbians, and it became one of the major sites for

the study of (homo)sexuality and gender transgression in the US academy.

Although this book does not invest in challenging queer theory at its core, the discomfort with the selective liberation it may inform creates a general mood for the reassessment of queer ontologies that the media propagate. The convenience of having *queer* as just another category, as a choice in the media spectrum, is one of these concepts that lands the queer brand in popular culture. Inventories of queer appearances in literature, media, film, and television have inevitably fallen short of more names and faces to explore, as they would do. When serializing queer presence in media and culture, as in Peele (2007), one finds highly diverse examples but permanently short of names that will be the next big thing or others that uneventfully fall into oblivion. In this case, one finds Israeli gender productions, the queer Blackness in *Noah's Arc*, and Taiwanese online communities. In some sense, the expectation that we hold to them is that they can also come to *globalize* their influence as opposed to being whatever these productions are, at their levels of influence, at their ways of informing or satisfying local queer publics.

As in *Calamity Jane*'s original Missouri plains, it is not only about verifying queerness as authentic but reaching it before the commodity cycle ends (McLaird, 2005). Localizing should seek the conditions and local repertoires of queer producers regardless of distribution and media power. It is like the Welsh pub attended by Daffyd Thomas from the BBC's *Little Britain* series. Dressed in stereotypical BDSM costume, Thomas challenged everyone by self-identifying as the *only gay in the village*. His uniqueness of being the *only one* and yet not leaving the town was part of the character's fun and charisma. Their queerness resided in being alone and together at the same time. He was always in the pub and yet distant regarding others' knowledge of himself.

Native texts and influences characterize unique traits from artists and media producers to their public without much effort. Halberstam (2011) expounded on how much queer knowledge has been left behind due to their being not academic or scientific enough or not resonating in a minimal space for debate. As they say:

How do we participate in the production and circulation of 'subjugated knowledge'? How do we keep disciplinary forms of knowledge at bay? How do we avoid precisely the 'scientific' forms of knowing that relegate other forms of knowing to the redundant or irrelevant?
Halberstam, 2011:10

Successful media making may have replaced the previous discussion on knowledge. For decades, one was assumed to lead to the other. But if knowledge on local queer is assumed to be available, in the West at least, it can still be limiting concerning expression and participation. Let's take the trans experience, for example. Decades of silence or prejudice are largely due to mainstream media channels reflecting deep societal concerns about the unknown. Once in the public recognition, the whole media spectrum, not only LGBTQ players, starts echoing about trans issues, including debates of those who can afford medical transition, challenge laws and get their voice through. As far as scholarly research remains and will remain rightly concerned with defining epistemic methodologies, pathways to localize queerness clash with the lack of media knowledge of these inner realities and the most profound divides between queer and heteronormative realities.

Within this vision of localizing queerness, much effort can be employed to spread a maximum number of allegories, including festivals, and reading weeks, that will *inform* on queerness with an eye to those living locally. Bao's (2021) idea of 'minor transnationalism' hints at how external queer influences inform artworks and somewhat condition artists and practitioners to a certain degree of opening their inner worlds to new vocabularies. I argue for a more galvanized and straightforward localization process that can boost possible homecomings by using global media, such as social media networks, which I discuss in the book's conclusion. For instance, local queerness that can live within communities through government efforts will increase a sense of tolerance and liberation that grows from the inside. Queerness as an ethnic venue should allow native vocabularies as the unmaking of colonizing, white-centric forms of belonging by projecting stories of success instead of relegating queerness to ableism and commercialism as the default.

In that sense, Chicana and Latinx epistemologies have established successful forms of pressure for inclusive queerness in multiple stages in the United States as elsewhere (Galván, 2014). Recently, the power of radical southern queer women transpires in illuminating figures that have emerged worldwide, such as Marielle Franco, who was tragically murdered in Brazil (Loureiro, 2020). Part of this dialogue has meant to illustrate other well-known or underexplored intersections between issues such as gender, race, Eurocentrism, and postcoloniality as models of local queerness (Nakayama, 1994; Milestone & Meyer, 2012). The case of disabled, religious, and intersectional individuals also sheds a light on features that are far less apparent in the mainstream, even though these are traits that bridge queer embodiments throughout an individual's life (Bohache, 2003; Pausé et al., 2016; Slater et al., 2018). New readings of postcolonial queer must encompass all forms of queer alterity, not only those available in big centres or favoured by the media. In effect, current media representations can still *colonize* on top of the traces left by ancient colonial empires either through relationships reinforced on camera or by unchanged north–south media flows.

Other approaches have taken a different route to consider queer culture somewhat less highbrow. To decolonize queerness, one must directly embrace what happens in mainstream culture, either in the West or the Global South. The 'pleasures' of pop culture include evoking a sense of feeling proud and connected to fandoms of several styles or trends (Jenkins et al., 2003), as not all queer culture is about heritage. To localize queer culture from the inside, one must acknowledge the self-identification with nations, cities, or groups that happens in tandem with one's circumscription to the 'gay', 'lesbian', or 'queer'. Queer artists and authors tend to reclaim this variety of links and put them on the map (Bartle, 2015), as shown in many studies in Ireland (Cronin, 2004), Spain (Barreto, 2017; Fernàndez, 2000), and in rural settings (Bell & Valentine, 1995; Sanchez & Sweetman, 2019). The focus on text and terms proves fruitful once we examine the number of transnational words that become queered up to fit momentous waves of recognition. These opportunities bridge less-known queer realities finally uncovered (Su, 2019; Massad, 2002).

From the audience's perspective, there are gains in localizing queer media and bringing it close to a sense of home. As a critical gateway to much reflection on Black spectatorship, media products are not innocent in keeping the audience captive or entirely outside their realms. Bell Hooks' *The Oppositional Gaze* (Hooks, 2012) remains an iconic piece and a powerful reminder of critical action:

When I returned to the films as a young woman, after a long period of silence, I had developed an oppositional gaze.

Hooks, 2012:96

Wouldn't it suit queer audiences the same *return* to the critical gaze? Doing it would invoke a few questions that entail existing in the real or fictional roles that compose globalized queerness. Where should these characters or producers belong to? Who are their neighbours? What are they *really* talking about? The more locally we conceive queerness today,

Figure 2 The casting of *My So-Called Life*. Wilson Cruz is the first from the left. © ABC Television. 1994. Image Courtesy of Alamy Stock Photo.

the more accurate remains people's portraits and the more influential the fight against localized homophobia is. Strategic silences are still allowed for and perpetuated by a rootless but ever-expanding queer media industry.

Therefore, questions about localizing merge with *locating*. Where are shows produced, where does artists' discourse come from, and which stages should one be looking at? Much less self-evident than the Welsh village of Daffyd Thomas from *Little Britain*, the *only gay in the village*, the sense of location comes very much racialized and problematized with other issues that are not found on the adequate level of recognition and analysis. In *My So-called Life* (1994–1995), the Latino actor Wilson Cruz played Rickie, a queer teen who was uninterested in women. The first ever HIV-positive gay character in MTV's *The Real World* series, aired in 1994, was a Cuban man called Pedro Zamora. In the UK, the 1959 series *South* featured a character named Jan Wicziewsky, played by Peter Wyngarde, a Polish retired soldier who fell for a fellow officer. The recent *L World* had the charismatic Carmen de la Pica Morales in seasons two and three.

These small parts do not suggest any causality between foreignness and homosexuality. Nevertheless, ancestry and stereotypes have helped shape characters even if they contributed to their incorporation by the white establishment. For instance, who could think of Ellen DeGeneres as an *Italian American* gay woman? She is just *Ellen*. These other smaller parts favour local queerness as an interactive concept with the issue of ancestry. These subtle attachments between queerness and accents, appearances, personal history, and locality (ethnic, visual, differential) have nonetheless served to *globalize* their queer presence in mainstream TV shows. The case of the 2014 Eurovision winner, Conchita Wurst, an Austrian representative, is another positive affirmation of the singer's motherland and international feedback. Wurst, played by Thomas Neuwirth, has sung in English as its globalized interface and toured worldwide because of her Eurovision status. Once fame faded Wurst returned to their Austrian roots and eventually became recognized by the country's president as a positive reference (Davies, 2014).

These cases of localized cum globalized queerness take this book's inquiry towards focusing on globalized queerness by addressing these omissions within the realm of mainstream culture. To amplify the discussion about the local and global aspects, the idea is to formulate hypotheses that imagine ideal settings of queer media as an open stance of political affirmation. For understandable reasons, there have been many expectations that queer media could represent the final liberation for such subjugated publics or if only, preserve its unruly, non-normative space of influence. As discussed above, queer media and culture have come a long way to entertain, mobilize, and empathize with queer liberation struggles (Ward, 2008). The book deepens into popular queer culture and media to inquire into the commodified structures of these appearances, their visual assets, and vocabularies. This study poses questions to elucidate this interplay between the materiality of queer presence, its traces, and historical backgrounds unnoticed globally versus the formulaic queerness of the media, which may hijack some of these local traits to form what I am calling globalized queerness.

A few hypotheses on globalized queerness

From the essential issue of sharing knowledge on minoritized sexualities to the contemporary panorama of globalized queerness as a homogenizing force, distinct levels of consciousness split one from the other. From Foucault's (1982) *aphrodisia*, the dietary protocols that Western societies adopted to ensure some level of ethics in sex to De Laurentis' (1987) *technologies of gender* on accessing knowledge imperfectly made available through language. This book's argument rests in seeing global queerness as another step blocking the advance of knowledge on queer realities through the media. As Jagose (1996:111) summed it up, queer theory also sees the limits of queer identity in society, which are fluid but not inapprehensible:

> It is not simply a question of where that community might be located – on the streets if the anti-intellectual tradition is to be trusted – but of how its interventions come to be 'political' in ways that are denied academic work.

A few hypotheses oriented this study in practical terms. They form an agenda that aims to understand globalized queerness based on the shortfalls of global media and cultural industries, including digital enterprises, without discrediting the undeniable advances in queer expression of recent years. Before laying out the hypotheses, some research questions are appropriate: Do global queer media acts contribute to the uprooting of queer artists and producers? To what extent does the global queer sphere of influence provoke and disrupt local queer communities? For example, is globalized queerness also a space of exclusion for those who cannot afford or understand international languages? Does the increase in the availability and profitability of queer discourses clash with current political debates involving LGBT rights? Is the process of globalizing queerness like the 'de-gaying' or 're-gaying' effects on forging a fitting version of homosexuality to mainstream society (Kitzinger & Peel, 2005; Visser, 2014)? What is the real participation of the Global South and other peripheral locations in the globalized queer industry? What is the role of local cultural industries in forging and maintaining indigenous queer cultures?

On the first hypothesis, one must acknowledge the remarkable potential for self-invention in the queer artistic community. Whether globalizing queerness is a quest to reaffirm queer non-territoriality, one should not deny that places of birth or upbringing are fertile for histories of shame (Sender, 2012). When taking this discussion to popular culture, the centrality of mediatized queerness in metropolises such as New York or London is unequivocally linked to relocation, settlement, and positive evasion sentiments. In short, what is the queer community if not a community in the physical or geographical sense? The queer experience transcends one form of existence or a single location – as queer personalities are made to be elusive in popular culture, a realm of Bakhtinian intersubjectivity (Peeren, 2008). In this hypothesis, queer territoriality relates to topics such as the gaze, the look, and performativity, which are constantly at stake in queer culture but can hardly be appreciated in their local settings and aesthetics, except in reinterpretations.

The second hypothesis sees globalized queerness as not about territoriality but authenticity. The case of RuPaul Charles is a paradigmatic one. In 1995, in *Wofoo To Wong Foo, Thanks for Everything! Julie Newmar*, the final scenes feature local drag queens, including then lesser-known *RuPaul Charles*, in a small part while the leading, global characters are played by straight actors such as Wesley Snipes and Patrick Swayze. Fast forward two decades, *RuPaul's Drag Race* has developed a semantics of its own 'codes of sisterhood', aimed at resisting negativity and upholding 'drag family values' (Simmons, 2014). The first

Figure 3 RuPaul in *Wofoo To Wong Foo, Thanks for Everything! Julie Newmar*. © Universal Pictures. 1995. Image Courtesy of Alamy Stock Photo.

RuPaul was not more authentic because he was not a mainstream media celebrity. Still, its famous metamorphosis left his queer portraits without a stronger relationship with whatever drag scene the artist had ever belonged to. His show has brought us queer characters that have, at best, worked as drag races advertising-boosted performances exported to various markets. Mass identification equated sellable dramas or charisma of whatever queerness was in the advertising. Similar phenomena may well be replicable elsewhere.

Thirdly, the highly loose borders between TV or film industries and the Internet, as well as the advent of micro-celebrity, influencers, and participative fandom, can blur national boundaries and ethnical backgrounds. It can become a formula for queerness that is easily replicable across markets. One example is the queer Italian artist Mahmood, the San Remo Festival winner. As an Italian-Egyptian singer, he came first in the traditional music festival, having emerged as an online act and fanbase. By rejecting the narrative of a victimized gay man with a migrant background, Mahmood designs his Arab queerness against a backdrop of Italian cosmopolitanism. One of his best-known lyrics says: 'You drink champagne during Ramadan, on TV there's Jackie Can, Smokes nargileh and asks me how I do it.' There might exist an element of 'utopic' capitalist reinvention (Cloud, 2001) in Mahmood's lyrics, which we shall see in further detail in Chapter 3. What stands out in his performance is the hyper-connectedness that being queer demands. In a country where racism is endemic and first-generation migrants are often denied citizenship, Mahmood inhabits a hybrid territory that does not always engage with such queer issues as such. In turn, he does not conform to a single version of himself.

These hypotheses can overlap or exist separately, but a structured investigation of the global expansion of queerness involves these points about territory, queerness, and media appearances. The institution of the international queer artist as the world-accepted citizen may crystallize an aura that leaves the stereotype of a funny, exotic, or parodic persona to evolve into the avant-garde brand expert who takes themselves seriously and profitable sponsorships. The limits of this process are much misunderstood. In the face of the explosion of queer media, crucial questions spring from the possibility of not seeing queer surroundings as supportive as they should be, in a world dominated by the *gay village* mindset (Weiner & Young, 2011). To investigate these or other regimes of globalized queerness, I have surveyed emphases found in different media contexts. In contrast, I do not imply an aligned consciousness around the wholesale of queerness. Instead, these discussions open a locus for seeing new infiltrations as queer lives are affected by this recent homogenization.

To conclude this section, I review the main areas of inquiry explored in the following sections. The book dwells on the ability of artists or media producers to stage self-reinventions, to disembody notions of sincerity or authenticity while embodying fame. It also highlighted the speed at which the Internet has expanded queer media into new discourses of global or local belonging. I contend that globalizing queerness consists of exogenous interests to everyday LGBTQ+ individuals in which situations of belonging or non-belonging are forged or invented for the benefit of popularity and profit. There are bonds and embodiments allowed or desired by popular culture that will likely create forms of self-identification that are not necessarily reflective of local queer cultures. This framework considers the different levels of queer artistry and media production, here problematized against early cultures or contexts before and after their mainstreaming. In the next section, I defend that a systematized approach must gather distinct datasets and methods that can benefit from Western and non-Western knowledge, as well as artists of separate branches and traditions to form a comprehensive, but not exhaustive survey of globalized queerness.

Main concepts, methods, and summary of the book

Globalized queerness draws on a vast spectrum of media appearances deemed as queer. Queer media and culture form an amalgamating expression for a broader scene of televised or non-televised spectacles and shows, including visual arts, music, acting, reality shows, dance, and other forms of gay, lesbian, bisexual, and trans crafting and archiving. It was essential to shelter all kinds of queer online and offline expression, not limited to online video making, modelling, celebrity, amateur singing and dancing, YouTubers, fandom acts, and paratexts related to mainstream acts. Culture is also used to refer to the intertwinement of these acts and artefacts conjugated with a storied impact on society. For example, controversial repercussions, news headlines, fashion trends, user-generated content, interviews by famous artists, and memes. These materials compose a truly eclectic and queered data set.

On the other hand, instead of trying to define *queer* or *gay*, *lesbian*, or *trans* as single terms that are either normative or limited to specific sexualities, this book engages with them as they come along but advances queer as an overarching identity (Dyer, 2002). Aware of the possibility of *gay streaming* (Ng, 2013): the excessive pointing to homosexuality as whitewashed, commercialized, and normative gayness, it is possible to embrace *queer* as a viable alternative. *Queerness*, instead, remains tied to an ultra-commercial and destabilizing term, while still faithful to how producers self-identify and place their affinities. There is enough literature to base the assimilation of queer as an interchangeable keyword for gay, lesbian, transgender, and categories in between. As far as individuals are affiliated with them, an increasing trend in queer theory or queer studies is to follow individuals in their non-conforming stances and the pronouns one can associate with. Therefore, queer is a functional choice for embracing the broadest number of initiatives and a critical alternative to place productions outside the heterosexual media narrative.

These choices beg the question of how to define queer culture and media. As discussed earlier, the interspersing between a broad sense of culture as topics, narratives, and public opinion projected on media productions gives enough space to know what queer popular culture and media mean without being too broad. This term has been used freely by numerous studies, compilations, annotations, and references on queer TV or film (Creekmur & Doty, 1995; Benshoff & Griffin, 2006; Gerstner, 2006; Driver, 2007; Peele, 2007; Lipton, 2008; Lovelock, 2019). This book's approach thrives on queer positions in popular culture that function as tailored queer media products, emphasizing the latter. For practical and analytical reasons, I needed a cut in time, here, it was the period (2010–2022) to find the most recent productions at the time of the research and level them alongside documentary evidence. Popular culture stems from music releases distributed by major labels, for instance, and alternative companies that have gained notoriety through more than one media platform. It is the case of photographers who have received attention on platforms such as Instagram or those who could have also appeared in the mainstream press or even in recommendations from other artists. It contemplates parody videos on YouTube but also drama characters in films, memes, or other forms of public display of queerness. This mix of highly commercialized and independent initiatives provided this research with both emerging and consolidated acts.

The book follows distinct methodological strategies defined by the chapter. Yet, they all point to purposive ways of identifying queer media producers and artists that problematize the local and the global in their language, coverage, and production. Methods to get to this contrast between global and regional discourses include archival research, cultural analysis, content and discourse analysis, and a small set of in-depth interviews with media producers and artists. The methods are meant to bring a distinct set of queer productions together and establish a critical view of them anchored on solid evidence that takes us through many stances. Dominick and Wimmer's (2010:64) guidelines to reach reasonable criteria using mass media choices have aided this study to concentrate on popular queer media that can be broadly accessible and count with a responsive audience. *Broadly accessible* can relate not only to mass media and millions of viewers or users, such as in the case of the Internet but also to media dressed in click-baiting and promotional framings. It would not be possible to know the extent to which queer media can be local or global without taking on this issue of availability and commercialization. The second criterion was approaching the audience not only as the viewer but also as a participant who can produce large pieces of content that characterize what queer media is today. Purushotma and Jenkins' (2009) ideas on participatory culture enlightened the performative aspect of queer fandom, without which it is impossible to verify acts, interventions, and repertoires that inform and deconstruct their mainstreaming. For example, slang and other local expressions become spreadable as they come up on shows, which, in turn, purport to represent the streets and communities.

Another preoccupation was to include both Western and non-Western contexts in line with a concerted effort in academia to decentre queer sexualities from West-based perceptions (Oswin, 2006; Halberstam, 2011). It was critical to open space for 'subjugated knowledges' that form layers of queer experience historically under-appreciated and overlooked by both Western academia and media enterprises (Robinson, Davies & Davis, 2012). On the other hand, while various academic compilations and encyclopaedic works have served as the source for names of LGBTQ+ artists, their careers, and periods of production, one must not isolate Western and non-Western in distinct spheres of perception. The unstoppable stream of media content and projects online have meant that audiences can be juxtaposed as productions go global or *glocal*. Most artists and producers from the Global South can today access the so-called mainstream stages through the Internet, and Westerners are growing more attentive to what happens in the south. Far from the ideal scenario of equitable contributions, it is fair to assume some ongoing exchanges across the Global South, as we shall see in the book.

Therefore, the issue of diversity still needs to be solved here. The book has included queer artists who got prominence through a string of mainstream English-speaking newspapers (*Guardian*, *New York Times*, *Washington Post*, *The Times*, and the BBC), as well as those featured in leading vehicles for LGBTQ+ artists and the public (e.g., Attitude, Pride. com). But to reach artists or producers with no media prominence, snowballing mentions and quotes were helpful. Besides alternative media articles, small social media accounts have served as essential sources. YouTube, TikTok, Instagram, and Facebook were platforms of choice for their breadth of users, but Twitter, Reddit, WhatsApp, Telegram, and smaller mobile-based networks have also been part of the effort to find them. At the last stage of data gathering, the pool of names reached the number of 300 artists from around the world, later shortened to 100 on the grounds of similar global representativeness in more than five languages. This number increased the feasibility of the work getting done. To search for emerging artists that could give their views on this research's topics, Instagram seemed a suitable choice given its popularity, broad coverage, and artistic variety, even though many acts will remain uncovered or censored by platforms because of these choices.

Once mapped and surveyed, these artists and media producers provided the study with texts and paratexts that informed most of the analyses. As discussed below, using mixed methods for content analysis was a natural choice as the amount of material on the Internet demands automated ways of analysing repetitions and trends rather than focusing on individual instances. For example, this was the case with news articles or Internet comments. For the in-depth interviews and case studies, it was possible to follow discourse analysis frameworks that could also privilege narratives and storytelling. As Catalano and Waugh (2020:289) pointed out, language has been an invaluable resource to gender and sexuality study as a reservoir of sexist tropes and homophobic ones, so much so to make it an essential resource for investigating it both as a threat and tool of resistance.

Ultimately, the data in this book consisted of retrieving and criticizing crucial passages in queer acts allied to cultural analysis. This reading is uniquely focused on the mechanisms of globalization of the queer experience juxtaposed with more significant tendencies in global media industries. The latter, I argue, stands opposite to local ways of understanding and mediatizing queerness while blinding other possible alternatives of conceiving one's queerness. This direction was undoubtedly followed to frame data as something that can also be queered and prevent *straightwashing* that has condemned queer folks to binaries encased as data choices (Guyan, 2022). In that sense, data can also present grouped saliences of local idioms that resist the commodification of queer media or demonstrate the *de-gaying* of queer idioms and the ultimate trivialization of queer lives. These methods do not seek to name single individuals as agents of negative or positive changes in that scenario. Following helpful exercises into queer research methods, as found in Nash (2016), this book's methods were queered up by dislodging *discourse* as an institutionalized societal event and levelling it as queer popular parlance and opinions. In brief, the quoted data appeared as discourses from genuine cultural participants, in line with academic or so-called authoritative voices. This effort aimed to offer scholarly knowledge, not as the only representative of verified queer knowledge but contextualizing it with material retrieved from the field, individual voices, and stories.

In sum, the book's scope comprises traditional mainstream media productions found on TV series or talk shows and films, as well as in the recent formats of online content, such as live-streaming, YouTube videos, and short clips. As the former gets much publicity via capitalized ways of press relationship and mass distribution, it also generates much data for research. The latter, otherwise, consists of self-made media producers, first-hand accounts, and influencer marketing, which are captured as they appear on each source. Thus, besides theoretical and foundational chapters, the book offers two chapters about these varieties of queer media production. From the conventional sense of stardom to very personal struggles that pop up in daily online streaming sessions.

Eventually, it was essential to keep the sense of media and popular culture as broad as possible to reflect *globalization* and *localization* as nuanced perspectives delivered by moments of exposure to large or small audiences. There was also an ethical aspect to be regarded, which amounts to the position one takes while watching queer media that can be as affection-driven and private as any testimonial and yet rendered into public, online content. As Mertens and Ginsberg (2009) debated, research involving LGBTQ+ individuals must abide by careful consideration regarding privacy, confidentiality, and protecting research participants. With that in mind, I have focused on potential readings that can reveal sexual or racial privilege when watching other groups' stories and narratives. As a gay man, I was entirely conscious that while critical spectatorship can be helpful to queer audiences hijacked by market forces, there is a degree of conscious or unconscious privilege that one should work on in a way to be as understanding as possible of others' affordances and needs of affirmation, regardless of these being encased in problematic or artificial media settings. Next, I outline each chapter's summary.

Chapter 1 charts several issues stemming from the commodification of queer media and culture. The problem of accommodating queer commodities has preoccupied authors for decades (e.g., Hennessy, 1994; Radin & Sunder, 2004; Kwon, 2016). They have nonetheless focused on the hegemony of prejudicial and heteronormative stereotypes resulting from commercializing images of queerness (e.g., Emig, 2000; Baştürk, 2016). Meanwhile, the global mediatization of pride parades has guaranteed that one type of outgoing queer individual stayed in the spotlight (de Jong, 2017). This chapter expands on local queer media in three spheres of queer influence: the community, the nation, and the city. After explaining the framework dedicated to *genealogizing* queer media, I developed commodifying, de-commodifying, and localizing as fundamental critical stances against the essentialization of gay and queer identities through globalized articulations. After putting forward ideas from Simone de Beauvoir, who saw the authentic agency as a synonym with authentic life, plus Lionel Trilling, Raymond Williams, and others, I settle on queer authenticity as the ultimate agency to the unpredictable and hybridism, against which commodification should be tested and analysed using concepts later explicated.

Chapter 2 presents the results from a Latent Dirichlet Allocation (LDA), which grouped the most frequently repeated topics-tracked media reports about queer arts and popular culture in outlets of the world's ten biggest media markets: the United States, the UK, Japan, South Korea, China, France, Italy, Germany, Brazil, and Canada. This survey was based on scraping news content through an API application that considered several global and local news sources over two years. A computational algorithm has identified unique news articles published in each market. A vocabulary was made up of words used to refer to queer artists in each of the languages/places based on direct terms such as gay, lesbian, transgender, and their equivalents in each of the languages. While not an exhaustive survey, it provides a path to engage with patterns of queer presence in global news. The survey's results (over 3,200 articles) named the countries where queer artists have appeared more often and examples of topics vis-à-vis examples of transnational or *glocal* coverage. Other conclusions and absences were quantified to understand the distinct flows that orient queer coverage to what concerns media and popular culture worldwide.

Chapter 3 explores the universe of queer artists in different generations of influence in popular culture. The chapter returned to the notion of the *queer artist* as an ephemeral and performative figure that was louder in the pre-Internet times. I proposed global and local readings that contrasted them with a recent harvest of pop stardom, following these artists' views of queer fame and national belonging. By drawing on a cultural analysis framework (Polzer et al., 2020), the study included the profile of Brazilian singers Pabllo Vittar and Linn da Quebrada, Hong-Konger weightlifter and speaker Siufung Law, South Korean pop artist Harisu, French performer Phia Menard, Italian singer and songwriter Cristiano Malgiolio, drag queen Crystal Rasmussen, among others. I revisit pieces of theories of queer cosmopolitanism conjugated with a few passages of debates on *mestizaje* and transculturation to critique constructed global queer identities juxtaposed with ideas of oppression and liberation. An extensive record of interviews given by these performers plus resurfaced paratexts evidence the ambiguous relationship between local and global contexts in modern queer frame.

Chapter 4 traces records of trans YouTube videos to investigate the growing scenario of online media produced by trans people. A quantitative analysis of words employed by these influencers, plus the application of an LDA analysis, tracked stories of trans men, women, as well as non-binary individuals who are on YouTube to communicate their struggles, disagreements, and victories. The Google-owned video website is often received with scepticism due to its hyper-commercialism, besides questions on authenticity and veracity. However, by hosting influencers who represent myriad references and ideological affiliations, the website has quickly become a career for many of these trans communicators using their life as raw material. Despite emphases varying according to regions and personal affordances, retrieved keywords mirrored a range of individual trajectories, including transitioning, de-transitioning, and clarifying audience questions about their bodies and social lives. Topics group a range of preoccupations that range from health care treatments, clashes within and outside trans communities, and general impressions on life and culture. This chapter ends with a reflection on this unprecedented takeover of trans narratives by trans individuals, which is a corollary to the growing capitalization of lives, vis-à-vis the censoring of their stances and the commodification of their own culture. The differences between global and local standards of trans repertoire are debated at the end of this chapter.

Chapter 5 dedicates to the semi-structured and in-depth interviews conducted with several self-identified queer media producers publishing their work or pursuing a career on the Internet. These interviews aimed to explore their relationship with early experiences in life and their view of global and local representations of queer culture. A total of

35 interviews and two profiles were drawn from long-term participant observations and approached many chapters of their personal, cultural, or artistic development. Furthermore, anonymized data from various social media profiles has allowed speculating about values and intimacies that these media producers share alongside plans for careers or living a public life. Down the line, I invited Goffman's facework theory to interpret these findings on the grounds of avoiding the topic, correcting current understandings, and making a point regarding one's queerness. These conclusions work as an integrative pathway to critically perceive the patches of queer lives and soundbites orienting one's position toward the world. The chapter concludes by taking these field notes and theoretical reflections as hints of attachment or detachment from globalized queerness.

The conclusion recaps previous chapters' discussions while acknowledging the challenging mission of striking a balance between local and global queer media in the wake of its cultural expansion worldwide. Weighing on the mainstreaming of queer popular culture, the advent of the news and the emergence of queer pop stats have shown how marketable the queer experience can be. More recently, the 'tiktokization of gender' reveals new challenges regarding the commodification of queer attention to the extent of exporting unheard slang and repertoires, remixing authenticity, as talent becomes entrepreneurial and tied to numbers. Back to the book's initial hypotheses, I argue that globalized queerness has had evident adverse effects, if not de-gaying or revisionist accounts, it includes the foreshortening of queer models of life and entertainment, but there is less space for realities that are not predicated on boosting algorithmic design. There is more to forming a common intellectual heritage that caters to all, in which I propose the notion of *possible homecomings*. I flesh out a series of proposals to appropriate modern technologies for agendas owned by local queer communities, circle back the name of local queer artists, and propose the exchange between local queer communities worldwide.

The book ends by acknowledging its conceptual and methodological limitations while making a case for further ties between queer popular artists, media producers, and their local communities. Globalized queerness has worked as an anti-stereotypical image to contain rainbow-like, pink-washed references and an alternative impression that offers a critical tool for the historically silenced public. This study has shown how to see the traces of local queer cultures that are easily dispersed. In contrast, others continue to resist thanks to grassroots ways of integration that work for and within frameworks of grassroots queer belongings. Moving forward, communities should battle more fiercely to own queer cultures using public ways of funding them. NGOs and community associations should channel notions of success as feedback into inbred forms of emancipation and funding that involve developing public policies specific to feed queerness on the local level. Less commodified forms of queer media will depend on renewed practices, but also bottom-up systems of acknowledgement, ownership, and recognition.

References

Adam, B. D. (1998). Theorizing homophobia. *Sexualities*, *1*(4), 387–404.
Ahmed, S. (2006). *Queer phenomenology*. Duke University Press.
Amin, K. (2020). Genealogies of queer theory. In S. B. Somerville (Ed.). *The Cambridge Companion to Queer Studies* (pp. 17–29). Cambridge University Press.
Altman, D. (1997). Global gaze/global gays. *GLQ: A Journal of Lesbian and Gay Studies*, *3*(4), 417–436.
Bao, H. (2021). *Queer Media in China*. United Kingdom: Taylor & Francis.
Barreto, D. M. (2017). Putting queerness on the map: Notes for a queer Galician studies. In B. Vizcaya & J. A. Losada Montero (Eds.). *Rerouting Galician studies* (pp. 25–38). Palgrave Macmillan, Cham.
Barnard, I. (1999). Queer race. *Social Semiotics*, *9*(2), 199–212.
Bartle, C. (2015). Gay/queer dynamics and the question of sexual history and identity. *Journal of Homosexuality*, *62*(4), 531–569. DOI: 10.1080/00918369.2014.983395
Baştürk, T. S. (2016). *What a drag? Popular culture and the commodification of 'feminine'- other bodies*. (Doctoral dissertation, Bilkent University (Turkey).
Bell, D., & Valentine, G. (1995). Queer country: Rural lesbian and gay lives. *Journal of Rural Studies*, *11*(2), 113–122.
Benshoff, H. M., & Griffin, S. (Eds.). (2004). *Queer cinema: The film reader*. Psychology Press.
Bersani, L. (1995; 2009). *Homos*. Harvard University Press.
Bohache, T. (2003). Embodiment as incarnation: An incipient queer Christology. *Theology & Sexuality*, *10*(1), 9–29.
Boyd-Barrett, O. (1998). 'Global' news agencies. In O. Boyd-Barrett & T. Rantanen (Eds.). *The globalization of news* (pp. 19–34). Sage Publications.
Browne, K., Banerjea, N., McGlynn, N., Bakshi, L., Banerjee, R., & Biswas, R. (2017). Towards transnational feminist queer methodologies. *Gender, Place & Culture*, *24*(10), 1376–1397.
Burgett, B. & Hendler, G. (2020). *Keywords for American cultural studies*.

(2007). United Kingdom: New York University Press.

Chauncey, G. (2019). *Gay New York: Gender, urban culture, and the making of the gay male world, 1890–1940*. United States: Basic Books.

Cloud, D. (2001). Queer theory and 'family values': Capitalism's utopias of self-invention. *Transformation*, 2, 71–114.

Corber, R. J. (2003). Nationalizing the gay body: AIDS and sentimental pedagogy in 'Philadelphia'. *American Literary History*, 15(1), 107–133.

Creekmur, C. K. & Doty, A. (1995). *Out in culture: Gay, lesbian, and queer essays on popular culture*. Cassel.

Cronin, M. G. (2004). 'He's My Country': Liberalism, nationalism, and sexuality in contemporary Irish gay fiction. *Eire-Ireland*, 39(3), 250–267.

Davies, C. (2014). Conchita Wurst pledges to promote tolerance after jubilant welcome home. *The Guardian*.

de Jong, A. (2017). Unpacking Pride's commodification through the encounter. *Annals of Tourism Research*, 63, 128–139.

Dominick, J. R., & Wimmer, R. D. (2010). *Mass media research: An introduction*. United States: Cengage Learning.

Dose, R. (2014). *Magnus Hirschfeld: the origins of the gay liberation movement*. New York University Press.

Doty, A. (1993). *Making things perfectly Queer: Interpreting mass culture*. University of Minnesota Press.

Dyer, R. (2002). *The culture of queers*. Psychology Press.

Driver, S. (2007). *Queer girls and popular Culture: Reading, resisting, and creating media*. Austria: Peter Lang.

Emig, R. (2000). Queering the straights: Straightening queers: Commodified sexualities and hegemonic masculinity. In R. West & F. Lay (Eds.). *Subverting masculinity* (pp. 207–226). Brill.

Fernàndez, J. A. (2000). *Another country: sexuality and national identity in Catalan gay fiction (vol. 50)*. MHRA.

Flew, T. (2018). Post-globalisation. *Javnost-The Public*, 25(1–2), 102–109.

Florêncio, J. (2020). *Bareback porn, porous masculinities, queer futures: The ethics of becoming-pig*. Routledge.

Fraser, N. (2007). Transnational public sphere: Transnationalizing the public sphere: On the legitimacy and efficacy of public opinion in a post-Westphalian world. *Theory, culture & society*, 24(4), 7–30.

Galván, R. (2014). Chicana/Latin American feminist epistemologies of the global South (within and outside the North): Decolonizing el conocimiento and creating global alliances. *Journal of Latino/Latin American Studies*, 6(2), 135–140.

Catalano, T., & Waugh, L. R. (2020). *Critical discourse analysis, critical discourse studies and beyond*. Springer International Publishing.

Giddens, A. (1990). *The consequences of modernity*. United Kingdom: Stanford University Press.

GLAAD (2022). *The 2022 GLAAD studio responsibility index*. Available at https://www.glaad.org/sri/2022 Access 28 March 2023.

GLAAD (2022B). *The where we are on TV report (2021–2022)*. Available at. https://www.glaad.org/blog/glaads-2021-2022-where-we-are-tv-report-lgbtq-representation-reaches-new-record-highs Access on 28 March 2023.

Gerstner, D. A. (Ed.). (2006). *Routledge international encyclopedia of queer culture*. Routledge.

Grangeia, M. L. (2015). *Brasil: Cazuza, Renato Russo e a transição democrática*. Brazil: Civilização Brasileira.

Guyan, K. (2022). *Queer data: Using gender, sex and sexuality data for action*. United Kingdom: Bloomsbury Publishing.

Halberstam, J. (2011). *The queer art of failure*. United Kingdom, Duke University Press.

Hames-García, M. (2011). Queer theory revisited. *Gay Latino studies: A Critical Reader*, 19–45.

Heinz, B., Gu, L., Inuzuka, A., & Zender, R. (2002). Under the rainbow flag: Webbing global gay identities. *International Journal of Sexuality and Gender Studies*, 7(2–3), 107–124.

Hennessy, R. (1994). Queer visibility in commodity culture. *Cultural Critique*, (29), 31–76.

Hooks, B. (2012). The oppositional gaze: Black female spectators. In M. Diawara (Ed.). *Black American cinema* (pp. 288–302). Routledge.

Jagose, A. (1996). *Queer theory: An introduction*. NYU Press.

Jenkins III, H., Shattuc, J., & McPherson, T. (Eds.). (2003). *Hop on pop: the politics and pleasures of popular culture*. Duke University Press.

Kinsella, J. (1989). *Covering the Plague: AIDS and the American media*. United Kingdom: Rutgers University Press.

Kitzinger, C., & Peel, E. (2005). The de-gaying and re-gaying of AIDS: Contested homophobias in lesbian and gay awareness training. *Discourse & Society*, 16(2), 173–197.

Kwon, J. (2016). Commodifying the gay body: Globalization, the film industry and female prosumers in the contemporary Korean mediascape. *International Journal of Communication*, 10, 18.

Lindner, K. (2017). *Film bodies: Queer feminist encounters with gender and sexuality in cinema*. Bloomsbury Publishing.

Lipton, M. (2008). Queer readings of popular culture. *Queer Youth Culture*, 163–180.

Loureiro, G. S. (2020). To be black, queer and radical: Centring the epistemology of Marielle Franco. *Open Cultural Studies*, 4(1), 50–58.

Lovelock, M. (2019). *Reality TV and queer identities: Sexuality, authenticity, celebrity*. Springer.

Lubitow, A., & Davis, M. (2011). Pastel injustice: The corporate use of pinkwashing for profit. *Environmental Justice*, 4(2), 139–144.

Massad, J. A. (2002). Re-orienting desire: The gay international and the Arab world. *Public culture*, 14(2), 361–385.

Maddison, S. (2000). *Fags, hags and queer sisters. Gender dissent and heterosocial bonds in gay culture*. London: Palgrave Macmillan.

Mann, W. J. (2001). *Behind the screen: How gays and lesbians shaped Hollywood, 1910–1969.* New York: Viking.
Martel, F. (2018). *Global gay: How gay culture is changing the world.* MIT Press.
McDonald, T. J. (2007). Carrying concealed weapons: Gendered makeover in 'Calamity Jane'. *Journal of Popular Film and Television, 34*(4), 179–187. DOI: 10.3200/JPFT.34.4.
McLaird, J. D. (2005). *Calamity Jane: The woman and the legend.* Oklahoma: University of Oklahoma Press.
Mercer, J. (2017). *Gay pornography: Representations of sexuality and masculinity.* Bloomsbury Publishing.
Mertens, D. M., & Ginsberg, P. E. (2009). *The handbook of social research ethics.* Sage.
Milani, T. M. (2013). Are 'queers' really 'queer'? Language, identity and same-sex desire in a South African online community. *Discourse & Society, 24*(5), 615–633.
Milestone, K., & Meyer, A. (2012). *Gender and popular culture.* Polity.
Nakayama, T. K. (1994). Show/down time: 'Race', gender, sexuality, and popular culture. *Critical Studies in Media Communication, 11*(2), 162–179.
Nash, C. J. (2016). *Queer methods and methodologies: Intersecting queer theories and social science research.* United Kingdom: Taylor & Francis.
Nicholus, S. (2020). Queer Anthropophagy: Building women-centered LGBT+ space in Northeastern Brazil. *Journal of Lesbian Studies, 24*(3), 240–254.
Ng, E. (2013). A 'post-gay' era? Media gaystreaming, homonormativity, and the politics of LGBT integration. *Communication, Culture & Critique, 6*(2), 258–283.
Oswin, N. (2006). Decentering queer globalization: Diffusion and the 'global gay'. *Environment and Planning D: Society and Space, 24*(5), 777–790.
Pausé, C., Wykes, J., & Murray, S. (Eds.). (2016). *Queering fat embodiment.* Routledge.
Payne, R. (2014). *The promiscuity of network culture: Queer theory and digital media.* Routledge.
Peele, T. (2007). *Queer popular culture: Literature, media, film, and television.* Springer.
Peeren, E. (2008). *Intersubjectivities and popular culture: Bakhtin and beyond.* United States: Stanford University Press.
Pheasant-Kelly, F (2013). Outlaws, buddies, and lovers: The sexual politics of 'Calamity Jane' and 'Butch Cassidy and the Sundance Kid'. In S. Matheson (Ed.). *Love in Western film and television* (pp. 141–160). Palgrave Macmillan.
Polzer, E. R., Nixon, W. C., Dengah II, H. F., & Snodgrass, J. G. (2020). *Systematic methods for analyzing culture: A practical guide.* United Kingdom: Taylor & Francis.
Pullen, C. (2016). *Straight girls and queer guys: The hetero media gaze in film and television.* Edinburgh University Press.

Purushotma, R., & Jenkins, H. (2009). *Confronting the challenges of participatory culture: Media education for the 21st century*. United Kingdom: MIT Press.
Radin, M. J., & Sunder, M. (2004). The subject and object of commodification. *Legal Studies Research Paper*, (16).
Rantanen, T. (2005). *The media and globalization*. Sage.
Robinson, K. H., Davies, C., & Davies, B. (Eds.). (2012). *Queer and Subjugated Knowledges: generating subversive imaginaries*. Bentham Science Publishers.
Rossi, V. (1981). *The celluloid closet*. Harper & Row.
Sanchez, L., & Sweetman, M. K. (2019). Book review: Queering the countryside: New frontiers in rural queer studies. *Teaching Sociology 47*(1).
Santos, B. de S. (2014). *Epistemologies of the south: Justice against epistemicide*. London: Routledge.
Sedgwick, E. K. (1990). *Epistemology of the closet*. United Kingdom: University of California Press.
Sender, K. (2012). No hard feelings reflexivity and queer affect. In K. Ross (Ed.). *The handbook of gender, sex, and media* (p. 207). United Kingdom: Wiley.
Simmons, N. (2014). Speaking like a queen in RuPaul's Drag Race: Towards a speech code of American drag queens. *Sexuality & Culture, 18*(3), 630–648.
Singhal, A., & Vasanti, P. N. (2005). The role of popular narratives in stimulating the public discourse on HIV and AIDS: Bollywood's answer to Hollywood's Philadelphia. *South Asian Popular Culture, 3*(1), 3–15.
Slater, J., Jones, C., & Procter, L. (2018). School toilets: queer, disabled bodies and gendered lessons of embodiment. *Gender and Education, 30*(8), 951–965.
Sontag, S. (1964). Notes on 'Camp'. *Partisan Review, 31*(4), 515–530.
Su, K. (2019). Queering the 'global gay': How transnational LGBT language disrupts the global/local binary. LSE Blogs. Available at https://blogs.lse.ac.uk/gender/2019/06/20/queering-the-global-gay-how-transnational-lgbt-language-disrupts-the-global-local-binary/ Access 02 February 2020.
Tan, J. (2019). Networking Asia Pacific: queer film festivals and the spatiotemporal politics of inter-referencing. *Inter-Asia Cultural Studies, 20*(2), 204–219.
Visser, G. (2014). Urban tourism and the de-gaying of Cape Town's De Waterkant. *Urban Forum, 25*(4), 469–482. Springer Netherlands.
Zebracki, M., & Milani, T. M. (2017). Critical geographical queer semiotics. *ACME: An International Journal for Critical Geographies, 16*(3), 427–439.
Ward, E. (2008). *Respectably queer: Diversity culture in LGBT organizations*. Nashville: Vanderbilt University Press.
Weiner, J. J., & Young, D. (2011). Introduction: queer bonds. *GLQ: A Journal of Lesbian and Gay Studies, 17*(2–3), 223–241.

Chapter 1

COMMODIFYING QUEER CULTURE

Whenever in this city, screens flicker
With pornography, with science-fiction vampires,
Victimized hirelings bending to the lash,
We have to walk ... if simply as we walk
Through the rainsoaked garbage, the tabloid cruelties
Of our own neighborhoods.
We need to grasp our lives inseparable
From those rancid reams, that blurt of metal, those disgraces,
And the red begonia perilously flashing
From a tenement sill six stories high,
Or the long-legged young girls playing ball
In the junior high school playground.
No one has imagined us. We want to live like trees,
Sycamores blazing through the sulfuric air,
Dappled with scar, still exuberantly budding,
Our animal passion rooted in the city
— Adrienne Rich, *The Dream of a Common Language*, I

The introduction has laid out all the book's main lines of inquiry: global and local aspects essential for understanding queer popular media and culture in contemporaneity. I approached the old problem of knowledge on queer culture vis-à-vis the significant development of means to learn about it. I argued that modern times had seen a growth in queer media production, leading to a cycle of spread and rejection of queer values, mainly due to commercialization and globalization. This chapter deepens this position by exploring legacy research that has warned on the ambiguities of globalizing queerness. As queer culture becomes increasingly visible, this success has been less problematized against notions of community, ethnic or political undertones it may have among local audiences. As we shall see, on the one hand, media industries sell queerness in the same shape of well-cut products and sensationalizing shows. On the other, this mix-up has never been so queer: the stir of local epistemologies and the heteronormative ones can easily have the buy-in from queer audiences from distinct backgrounds.

The problem here lies in the *authentication* of queerness as a media enterprise. *Queer* has inspired streaming playlists, TV series, and other acts. However, queer as a multibillion-dollar industry is not interested in being the unclassifiable or norm challenger. One can argue that by multiplying the means of eliciting queerness, one puts it behind commercial barriers. The captive queerness demands questions about its challenges, mainly addressed to the prominent industries that propel it. As I mentioned in the introduction, the unmaking of modern queerness consists of deconstructing its forms of commercial distribution. If it took decades to arrive at a scenario of moderate acceptance of queerness in mainstream society, globalizing could quickly affect people's learning about fluidity and the right to subjectivity. I propose three fronts to unpack the globalization of queerness and point to the scenario of investigation that has based this book.

First, the debate on the locality of queer culture is reconnected to the critique of modern sexualities that stems from Foucauldian ideas of genealogy. I do this by repurposing *genealogy* into *genealogizing*. That means restoring the queer commodity to three levels of relevance: the community, the nation, and, ultimately, the culture. More than erecting fences or seeing queer acts performed in farmlands or rural settings, localizing queerness is to make queerness open, mutable and different everywhere. It ensures its quintessential spontaneity and chaotic transformability. Second, notions of *authenticity* and *sincerity* assist in deconstructing the vagueness around visions of queer as a permanent blurring of reality or evading normativity. Authenticity lies in issues of agency and autonomy that emerge from media practitioners. It embeds in the way audiences conceive popular artists and their artistic persona. Third, the last section settles restoring *localization* of queer artists by surveying actors that have somewhat dodged the market logic and remained true to their communities. As a framework for studying globalizing queerness, this threefold analysis thus seeks to reinterpret queer appearances, whether resisting or accelerating queer commodification, as we see next.

The community, the nation, and the culture: In search of queer territories

Many questions can be posed about what queer belonging means, primarily if directed to queer artists and media producers. Where are they? Jargons such as LGBTQ community or Trans Lobby may have helped notions of unity and power, but also helped to feed harmful tropes based on reductionist readings. They can drag the political movement behind gender and sexuality acceptance into a niche existence that does not ring true to the size and blended presence of queers in society. The heterosexual society, otherwise, continues to frame itself with terms associated with the nation, as far as queerness, to a large extent, proposes a unified mode of existence, foreign and national, local and global. But should queers leave the nation, the fatherland, behind?

The primordial question of location remains in queer thought the one of 'being *in or out* of the closet'. In effect, location has remained critical for evading persecution and stigmatization. One needed a place to belong in the community or to defend oneself from aggression or miscategorization. It has been a thorough physical or epistemological struggle. As Carol Warren (1974) argued about gay environments: 'Gay inner time and gay interaction are protected from the invasion of outsiders by other kinds of walls: the refusal of entry to strangers, the concealment of gay bar entrances, and the palpable change that happens in a gay crowd on the entry of straights.' Seidman (1991) criticized the epistemological barriers that come with affirmative identity. A 'postmodern anxiety', according to him.

From the state and its institutions, modern queers retrieve many notions of location. It is the nation-state that hosts queer refugees or proceeds to examine them for that matter; a country's parliament drafts the laws that must include millions in decades. The state has also created the legal apparatus or the socioeconomic conditions to allow queer media industries to thrive within legal or social frameworks that are still up for criticism today. As both the haven for queer refugees escaping hostile societies (Munro, 2012; Raboin, 2013) and the heterosexual territory in which queers fail to integrate (Smith, 2010), the limits of this national accommodation of queerness are less understood. Instead, the use by the state of queerness in its propaganda has sounded the alarms, as the case of Israel suggests. To many national audiences, though, having *their* queers abroad still represents a shameful fact, a threat (Kamenou, 2012), such is the case of recent Poland (Kulpa, 2013).

Facing the nation as an incubator for popular culture makes another pathway to see queer territories. It is indubitable that queer passions are usually framed according to national institutions: The gay romance in the American army has become a popular narrative (Caserio, 1997). On television, queerness has often clashed with rigorous standards of broadcasting, morality, and, more recently, the urge for diversity. Baker

(2017) saw the 2014 Eurovision Song Contest, won by Austrian drag queen Conchita Wurst, as playing into the 'politics of LGBT and European belonging', in which goals were to project the image of gay friendliness over the countries of the bloc. Transgender singer Dana International won the 1998 award on behalf of Israel (Gross, 2014).

While the queer's own country triggers discussions of power, pinkwashing, and politics of acceptance/rejection, local cultures, wherever they may be, inform a more positive, less institutionalized form of blending. In China, lesbian networks of resistance formed through Taoism, folklore, and working-class solidarity (Zhao & Wong, 2020). The Filipino queer *aswang* depictions thrive on different media platforms (Lim, 2015). The queering of the French language among the youngest generations is a reality (Provencher, 2016). These few examples shed light on many others that exist but fail to fit mechanisms of national inclusion. The biggest challenge remains not relative to the national borders, at least for the majority, but one that constantly returns to the city and the urban bias of queer politics.

The persisting *metro-normative* flattening of queer belonging raises a lot of suspicion about what kinds of partnerships are made and where these actors are based. The mechanisms that spread queerness through the media have transfixed almost all resistance by selling themselves as the only possibility of divergence. Hence, the modern façade of contemporary queer culture is mainly written in English and adorned with West-based superstars. Queer media producers, perhaps unwittingly, work as interlocutors to the minds and the eyes of the metropolis, which begs the question of how possible or impossible it is to be queer in other realms of belonging, as a few studies have exposed such contradictions (Bell & Valentine, 1995; MacArthur, 2018). The critique of the metropolitan queer in the media slowly shifts from its emphasis on space, the size of the spaces available, to posit the quality of such locus. Featured in series such as *Sex in the City*, being talk show hosts, or becoming friends with celebrities, the same set of characters and idioms, either real or fictional, stabilizes queer appearances as a kind of fixture. Queer folklore, or the queerness that embeds old forms of expression, is rendered unsuitable if not adaptable to appear on modern media outlets and replenish such audience expectations (Bravmann, 1997).

In that scenario, neither the community nor the nation or the metropolitan culture works to lodge queer individuals without imposing commercialization as a condition. The wholesale of the broadest and biggest stages to queer spectacles nowadays follows the workflow of public policies (pink-washed, media mogul-sponsored), think-thanks, and modernization ideas. While minor acts try to survive under the most unpredictable circumstances (university halls, rural clubs, historically homophobic territories, radical and outlawed spaces), market institutions privilege the *gay niche* as a large string of middle-class viewers, forming an imagined queer unanimity. The advent of *gay villages* and similar enterprises have already led to many cases of removals and gentrification of the urban fabric (Knopp, 1990; Hess, 2019). Advertising profits from market research have profiled gays since early on (Bowes, 1996; Fejes & Lennon, 2000), either for tourism (Hughes, 2005) to surrogacy (Jacobson, 2018) or to feed a normalized sense of community (Richardson, 2005; Lewis, 2017). It invents the presence of the 'bear' in gay representations and forges the acceptance of 'bareback' sex (Mercer, 2017), or dresses pornography as culture (Maddison, 2013; McNair, 2013).

In a nutshell, the entire landscape of making queer commodities has benefited from queer national epistemologies. This repertoire eventually becomes part of an urban bias of queer culture, largely based in America. *Globalized queerness* is, therefore, this continuum between the commodification of the city and the community as the utmost colonization of the *culture*. To contemplate the localization of queer culture, one must delve into conceptual alternatives more seriously. The following section tries to dig in for an alternative genealogy. Not the genealogy of sexuality, a buzzword in queer studies, but the genealogies of the queer commodity. This Foucauldian, post-structuralist concept is arguably overused in queer theory. Still, it yields good points for thought if one can employ more effort in its discontinuities and in understanding power struggles.

Genealogizing queer commodities

As Michel Foucault contended (1976:61), the actual transformation of sex over time consisted of a gradual but helpless transformation into discourse. To study genealogies of queerness is, likewise, to question this rendering from homosexual, gay, lesbian, trans into queer, its inevitable detachment of sex and approach to product. Foucault's famous proposition that there is a repressive theory to be revisited, i.e., the construction of sex from a freed practice into a forbidden one, inspires a similar analysis of how globalized queerness could, potentially, divert the unauthorized and subversive queer into happy, but authorized *queerness*. Before and after mass media, organized queers have seen silence as the *last thing we need*. The following developments, nevertheless, have seen the license to exploit queerness without the queer. From expensive bags flying in East Village, New York, to Harry Styles' straight-being-gay queerness. To a large extent, the notion of genealogy injects some rationale into the constant naming, renaming, and enacting of queer popular culture vis-à-vis the current logistics of media representation.

Of course, there can be no reliable historical account of commodity queer. Yet, a few elements assist in examining the ontological properties of queer theory that have eased the conditions to market queerness. It is worth reminding that the studies of other genealogies have informed queer studies in feminist, gay liberation, psychoanalytic, and queer desire branches (e.g., Turner, 2000). Turning the page, genealogy can still challenge the assumption that queer commodities always mirror the truth in society. More recently, postcolonial accounts have re-contextualized the presence of exploited bodies in local cultures to find divergence concerning where they always lived and thrived (Romanow, 2009; Chiang, 2013). While not entrenched in postcolonial critique, this de-naturalization of queer commodity helps by recognizing that the Western 'queering' of facts and characters may often sound alien to genuine indigenous knowledge on queerness. And yet, the Western queering is the one to sell products worldwide (Alexander, 2008). Moreover, queer disability and deviant queer remain silenced at best and, at worst, bound to frame individuals only through their oppression and, therefore, continuously part of the commodity cycle (McCormack, 2018; Jones, 2020).

In this panorama, genealogies of queer commodities can revisit the introducing and re-introducing of world-imported images and characters. It should be conditioned to the post-materialistic order it inserts itself in everyday life. Butler's (Butler, 2011) influential idea of queer as the uprooting of labels and normative identities has essentially paved the way for the reconstitution of queer subjects based on new terms, ideally one of queer individuals' own making. But to what extent isn't this blurring of boundaries in the 21st century the legitimization of the forces of consumerism needed, for example? Indeed, in the books, the study of genealogies has certainly missed several discontinuities between queer and heterosexual societies and within queer societies as well. In the legendary documentary, *Paris is Burning* (1990), directed by Jennie Livingston, most participants of the legendary New York balls depicted were originally from the city's periphery. In many parts of the documentary, the inspiration voiced comes from American-made dreams, and commodities come to the fore, as some interviewees tell (my italics):

> The ball to us is as close to reality as we are going to get to all of that *fame, fortune, stardom, and spotlight*.
> (4'42")

> I used to see the way that rich people live, and I feel it more ... you know ... I used to slap me in the face and say: 'I have to have that.' Because I never felt comfortable being poor. Even middle class doesn't suit me. Seeing the rich is seeing the way people in *Dynasty* lived. These huge houses! (...)
> (4'47")

To study the genealogy of the queer commodity is to summon all these references and track the affordances and miss-outs. Many studies have precluded factors such as popular culture, nation, and heritage as oppressive and contrary to a rather conventional ideal of queer community and solidarity. In the documentary's case, the wealth and power displayed in TV series, more blatantly visible in a city such as New York, still pertains to American queer as one can get it. The problem is the whiteness of this wealth which, at the same time, oppresses and excludes ball attendees even though exclusion created a plethora of brilliant representations.

In the 21st century, these values of wealth boasting have not only been implanted into queer culture of all ethnicities and social classes but are also constantly revived in popular discourse. Taking American series, for example, there has been much less discussion on how economically poor queers are or, better framing it, most queer discourse after the 2000s has been founded on wealth and privilege. In 'pink dollars, white collars', Peters (2011) fleshed out the fabric of queer affluence in *Queer as Folk*, interspersed with a culture of exclusion of gays and lesbians who are less able to afford what TV shows deem as the basics for being queer. This early naturalization of gays as turned by default into white, wealthy, well-educated, has left a footprint that, arguably, made easier the *normalization* of gay rights as material and institutional rights, on the one hand. It might have made it more difficult to prove and legitimize other intersections of queer existence on the other.

The appreciation of globalized queerness does not necessarily lie in being adamant about the glories of queer entrepreneurship (nor the 200,000 dollars awarded to the winner of *RuPaul's Drag Race*). Queer entrepreneurship has been, in reality, much less acknowledged or understood outside the shape of excellent cultural forms. Maddison (2013) charted some signs of gay entrepreneurship as akin to an exercise of affection and desire, which also contains a political expression. In other words, it can be favourable to the extent that it takes alongside the values and contradictions of many communities. The issue with globalized queerness is that it *contains* inequality. Irreparably interwoven in brands and paid Instagram postings, modern showcases of replicable queerness worldwide may never know or make any sense of deprivation as true or legitimate. The queer commodity is born from this negotiation between forms of the Impossible while denying other kinds of existence.

To genealogize queer commodity is, therefore, locating its origins back to the heart of liberation movements but detaching the product and the grand scene from a universe of unauthorized, unpaid, precarious stories of queer existence. It is seeing vocabulary as a cue for before and after media consumption. What can audiences know about queer communities beyond this frame in a world of aggressive and intrusive digital advertisement? Millions of dollars later, what is up for queer producers seeking any notion of thriving that does not depend on funding the same lifestyles? What has the recent platformization of queer culture represented to individual media producers? How about the selective nature of algorithmic censorship splitting good or bad queers? How about the media giants keen to sign deals that perpetuate queerness as a style devoid of political expression? Not all these questions belong in this book, but to debate commodification and decommodification is to somehow place alternatives of localization in the face of issues that silence any possible return to liberation.

Commodifying, de-commodifying, localizing

The close link between queer culture and processes of commodification has inspired numerous scholarly debates for decades (e.g., Hennessy, 1994; Radin & Sunder, 2005). Commodification is also seen through the prism of heteronormative stereotypes queer culture helps to perpetuate (Emig, 2000). Commodity queer has also thrived in the spaces it occupies, the time it allows for artists fitting certain standards, and the budget it allocates to some shows and not others. In other niche environments, like rap and hip-hop scenes, queer culture remains stigmatized, as gay, lesbian, trans and non-binaries imaginaries do not make to the genre's lyrics or aesthetics (Li, 2018). Queer guys have achieved greater prominence in circumstances that involved straight girls, whose appearances often mould light entertainment and permissiveness. The bottom line is one of heterosexual gaze to queer manners (Pullen, 2016). In popular culture, queer as this 'feminine other' played very well into patriarchal ideology (Basturk, 2016). Mediatized pride parades have seized upon encounters that purport to show harmony with the rest of society (de Jong, 2017), and so is the effect of mainstreaming televised drag races (Collins, 2017).

Amid this pessimistic scenario, a counter-effort has tried to assign positive features to queer popular culture. Most theses, in understanding commodification and decommodification, focus on linguistic, pedagogical, or behavioural fronts, in which *decolonization* is the most appropriate term. Hunt and Holmes (2015) saw 'everyday decolonisation' as the practice of acknowledging backgrounds and privileges towards chartering 'geographies of allyship'. Similar accounts see synergies directed at the realm of queer pedagogies (Smith, 2013), indigenous autonomy (Driskill et al., 2011), and promoting critiques from queers of colour (Salas-Santa Cruz, 2021), in which the black queer woman should assume a central role (Amin, 2020). All these concerted efforts have established determinations that are very much possible to achieve, either via community activities, meetings, councils, schools, and academia. However, these same struggles have arguably missed further consideration of how the mainstream media has also embarked on a mission to sell and, somehow, hijack this journey.

A subtle awareness of the hard work necessary to change queer media out of commodification has started to appear. Atay (2021) argues for networks that focus on transnational and decolonial accounts to disinvest from whitewashed queer finally. Oswin (2015) saw the city as the stage where queer lives can be effectively led towards open grounds of acceptance and decolonization. Bao (2020) instead mapped much cooperation in the global south, with grassroots groups organizing in China and Africa. Trans presence in sports has attracted broader attention, but so far, the topic has been, at best, exoticized and nowadays finds itself battling for space in cis-gendered competitions (Matthews, 2016). In the entertainment realm, less research covers fresh ways of localizing queerness on distinct terms. The *gay friend* or the *dying homosexual* are still common places exploited in the media. Fewer mentions relate to *everydayness* and the long history of LGBTQ+ populations.

Between silence and commodification, one can still learn from decades of queer media representations. For example, in deeply repressive environments, Western representational practices could have promoted undesired conversations about lesbian and gay communities (Hayes, 2000; Martel, 2013). Media commodities could add to the subversion of stereotypes of masculinity beyond the emphasis on lifestyles (Forrest, 1994; Bateman, 2005). Observing queer stereotypes can enlighten on paradoxical relationships, but is this also feeding marketization? Queer stereotypes that lead to heterosexual profit and audience growth could eventually boost universalization and positive knowledge. Decommodification, otherwise, while not entirely charted yet, has amounted to the prioritization of choice that stems from an LGBTQ audience. Decommodification would primarily consist of restoring role models for queer individuals without alienating them from the production and profiting from such images.

Bersani's (1987) controversial essay *Is the rectum a grave?*, published in the tragic context of AIDS, has the author pondering the implications for the gay self in a culture that privileges sex and entertainment. In *Homos* (Bersani, 1996) and later in an essay entitled *Gay Betrayals* (Bersani, 2010:13), the author expounds on the defeat of gay and queer cultures of modernity when trying to earn a place of their own as opposed to conforming with normalization. Instead of blurring gender divides as reinventing sexualities, queer folks have submitted to normalized alternatives, as he explains:

> Queer politics has been mainly a micropolitics focused on particular issues which there is no reason to believe will ever be exhausted if the fundamental types of community and relationality out of which such issues spring are not in themselves questioned and redefined.

Indeed, while some critique of Bersani's point applies directly to this book's argument, it is resonant, especially with the relatability of queerness today, which, in society, finds other forms of reasoning. For instance, the possibility of *de-gaying* or de-sexualizing queerness that would come as a result. In that case, commodification can also amount to this detaching of queer identities, seen as strictly sexual or asexual, repelling what is perceived as damaging toward mainstream society's sensitivities. Comparably, asexuality has appeared as an escape from gender performance, except if it is commodified and used for capitalist reinvention lifestyles (Vance, 2018). While analysing sexual identities in capitalism, Rosemary Hennessy (2017) outlined the structures of consumption of these sexualities. One of them transpires from social reproduction, which becomes a determinant for materialist approaches to love, resulting in such dissemination that becomes opposed to an original conception of solidarity and care. One way out from the fetishized commodity in its neoliberal facet consists of de-escalating the presence of these goods from the global mainstream.

In tandem with these ideas, I prefer to call *localizing* an attempt at dismantling queer commodities by apprehending their conditions of social reproduction. In 'recasting commodity', Gilbert and Gleghorn (2014) catalogued multiple indigenous initiatives that have reshaped their original condition of a commodity by remixing and transcending circulation cycles to increase awareness and access. Aligned to the Marxian notion of *exchange* value, the globalized queer commodity finds distinct and complementary orientations, but which do not end in benefits for queer people. In a world bursting with references, many attempts have sought to recast queer commodities as something accessible, democratic, and affordable. From commoditized gay cowboys (Nast, 2002) to *tango* as a non-heteronormative dance style (Savigliano, 2010), or the old Portuguese style, the *Fado*, which has transcended into *Fado Bicha* and later became a queer group (Da Silva, 2019). Conversely, the option to de-commodify via an extensive indigenous vocabulary seems the most viable option at this point. Not least because of the impenetrability of global cultural industries but also the prospects that the infinite imagination of queer producers can, one day, dry the systems out of its references (Kirsch, 2000).

In this way, it is more sensible to speak of a queer presence in popular culture that lacks local recognition than one that is not entirely commodified. The possibility of queerness in popular music (Parahoo, 2020) or queer interpretations for non-queer texts (Grossman, 2020) can take small-scale producers to many episodes of prominence and healthy profit. In such queer adventures, though, not all texts are meant to be globally understood as part of a mutually recognizable queer language. These texts may even lack the sensitivity to Western preferences in queer popular culture, and, therefore, stand far from the public savviness and global market orientation. In short, not all successful media products can be or will be *Queer Eye for the Straight Guy* (Lewis, 2007). Essentially, there are many queer eyes and many eyes that are not necessarily queer that do acquiesce to the heteronormative culture due to the lack of a more appropriate framework to receive them.

In queer *disidentifications*, Muñoz (1999) saw the upshot of frames that have kept queers of colour out of the main picture for a long time. It is not about rejecting political images that run outdated. Mainstream productions have, one way or the other, helped define the queer individual and somehow blazed the trail for many shows today (Edelman, 1998). Instead, the key to decommodification lies in leveraging more urgent images regarding local queer expression. In Latin America, popular music and cinema has long served to gather support against authoritarian forces and inequality (Shaw, 2013). In many cases, this influence from popular music inspired a mindset of social change across borders in a rule of regional solidarity (Palomino, 2020). In sum, these populations have regarded these local manifestations as utterly essential to their parlance and culture in a time of American expansionism.

This book aims to advance localizing queerness by leveraging an understanding of queer cultural goods beyond prominence, profit, and popularity. It does not happen as a miraculous form of transcendence from the excessively global to the authentically local. Between the commodity and the non-commodity exists a process of slow recognition and blending of local features founded in notions of sincerity and authenticity. As seen above, media producers and artists have invested lately in *globalizing* queerness to the extent that artists and media producers can, for example, sing in more than one language, promote co-nationals, or improvise in lyrics or rhythms of different countries. But to what extent can these products be deemed as fundamentally queer or only representations of *queerness* to suit audiences and investors? Before delving into other questions and materials of this book, I propose a last reflection on how notions of sincerity and authenticity can assist us in facing various queer dilemmas in contemporaneity. Not least, to see queer popular culture as a system of agencies and decisions rather than sheer spectacle. As I discuss next, the decolonization of queer culture is not a stand-alone process.

Sincerity, authenticity, and the queer commodity

One of the possible and yet under-explored efforts for drawing genealogies of queer commodities lies in the notions of sincerity and authenticity. Since the 1970s, queer films, documentaries, and activist media have benefited from deeply personal stories, people's trajectories and intimacies. It reinvents, mocks, and mixes the lines between truth and the ideal. 'I am strong enough', sang Cher in the iconic queer anthem of the late 1990s. 'I Will Survive', Gloria Gaynor's gay liberation song, prefigured myths of fight and survival. These are not only profoundly confessional songs, but these statements also excite queer spectators if taken wholeheartedly. Authentic as they can be, these lyrics have garnered genuine expectations. Despite their commodity aspect, in queer terms, these songs showcased values related to personal struggles, which are sincere in their reception.

As Maddison (2018) argued regarding the Internet, much anxiety goes unattested, even when gay performers or speakers seem to 'design life'. In the age of live-streamed acts, dubbed franchised shows, and mass slang replication, it is legitimate to enquire into queer commodities being genealogically and affectively tied to home-grown values, even under fake lyricism, mockery, or exaggeration. Let's take drag culture. One of the world-most famous queer artists of recent times, RuPaul Charles, has given very telling remarks about his background. In interviews with the mainstream press, Charles reflects on the many events that helped the concoction of his artistry and his way into the globalized stage persona. This passage from early life to the world of spectacle is mentioned as 'the new life':

> I enrolled in the Northside School of Performing Arts, and it changed everything for me. I really did find my tribe. I wasn't weighed down by what I was supposed to be in San Diego, by all the people who knew me there. I was free to create a new life for myself (...) I knew that I loved David Bowie, Diana Ross, Cher and James Brown. My first inclination was to just copy David Bowie. In my tribe in Atlanta, that was the common denominator. All us kids were devotees of David Bowie.
>
> Delaney, 2019

Later in the interview, Charles, already the famous drag queen and *VH1* TV host, vows at the other side. The global *RuPaul* acknowledges his [global] tribe while clearing the connections to the Atlanta times and his early self, while both selves fight at some point:

> It didn't feel like a burden. Because when I was 13 and made that pact with myself to never put myself in that box, I always felt like the *Boy Who Fell to Earth*. I was looking for others like me. I always thought my people were out there somewhere (...) A lot of what I had done before was because I wanted my father's attention and to be validated by him. Through therapy I realized, 'No, my motivation was to be that. It has to be laughter, colors, music, dancing, beauty, love — all of the things that make life worth living.'
>
> ibid.

Importantly, Charles also puts his characters as this continuum between global and the local selves:

> That's what I've done, but never once thinking, 'Oh, that is me'. It's a part of me, but the me is still that introvert who is masquerading as an extrovert. I feel very comfortable with that.
>
> ibid.

The fact that such an influential star as RuPaul Charles can openly discuss this confluence between the native self: the introvert and impressionable boy, and the later self: the extrovert and mighty blond, black, and queer, means a lot to this genealogy of queer commodity. His acknowledgement of himself as a constructed self, the latter coming through entirely from television stars, place the distinction between the local and global very apparent. All of Charles' quotes were known in America and the whole Hollywood-watching world. This way of *confessing* one previous or past lives of queer performers leaves the spectator or RuPaul's follower facing sincerity as an utterly critical value to understanding queer trajectories in popular culture.

Indeed, queer artists have increasingly explored such a position. In literature, queer writers exercise the same ability to revisit memory and use it as their raw material while distancing themselves from it. In the last decade, both Abdellah Taïa and Edouard Louis have become well-known Francophone writers bearing stories of survival as gays living in small towns or repressive countries. Taïa is from Salé, Morocco, and Louis is from Picardy, France. In both writers' works, their experiences and early images have made their writing instantly recognizable to the public. The discourse of persecution, but also affectivity about the places they grew up in and the discovery of their sexuality, embeds their existence as artists and public characters. Writing is an exercise to localize their presence, but their later emergence as prominent writers binds their escape not only as a runaway act but from anonymity and, to a certain extent, from any possibility of intimacy or belonging.

In his work about sincerity and authenticity, Lionel Trilling (1971) paid much attention to sincerity as this 'congruence between avowal and actual feeling' (Trilling, 1971:2). Trilling's observations may lie miles away from queer sensitivities. Still, it rightfully places this Rousseau-esque sincerity in *confessing* something that accessorizes one's current identity. Trilling's main distinction between sincerity and authenticity is that the former equates the truth to others, while the latter is about being true to oneself. In the case of queer culture, sincerity can relate to being true to the public, other artists, celebrities, and vlogs through many forms of confessions. From risky admissions such as leaving the closet to recent TikTok-like baroque queer: all become confession. Sincerity materializes in replicating fresh trends, viral performances, and new gender breakthroughs (Fernández Carbajal, 2021). The 'others', as a result, prompt one's return to authentically queer. Although queer politics have been making a case for the anti-authentic queer for a long time, globalized queerness has meant having the security to live, consume, and fight for affirmation through the connection to this sincere self.

When it comes to culture, the authenticity discussion has had many other undertones. At the same time, the expectation of authenticity from the artist's side stems from multiple artistic, cultural, and capitalist sides. Trilling (1971) summed up the challenges of the authentic self as one of not being everybody:

> The commonplace belongs to everybody, and it belongs to me; in me, it belongs to everybody; it is the presence of everybody in me.

To better explain it, Trilling then cites the case of Madame Bovary, the French woman who cheats on her modest husband in search of the high life, by Edouard Flaubert:

> The Hell that was the commonplace of Yonville, enters the Hell that was the commonplace of the high culture of her nation.
>
> p. 71

The 'queer' gaze of Madame Bovary over the male body (McCollum, 2014) is not part of Trilling's exploration, so he suggests it regarding the 19th century's Oscar Wilde. The latter's challenges against societal masks appear in George Eliot's 'mercurial and improvisational' mood (p. 121). Flaubert and many anglophone authors a century later attempted a gender crossover, but which remained *locally* queer. The bottom line lies in the two levels of sincerity and authenticity vis-à-vis one keeps to themselves or the world: Very confessional and timid on a personal note, and very loud and controversial to the rest: a collection of authentic proofs offered to society. Both levels of truth are found in this book's actors and media producers, as we shall see in Chapters 4 and 5.

The case for sincerity and authenticity in queer culture also offers room for debate on commodification. Based on what Raymond Williams (2013) argued about the state of culture, the fear of being inauthentic has its capitalist roots. The authentic is expensive, inaccessible, and inappropriate for most people. In music, for example, queer sincerity has emerged from the roles assigned to queer practitioners at their time. From the mythical figure of the *castrato* (Wilbourne, 2013) to the 'pseudo-nostalgia' of the Americana style (Goldin-Perschbacher, 2018), these examples prefigure this expectation of being here and there as being with products. Lately, debates around the truth in trans voices are recurrent, whether the right to be trans pertains to any guarantee or legitimacy to medically transitioning (Pennington, 2019). In its most visible, queer appearances on reality TV have also produced a spectrum of personalities that are only to confirm stereotypes (Lovelock, 2019). Authenticity as unaffordable uniqueness has yet inspired debates on the culture of beauty on Instagram, in which the *post-queer*, that is, the peaceful rest on top of diverse and interchangeable identities and sexualities, becomes trapped in a hole of standards, filters, and layers of body performativity among gay males (Chen & Kanai, 2021).

A third way of seeing authenticity lies in Simone de Beauvoir's ideas of a *genuine man*. Drawing on feminist critiques of society is a win-win game for queer studies. It enriches the possibility of coalition thinking and bridges thoughts from non-normative ways of conceiving life. De Beauvoir has also not thought directly about the experience of gender that destabilized her womanhood as a straight, cisgender female. Yet, she has worked on examples of structural oppression regarding acquiring freedom through authenticity. For example, the life of Saint Teresa of Avila (1515–1582) is one of an authentic mystic because of her fierce agency toward thinking by herself and allowing others to do so (Cleary, 2022). Avila can encapsulate much queerness with her visions of angelical penetration and unconfirmed ardour for her faith. I stick to de Beauvoir's work on authenticity or genuineness as the critical existentialist component that supplies life with making sense of imperfection and silence. She argued in *The Ethics of Ambiguity* about the usefulness of *lacking* things in life. Debating the genuine man and his quest for being authentic before God, de Beauvoir says:

> He will understand that it is not a matter of being right in the eyes of a God, but of being right in his own eyes. Renouncing the thought of seeking the guarantee for his existence outside of himself, he will also refuse to believe in unconditioned values which would set themselves up athwart his freedom like things. Value is this lacking-being of which freedom makes itself a lack; and it is because the latter makes

itself a lack that value appears. It is desire which creates the desirable, and the project which sets up the end.

de Beauvoir, 2018:33

The display of queer authenticity and sincerity depends on these multiple modes of confession increasingly available in new media. This interplay between the authentic, home-grown, *everybody knows that he/she is*, or that *he/she/they are queer* to encase the ambiguities of being queer contrasts with castings, contracts, and other certainties of the mainstream media making. From Trilling, Williams, and de Beauvoir, one learns that authenticity and sincerity point to confessing and performing but demonstrating agency. In this book, globalized queerness can appear as channelling, instead, inauthenticity as a weakness of agency and thinking. RuPaul's early life as an adorer of all things television shows a unique space of personal experimentation that, no surprise, gets globalized and conquered by lucrative media industries. The sincere but inauthentic embrace of the global capitalist authenticity enterprise. The case of Caitlyn Jenner being outed as a transwoman on the cover of Vanity Fair, photographed by prestigious lesbian Anne Leibovitz, leads to assumptions that she *needed* Vogue, such a prestigious publication, as much as the magazine needed her, in her *authentic* identity, hidden for decades within herself.

That being the case, sincerity and authenticity are encased in *confessional* materials that belong in the spectrum of the global queer media. Secondly, sincerity and authenticity occur beyond queer actors' control but depend on profitable media circumstances. Finally, *genealogizing* commodity queer seeks regimes of sincerity, authenticity, and capitalism that turn globalized queerness into viable and desirable. If, in the present, brands might colonize the quest for authenticity in pursuit of profit (Södergren & Vallström, 2021), media producers fall short of finding their way out of commodity due to their lack of awareness. Beyond commodity, queer media and culture could work as resources for 'identifying today's emotional cultures' (McCarthy, 2016), developing independence and suspicion regarding globalized realities. As we shall see in the following four chapters, much data favours analysing the constant media flow of confessions, proofs of authenticity, and antinomian statements of freedom in queer discourses. The current queer media ecology otherwise lacks the language, images, and historical or political values that could forebode the closure of queerness into such regimes of commodification. Next, I end this chapter by discussing strategies that made this investigation into queer commodities feasible.

Surveying local and global aspects in queer commodities

In dialogue with all the points expounded above, the book targets a spectrum of global and local references that illustrate the expansion of queer media and culture worldwide. By fixating on traditional media platforms and the Internet, this study has perused available materials that evidence the impact of globalized queerness on forms of sincerity, authenticity, commodification, and decommodification. Queer media producers and artists can be brilliant memorialists; they drop cues of their past or treat it as performatively as if they were mere visitors of their local self. When examining the existence of queer roots in a diaspora, Jarrod Hayes (2016) has pointed to some diasporic discourses that stabilise individual identities around a common origin. In line with that approach, this book seeks to destabilize the same discourse of queer roots that breaks with or remakes any possible relationship with the past, as the author states: 'Conversely, the notion of roots has allowed several lesbian and gay writers to establish a connection to their "forebears hidden from history" (...) What would a queer family tree look like?'

To investigate globalized queerness is to inquire into multiple dilemmas of belonging too. Price (2015) has used Christopher Isherwood's books to argue about queer attachments and detachments from history or the world surrounding them. Even seeing globalization as a 'residual' influence from broader culture onto queer culture, Price claims that the existence of positivity toward the world is what others have seen as decadence only. Queer artists can engage with these systems of social or philosophical belonging, even if just marginally known. Hong (2013:150) saw a continuum between bathhouses and movie houses as shared queer spaces in the films of the Chinese director Tsai Ming-Liang. This aesthetic, the author contends, rests much in line with Roland Barthes' poetics of cruising, which problematized queer practices in France, believed to exist only in the West.

In time, this continuum with the East puts the queer universe of 'seeing and being seen' concurrently with local subtleties and the *genealogist* perspective discussed earlier. In practice, this book translates these insights into seeing discourses of belonging on larger platforms, touring confluence areas in queer media and recognizing 'gaps' between global and local queerness. This discussion links to the genealogical aims also because it considers our (mine and the readers') views about where lies queer sincerity and authenticity in these emotional testaments. This material is to be located not in grand statements, ads, or world tours but in short visits to blind spots, word mentions, topics, and opinions voiced in interviews. After all, as we shall see, there is an imminent discussion on belonging to be taken that stems directly from artists' views and will to acknowledge these roots. This analysis' final goal is to verify the extent to which local queer selves can destabilize commodity culture or confirm its pattern of uprooting.

This effort of mixing and remixing ancestry as a cultural currency opens many opportunities to interpret queer production of the last decades. Matt Bernstein Sycamore, a.k.a. Mattilda Bernstein Sycamore (2008), organized a series of essays called *That's Revolting*, in which queer authors challenged comfort zones of dialogue with heteronormative society by putting up with ideas that went against the grain. For instance, *Dr Laura, Sit on My Face* or *Legalized Sodomy is Politically Legalized* are some of the titles that transformed political goals of acceptance into outright humour. While these were excellent ideas to play with, there is also an idea of the transgression of titles such as *Dr Laura* or the word 'legalized', which recalls forms of institutional membership and approval for the universe of gay porn. Another example of queer infiltration into global recognition happens in the black rap or hip-hop scene. Whenever a musician raps about sexual liberation struggles, they can also speak about stressful episodes of queer liberation, for example (Li, 2018). Both streams portray the lack of visibility as feedback that lies beyond parody. Here, the possibility of returning home is placed against these anti-queer realities, namely, the legalized political game and male gaze traditions.

Again, the solution to this impasse is seeing *localized queerness* as a repertoire tool that allows for expression, references, and nostalgia. It is, more notoriously, carried upon by fine queer productions and user-generated content. Eventually, queer artists and media producers generate the terms through which they design new attachments that do not necessarily conform with the nation, the city, and the community. When juxtaposed with commodified names, local expressions problematize the commodity cycle because they can derail the expectation of replicability and certainty about actors. In this book, the proposal is to investigate these new possibilities for the queer commodity within the milieu of cultural industries, including outputs such as books, films, and TV in addition to Internet-based productions as markers of *local culture* that springs from within LGBTQ+ communities.

These and other examples will show that an enormous part of the scholarship on queer cultural production has stayed at the ontological consequences of *destabilizing* hetero-centric narratives or penetrating cultural realms such as rap or cinema. Another stake of literature focuses on other nuances of queer disenfranchisements, such as the absence of history and the re-conquest of autonomy and authorship. This book articulates both branches by listing various cultural geographies, including those based on the Global South, in line with conventional ways of conceiving queerness based on Western historical settings and events. This method takes us to a collection of cases, meaning the intersection of cultural, national, ethnic, religious, and regional appearances and many forms of heritage.

The crux of a repertoire cut goes across nations and cultures to bring knowledge from several cultural insiders and cultural outsiders in need of recognition (Browne & Nash, 2016). Here, this repertoire arises from the knowledge materialized in their artworks, media products, interviews, reviews, and artistic vision. The book prioritizes discourse and cultural analysis methods focused on reconstructing repertoires to investigate artistic intention (Wetherell & Potter, 1987). It allows for isolating as well as categorizing mentions of many kinds. For example, contemporary queer artists such as drag queen Pabllo Vittar and French singer Christine and the Queens, whom I discuss in Chapter 3, have blurred the boundaries of language, nationality, and culture. These artists have been featured in mainstream magazines such as Vogue and have achieved recognition in the mainstream. Still, their repertoire stems from a broader intent of bringing back their local cultures while staying loyal to the aesthetic and cultural elements of their upbringing.

With that in mind, this research has used queer repertoire from many loci worldwide. Research departed from queer appearances both in English and in one of the languages spoken in the following countries: the US, Japan, China (Simplified Chinese), Germany, the United Kingdom, France, Brazil, South Korea, Canada, and Italy. These countries encase the world's largest media markets according to surveys from PriceWaterhouseCoopers (PWC, 2017, 2021). Regardless of the actual weight of these countries in the world's media, these nations have represented a fair supply of linguistic and cultural diversity. Moreover, conjugating qualitative and quantitative research methods has served multiple purposes here. Firstly, it reaches queer culture in different circumstances while covering several generations. Secondly, it informs the circulation of queer media and culture. One that prioritizes cultural products and artefacts circulating freely across wealthier markets. Hence, this list challenges many realities in places with fewer restrictions and those with firewalls against LGBTQ content, such as China. Others that are not strange to queer commodities, such as European countries, still pose questions about affordance and language divides. The potential for translations and the possibility of accessing original and translated versions of the material was another point of interest in this exploration.

On the other hand, this book's approach does not evade the phenomenological search for queer fluidity and reinvention. In some instances, it centres on the materiality of *queerness* as expressed in the heavily quantified realm of social media and the Internet. The number of occurrences and appearances in queer culture does not inform the quality of these mentions of globality or locality. Still, it helps understand the meanders of conversations in podcasts, videos, and social media postings. To quantify these occurrences is essential to uncover forms of queer expression according to the same criteria the market looks at them. That includes user-generated content, YouTube videos, artist interviews, and TV or streaming scripted series. Furthermore, incursions in queer culture by heterosexual celebrities, so common in large media markets, can yet be a marker for the boundaries of queer culture and the whole process of commodification discussed earlier.

This sample election is not without its limitations and problems. The measure of any media market will fail as it can vary by aspects such as the salience among diverse publics. The degree to which that population is connected or not to the Internet and not censored or put behind firewalls, such as in the case of China, determines the degree of success obtained here. For this book's illustrative purposes, it suffices to get a glimpse of popular culture in its most accessible and reproducible way. This effort may still stay miles away from the local queer culture at its unmediated aspects and inaccessible formats. However, it still appears in para-texts, online comments and mentions by well-known queer artists, featuring on queer festivals, and smaller scenes coming in the last chapters.

Rather than the exhaustiveness of acts, languages, and cultures, the sincere and confessional appearances of queer actors will naturally be probed against audience reaction and producer longevity. This insight seeks to study cultural contributions and artworks that can also be based on their artistic merits and recognized in heterosexual society. Nonetheless, it is not only possible to depend on the latter; therefore, single acts of confession or unique moments of creative performance can generate a combination of the genuineness and relevance of the questions raised in the research. The sample's breadth ultimately resulted in over 500 pieces of news, commentary, and interviews by queer artists, comprising written or recorded profiles, reviews, retrospectives, visiting artists, and commercial and experimental queer acts.

Once all this repertoire was surveyed, catalogued, and coded, notes were split according to chapters that privileged their format and specificities. *Global, local,* or, *glocal* were the main criteria of coding. The main challenge comprised queer appearances as a range of non-visible strategies to reach prominence, such as publicity stunts and paid ads disguised as news. Some buffer of time has been allowed for the cases in which queer acts have not yet reflected either case of globalization or localization or even have not lived up to their artistic potential. This reason explains the preference for less recent acts to give the necessary space for critique. Moreover, studying queerness demands being conscious of a character's alterity and allowing time for this conscious bypassing of current artistic or cultural references. When discussing *gay bonds*, Weiner and Young (2011) mentioned zones of self-exemption from 'homophobic regimes of knowledge and normalization'. Taking these ideas forward, the analysis will happen when artists self-exempt from or immerse in questions about their background, that is, when media appearances relate directly to themselves, their past, or their *true* person.

Furthermore, as I discuss in Chapter 5, the idea of prominence sums up expectations voiced or assumed on any social or mainstream media coverage level. Prominence can also establish an assessment of how actors' interventions, music lyrics, or cultural output can create a sense of pride in those who stay behind (Latané, 1996). According to this idea, individuals are held accountable for their influence on each other. It could be argued that popular culture is about tacit aspects of an actor's appearance and discourse. The embeddedness of these local or global references relates to the degree to which one tracks down local features in their repertoire. The notion of 'weight' in this influence is verified through the upstream from the user/consumer level back to these actors, as well as expressed on the multiplicity of other forms of publicity, i.e., YouTube comments, fans' comments on social networks, and presence in events.

To finalize this discussion, this conceptual package was designed to cover *commodifying, de-commodifying,* and *localizing* based on the intersection of sincere or authentic values and the genealogical possibilities of queer commodities. It sets queer popular culture and media as sheer characterizations of one's artistry, outspokenness, parody, and spectacle. Cultural actors emerge as practitioners, artists, media producers, and influencers. Sources to them are included, comprising academic and non-academic citations. Several volumes that list queer appearances have had similar criteria in their treatment of popular culture (e.g., Gerstner, 2006; Lovelock, 2019). Popular culture remains a fluid advent that pertains to many publics and expectations. It covers a vast amalgam of productions that only exist on the web as the latter becomes increasingly relevant. As covered in the following chapters, the main realms are the news, pop culture (e.g., music, TV, film), YouTube, and social media. These realms have been carefully picked upon based on the fluency of queer culture in them, as well as the possibility to approach both inherited narratives on queer individuals and self-made content that covers inbred, even if highly capitalized, interests of LGBTQ+ communities.

Conclusion

This chapter has given the reader a logical sequence for approaching queer popular culture through the prism of the commodifying processes that boost globalized queerness. In the Introduction, I first delimited what can be considered local in the global queer culture based on multiple platforms and the growing capitalization of queer cultures. Then, the discussion flew into highlighting a set of queer loci where the sell-off of identities and queer media products takes place, including the community, the nation, and the city. It is argued that commodifying and de-commodifying queer media has composed a nuanced scenario of compliances to and disruptions of global media industries, the display of local values, and rooted feelings of belonging. Later, the idea of genealogies of queer commodities draws on Foucauldian heritage to amplify its quest to track commodity cycles and what informs them. Raymond Williams' commodification as capitalist reinvention and de Beauvoir's ideas of authenticity as an agency inspires future analyses. The case of RuPaul Charles, pre and post-celebrity, illustrates the dynamics between locality or globality that encompasses fame and successful media businesses with sincerity and authenticity debates. The chapter ends by probing notions of sincerity and authenticity into values that queer media have articulated, which can be honest and capitalized, but also affective and transformative to varying degrees. Next, I start presenting a survey into queer news.

References

Alexander, B. K. (2008). Queer(y)ing the postcolonial through the West (ern). *Handbook of critical and indigenous methodologies*, 101–133. London: Sage.

Amin, K. (2020). Genealogies of Queer Theory. In S. B. Somerville (Ed.). *The Cambridge companion to queer studies* (pp. 17-29). Cambridge University Press.

Atay, A. (2021). Transnational and decolonizing queer digital/quick media and cyberculture studies. *Communication and Critical/Cultural Studies, 18*(2), 183-189.

Bao, H. (2020). The queer Global South: Transnational video activism between China and Africa. *Global Media and China, 5*(3), 294-318.

Baker, C. (2017). The 'gay Olympics'? The Eurovision song contest and the politics of LGBT/European belonging. *European Journal of International Relations, 23*(1), 97-121.

Baştürk, T. S. (2016). *What a drag? Popular culture and the commodification of 'Feminine'-other bodies.* Diss. Bilkent University, 2016.

Bateman, R. B. (2005). What do gay men desire? Peering behind the queer eye. In J. R. Keller & L. Stratyner (Eds.). *The new queer aesthetic on television: Essays on recent programming* (pp. 9-19). United Kingdom: McFarland.

Bell, D., & Valentine, G. (1995). Queer country: Rural lesbian and gay lives. *Journal of Rural Studies, 11*(2), 113-122.

Bersani, L. (1987). Is the Rectum a Grave? *October, 43*, 197-222. doi:10.2307/3397574

Bersani, L. (1996). *Homos.* Harvard University Press.

Bersani, L. (2010). Gay Betrayals. In H. Quinlan & R. Hastings (Eds.), *Two words.* Afterall Books.

Bowes, J. E. (1996). Out of the closet and into the marketplace: meeting basic needs in the gay community. *Journal of Homosexuality, 31*(1-2), 219-244.

Bravmann, S. (1997). *Queer fictions of the past: History, culture, and difference.* Cambridge University Press.

Browne, K. & Nash, C. J. (2016). *Queer methods and methodologies: Intersecting queer theories and social science research.* United Kingdom: Taylor & Francis.

Butler, J. (2011). *Gender trouble: Feminism and the subversion of identity.* London: Routledge.

Caserio, R. L. (1997). Queer passions, queer citizenship: Some novels about the state of the American nation 1946-1954. *MFS Modern Fiction Studies, 43*(1), 170-205.

Chen, S. X., & Kanai, A. (2021). Authenticity, uniqueness and talent: Gay male beauty influencers in post-queer, postfeminist Instagram beauty culture. *European Journal of Cultural Studies, 25*(1), 97-116.

Chiang, H. (2013). (De) Provincializing China: Queer historicism and Sinophone postcolonial critique. In Chiang, H., & Heinrich, A. L. (Eds.). *Queer sinophone cultures* (pp. 39-71). Routledge.

Cleary, S. (2022). *How to be you: Simone de Beauvoir and the art of authentic living.* New York: Random House.

Collins, C. G. (2017). Drag Race to the bottom? Updated notes on the aesthetic and political economy of RuPaul's Drag Race. *Transgender Studies Quarterly, 4*(1), 128–134.

Da Silva, D. (2019). *Trans tessituras: Confounding, unbearable, and black transgender voices in Luso-Afro-Brazilian popular music*. Columbia University.

Delaney, J. (2019). The interviews: RuPaul Charles. The Emmy's. Available at https://web.archive.org/web/20210803095013/ https://www.emmys.com/news/interviews-archive/interviews-rupaul-charles Access 03 August 2021.

De Beauvoir, S. (2018). *The ethics of ambiguity*. London: Open Road Media.

de Jong, A. (2017). Unpacking Pride's commodification through the encounter. *Annals of Tourism Research, 63*, 128–139.

Driskill, Q. L., Justice, D. H., Miranda, D., & Tatonetti, L. (Eds.). (2011). *Sovereign erotics: A collection of two-spirit literature*. University of Arizona Press.

Edelman, L. (1998). The future is kid stuff: Queer theory, disidentification, and the death drive. *Narrative, 6*(1), 18–30.

Emig, R. (2000). Queering the straights: Straightening queers: Commodified sexualities and hegemonic masculinity. *Subverting masculinity: Hegemonic and alternative versions of masculinity in contemporary culture, 1*, 207.

Fejes, F., & Lennon, R. (2000). Defining the lesbian/gay community? Market research and the lesbian/gay press. *Journal of Homosexuality, 39*(1), 25–42.

Fernández Carbajal, A. (2021). Hipsters end: Queer time, and imitation versus authenticity, in Matthew Lopez's the inheritance. *Journal of Homosexuality*, 1–21.

Forrest, D. (1994). We're here, we're queer, and we're not going shopping. *Dislocating masculinity: Comparative ethnographies*, 97–110.

Gerstner, D. A. (Ed.). (2006). *Routledge international encyclopedia of queer culture*. Routledge.

Gilbert, H., & Gleghorn, C. (2014). *Recasting commodity and spectacle in the indigenous Americas*. Institute of Latin American Studies, p. 275.

Goldin-Perschbacher, S. (2018). Gay country, TransAmericana, and queer sincerity. In F.E. Maus, S. Whiteley, T. Nyong'o, & Z. Sherinian (Eds.). *The Oxford Handbook of Music and Queerness*. Oxford University Press.

Gross, A. (2014). The politics of LGBT rights in Israel and beyond: Nationality, normativity, and queer politics. *Colum. Hum. Rts. L. Rev., 46*, 81.

Grossman, D. (2020). Sexuality and popular culture. In N. A Naples (Ed.). *Companion to Sexuality Studies* (pp. 279-298). Wiley.

Hayes, J. (2000). *Queer nations: marginal sexualities in the Maghreb*. University of Chicago Press.

Hayes, J. (2016). *Queer roots for the diaspora: Ghosts in the family tree*. University of Michigan Press.

Hennessy, R. (1994). Queer visibility in commodity culture. *Cultural Critique*, (29), 31–76.

Hennessy, R. (2017). *Profit and pleasure: Sexual identities in late capitalism*. Routledge.

Hess, D. B. (2019). Effects of gentrification and real-estate market escalation on gay neighbourhoods. In *Town Planning Review*. Liverpool University Press.

Hong, G. J. (2013). Theatrics of cruising: bath houses and movie houses in Tsai Ming-liang's films. In C. Howard & A. L. Heinrich (Eds.). *Queer sinophone cultures* (pp. 169–179). Routledge.

Hughes, H. (2005). The paradox of gay men as tourists: privileged or penalized?. *Tourism Culture & Communication*, 6(1), 51–62.

Hunt, S., & Holmes, C. (2015). Everyday decolonization: Living a decolonizing queer politics. *Journal of Lesbian Studies*, 19(2), 154–172.

Jacobson, H. (2018). A limited market: the recruitment of gay men as surrogacy clients by the infertility industry in the USA. *Reproductive Biomedicine & Society Online*, 7, 14–23.

Jones, A. (2020). Queer performativity: A critical genealogy of a politics of doing in art practice. In B. Ferdman, & J. Stokic (Eds.). *The Methuen Drama companion to performance art* (p. 58). London and New York: Methuen Drama.

Kamenou, N. (2012). *Cyprus is the country of heroes, not of homosexuals: Sexuality, gender and nationhood in Cyprus*. (Doctoral dissertation, King's College, University of London).

Kirsch, M. H. (2000). *Queer theory and social change*. Psychology Press.

Knopp, L. (1990). Exploiting the rent cap: The theoretical significance of using illegal appraisal schemes to encourage gentrification in New Orleans. *Urban Geography*, 11(1), 48–64.

Kulpa, R. (2013). *Nation queer? Discourses of nationhood and homosexuality in times of transformation: Case studies from Poland*. (Doctoral dissertation, Birkbeck, University of London).

Latané, B. (1996). Dynamic social impact: The creation of culture by communication. *Journal of Communication*, 46(4), 13–25.

Lewis, T. (2007). 'He needs to face his fears with these five queers!' Queer Eye for the Straight Guy, makeover TV, and the lifestyle expert. *Television & New Media*, 8(4), 285–311.

Lewis, N. M. (2017). Canaries in the mine? Gay community, consumption and aspiration in neoliberal Washington, DC. *Urban Studies*, 54(3), 695–712.

Li, X. (2018). *Black masculinity and hip-hop music: Black gay men Who Rap*. Springer.

Lim, B. C. (2015). Queer Aswang transmedia: Folklore as camp. *Kritika Kultura*, 24.

Lovelock, M. (2019). *Reality TV and queer identities: Sexuality, authenticity, celebrity*. Springer.

MacArthur, G. (2018). Queer as folklore: How fun home destabilizes the metronormative myth. Available at https://openscholarship.wustl.edu/cgi/viewcontent.cgi?article=1005&context=mcleod Access 04 October 2020.

Maddison, S. (2013). Beyond the entrepreneurial voyeur? Sex, porn and cultural politics. *New Formations, 80*(80), 102–118.
Maddison, S. (2018). Designing life? Affect and Gay Porn. In T. Sampson, S. Maddison, & D. Ellis (Eds.). *Affect and social media: Emotion, mediation, anxiety and contagion.* United Kingdom: Rowman & Littlefield International.
Matthews, T. R. (2016). *Decolonizing transness in sport media: The frames and depictions of transgender athletes in Sports Illustrated.* (Doctoral dissertation, Colorado State University).
McCarthy, E. D. (2016). Emotional performances as dramas of authenticity. In: J. P. Williams (Ed.). *Authenticity in culture, self, and society* (pp. 257–272). London: Routledge
McCollum, J. (2014). Morsels of body: photographic love and the queer gaze in Madame Bovary. *Journal of Gender Studies, 23*(2), 155–166.
McCormack, D. (2018). Queer disability, postcolonial feminism and the monsters of evolution. In C. Åsberg, & R. Braidotti (Eds.). *A Feminist Companion to the Posthumanities* (pp. 153–164). Springer, Cham.
McNair, B. (2013). *Porno? Chic!: How pornography changed the world and made it a better place.* Routledge.
Mercer, J. (2017). *Gay pornography: Representations of sexuality and masculinity.* Bloomsbury Publishing.
Muñoz, J. E. (1999). *Disidentifications: Queers of color and the performance of politics* (vol. 2). University of Minnesota Press.
Munro, B. M. (2012). *South Africa and the dream of love to come: queer sexuality and the struggle for freedom.* University of Minnesota Press.
Nast, H. J. (2002). Queer patriarchies, queer racisms, international. *Antipode, 34*(5), 874–909.
Oswin, N. (2015). World, city, queer. *Antipode, 47*(3), 557–565.
Palomino, P. (2020). *The invention of Latin American music: A transnational history.* Oxford University Press.
Parahoo, R. (2020). *Exploring being queer and performing queerness in popular music* (Doctoral dissertation, The University of Western Ontario (Canada)).
Pennington, S. (2019). Transgender passing guides and the vocal performance of gender and sexuality. In F. E. Maus, S. Whiteley, T. Nyong'o, & Z. Sherinian (Eds.). *The Oxford handbook of music and queerness.* Oxford University Press.
Peters, W. (2011). Pink dollars, white collars: Queer as Folk, valuable viewers, and the price of gay TV. *Critical Studies in Media Communication, 28*(3), 193–212.
Price, M. B. (2015). A genealogy of queer detachment. *PMLA, 130*(3), 648–665.
Provencher, D. M. (2016). *Queer French: Globalization, language, and sexual citizenship in France.* Routledge.
Pullen, C. (2016). *Straight girls and queer guys.* Edinburgh University Press.
PWC (2017). *The largest media markets ranked by revenue.* PriceWaterhouse Coopers.

PWC. (2021). *Perspectives from the global entertainment & media outlook.* Available at https://www.pwc.com/gx/en/entertainment-media/outlook-2021/perspectives-2021-2025.pdf Access 11 August 2021

Raboin, T. (2013). *Constructing a queer haven: Sexuality and nationhood in discourses on LGBT asylum in the UK.* (Doctoral dissertation, University College London).

Radin, M. J., & Sunder, M. (2005). The subject and object of commodification. *Legal Studies Research Paper*, (16).

Richardson, D. (2005). Desiring sameness? The rise of a neoliberal politics of normalisation. *Antipode*, 37(3), 515–535.

Romanow, R. F. (2009). *The postcolonial body in queer space and time.* Cambridge Scholars Publishing.

Salas-Santa Cruz, O. (2021). Queer and trans* of color critique, decolonization, and education. In *Oxford research encyclopedia of education.* Oxford University Press. Available online at https://oxfordre.com/education/view/10.1093/acrefore/9780190264093.001.0001/acrefore-9780190264093-e-1336

Savigliano, M. E. (2010). Notes on tango (as) queer (commodity). *Anthropological Notebooks*, 16(3), 135–143.

Seidman, S. (1991). Postmodern anxiety: The politics of epistemology. *Sociological Theory*, 9(2), 180–190.

Shaw, D. (2013). Sex, texts and money, funding and Latin American queer cinema: The cases of Martel's La niña santa and Puenzo's XXY. *Transnational Cinemas*, 4(2), 165–184.

Smith, A. (2010). Queer theory and native studies: The heteronormativity of settler colonialism. *GLQ: A Journal of Lesbian and Gay Studies*, 16(1–2), 41–68.

Smith, K. (2013). Decolonizing queer pedagogy. *Affilia*, 28(4), 468–470.

Södergren, J., & Vallström, N. (2021). Seeing the invisible: brand authenticity and the cultural production of queer imagination. *Arts and the Market*, 11(3), 275–297.

Sycamore (2008). *That's revolting! Queer strategies for resisting assimilation.* United Kingdom: Soft Skull Press.

Trilling, L. (1971). *Sincerity and authenticity.* United Kingdom: Harvard University Press.

Turner, W. B. (2000). *A genealogy of queer theory* (vol. 12). Temple University Press.

Vance, C. (2018). Unwilling consumers: A historical materialist conception of compulsory sexuality. *Studies in Social Justice*, 12(1), 133–151.

Warren, C. (1974). *Identity and community in the gay world.* New York: Wiley.

Weiner, J. J., & Young, D. (2011). Introduction: queer bonds. *GLQ: A Journal of Lesbian and Gay Studies*, 17(2–3), 223–241.

Wetherell, M. & Potter, J. (1987). *Discourse and social psychology: Beyond attitudes and behaviour.* London: SAGE Publications.

Wilbourne, E. (2013). The Queer History of the Castrato. In F. E. Maus, S. Whiteley, T. Nyong'o, & Z. Sherinian (Eds.). *The Oxford handbook of music and queerness.* Oxford University Press.

Williams, R. (2013). *The long revolution.* United Kingdom: Parthian Books.

Zhao, J. J., & Wong, A. K. (2020). Introduction: Making a queer turn in contemporary Chinese-language media studies. *Continuum, 34*(4), 475–483.

Chapter 2

QUEER NEWS

10 May 1993 – Sullivan published a special issue called *Straight America, Gay America*. The *New York Times* is almost overcompensating for its former reticent by giving startingly generous news and editorial coverage to gay subjects.

— Bersani, 1995:13

The previous chapters explored how globalized queerness emerges as a concept that stretches over different cultural industries and their commodities. Globalized queerness excels at informing and forging stylistic connections to construct being queer as consonant with products and shows. The last chapter discussed commodification as something beyond the normalization or acceptance of queerness in society. The reader learns that commodifying queer culture includes accepting the exchange of a simplistic form of queer knowledge through the media. In this way, sincerity and authenticity are values that should be seen alongside queerness as much as one can learn local stories about queerness, such as leaving one's home, escaping oppression, and finding allies that are not necessarily depicted in global queer media. In sum, globalizing queerness has oftentimes meant that queer artistry, productions, and queer knowledge feed into a multi-million-dollar industry without showing the less marketable sides of being queer. The next question to be approached in the book is about who informs the whole industry and consumers. Who are the partners or the entrepreneurs of globalized queer media and culture?

To a large degree, queer culture is much indebted to journalism to the extent that the news informs on the events, politics, and epistemologies of LGBTQ+ communities to the broader society and among itself. This chapter dedicates to the realm of digital journalism as the natural habitat of queerness around the world. It tracks down the local and global emphases of queerness as topics allotted to online news articles of everyday life. Whenever queer culture and artistry are the topic of the reporting, this survey enquires into occurrences of articles that refer to queer artists and media producers (henceforth, queer news) as they appear in the world's ten biggest media markets. The intention was to analyse them according to their cross-citations of national or foreign names. By scraping news API data (n=3851) from numerous sources, it is possible to compare the digital coverage of queer culture based on a threefold criterion, namely the topics, the actors, and the locations that drive journalistic interest into queer affairs daily. The extent to which online reports in distinct news contexts have prioritized global queer media productions over the presence of local, non-Western LGBTQ+ communities. Results offer fresh ground for the visualization of the emphases and absences of digital journalism in its role of informing about the queer culture.

Queer culture and digital journalism

As seen, the subject of queer popular culture and its unstoppable commodification has spanned many realms, not limited to social media, dating apps, and urban life (Radin & Sunder, 2005; Light et al., 2008). Even if online newsgathering can be included in this process, less criticism applies to the news as it remains a fundamental source to learn about LGBTQ+ communities, their events, and politics (Barnhurst, 2003; Moritz, 2009). Let us take the example of online tabloids and how they break the news of sportspeople and singers who 'come out' as non-heterosexual or non-gender conforming (King, 2017; Motschenbacher, 2019; Stott, 2019). On a positive note, inasmuch most of the audience can label this piece of news as just gossip, it will still aid several anti-homophobia campaigns, help sell LGBT and singers in a shift from derogatory narratives of previous decades (Cleland et al., 2018; Kian, 2019). The promotion of gay memes, another case, has bridged gay slang and pop culture into heteronormative environments (Buckledee, 2020).

The daily news has counted on websites such as *Advocate.com, Gay Times* or *Them.us* for years to provide readers with dedicated coverage of LGBTQ+ affairs. In effect, major global, mainstream news portals such as *BBC.com* or *Reuters*, among many others, have started with sections aimed at the queer public. Websites like *BuzzFeed* have innovated by appointing 'LGBT Chief Correspondents' (Beaujon, 2013). The ubiquity and consequent organization of the news in that direction may lead to an assumption that, at least in the West, that online news, queer life, and popular culture have walked towards a scenario of acceptance and consolidation (Betancourt, 2020). Essentially, it does so by forging mass 'gay media representation', which sums up all topics that concern behaviour and sexuality in a sort of digest to society (Mowlabocus, 2017).

The ecosystem of digital queer news outlets plays a broader role in what Siebler (2016) referred to as *learning* about queer identity. There has been a series of calls to hold digital journalism to account concerning the public oversight of marginalized communities (Burgess & Hurcome, 2021; Zelizer, 2019) and the assessment of contextual sensitivity (Humprecht & Esser, 2018; Robinson et al., 2019). Recently, mainstream queer journalism has, at the same time, faced issues of genuineness and suspicion from commentators on whether high-profile editors are indeed echoing queer voices or only bending to profits and social pressure (Bendix, 2019). In the following sections, I discuss the growth of queer news as a recent advent that affects both global and local queer culture, as it consequently amplifies the spectrum of globalized queerness. The consistent growth of queer media products made available everywhere also poses challenges to journalists in terms of informing on queerness as a global phenomenon instead of detaching locally based queer individuals as *less* queer or delegitimized actors. By inquiring into these two expectations, the local and the global, plus the globalized side of queerness – i.e., the standardized queer interface that goes public thanks to the news – one can recognize, support, and advance the kind of knowledge that builds queer culture on an everyday basis.

Queer appearances as global news

In *Global Gay: How gay culture is changing the world*, Frédéric Martel (2019) argued for the multipolarity of gay presence worldwide. Martel cites field research conducted in countries such as Iran, Brazil, and Algeria, whose queer populations seem at the same time to fight local homophobia while exposed to debates seen in the West. Arguably, US-based media may lead the way by providing several audiences with a queer repertoire of TV series and expressions. Still, there is also an inbred process of developing queer parlances among non-Western cultures. The news can play a role in 'changing the world' toward gay culture to the degree of its global outreach, boosted by an increasing queer fluency on the Internet. For example, in 2019, 28% of US LGBTQ interviewees said they had increased their consumption of queer news websites. This number can be even more significant if one looks at regional newspapers and magazines readership (Watson, 2019), which may have increased after the Covid-19 pandemic. At least the scenario of escalating interest in the news grows as an instrument for diversity in mainstream publications (Bodó et al., 2019) starts to guide newsrooms to explore ethnically and sexually diverse agendas (Wallace, 2020: 11).

From a news perspective, queer culture has received considerable attention. English-speaking programmes, such as *Queer Eye* and the rising stardom of transgender celebrities, have inspired fresh narratives in bulletins and cultural digests (Kerrigan & Pramaggiore, 2021). Over the years, *RuPaul's Drag Race* has become one of the most commented TV series distributed worldwide. As a result, the *New York Times* published an article entitled 'Is "RuPaul's Drag Race" the most radical show on TV?' (24 January 2018), as the artist appeared on the 'Most Powerful Drag Queens in America' list published by the online news website Vulture (10 January 2019). While these occurrences are not suggestive enough of an enduring influence worldwide, there is surely a link between the success of global queer media commodities and their mirroring and positive reviewing by online headlines. Appearing in translation elsewhere, *RuPaul's* TV franchise paves the way for new communicative avenues, even in countries proud of their own languages' specificities such as France (Fusco, 2020). *RuPaul* has pushed for local audiences to contrast the American artists with thriving local transgender scenes, as it happened in Brazil (Leite, 2017).

Investigating the space granted for queer culture in digital journalism means inevitably engaging with its role in boosting queer English-spoken, American-based queer media productions. In short, what one could call *global* queer news. US-chroniclers can generate facts and interests that are not necessarily American-made. Still, once this material appears written in English, it suffices the claim of Western populations and creates an agenda around a specific issue. Hollywood celebrities who 'come out' or 'transition' or UK or US productions that reach Asian or Latin American markets generate an echo on queer populations elsewhere. These media repercussions, on the other side, can create controversy among public opinion miles away. By contrast, the vibrancy of local queer scenes contrasts with the reduced attention paid to these local outlets and languages. Next, I discuss queer news as featured in small or medium-sized outlets. The view of queer culture as utter commodities clashes with the continuous stream of queer artists in non-Western countries or those uninterested in the global media affairs, as we shall see. These actors seem to be growing more attached to their ethnicities and shimmering their societies in unexpected ways, as we shall see.

Queer appearances as local news

The newsworthiness of queer culture on a global level has followed an intricate relationship between the repackaging of local visual and language repertoires, the market investment, and an idea of public acceptance. It is clear from what has surged as the re-interpretation of old styles: from commoditized gay cowboys (Nast, 2002) to a new perception of *fado* as the queered-up version of the Portuguese music style. News reports spread *events* that create momentum around local actors, sponsors, and connections with queer communities that see it as a unique chance to *appear* in the media (Savigliano, 2010). In 'recasting commodity', Gilbert and Gleghorn (2014) saw it as a subversion of the regular media cycle that can be diverted for other kinds of publicity. Indigenous communities could seize that space to voice things differently, at least once. That being the case, the focus on local queer news should be on the awareness about destabilizing latent vocabularies that dared not to be said or appear at the local level. Away from global news readers, these new frames could blaze the trail for local queer relationships, which could shun forms of persecution or, otherwise challenge normative limits of acceptance in conservative media making (Copeland, 2018; Ula, 2019).

In this way, local queer affairs may or may not exist as the *news*. In the global news media cycle, the matter is one of de-escalating or de-prioritizing queer people's facts in the name of conventional interests from globe-trotting media. Whether in popular music (Parahoo, 2020) or re-interpretations of non-queer media texts (Grossman, 2020), one might also ponder what kinds of queer manifestations may still skip the news cycle entirely to *instead* figure as announcements, Facebook posts, letters, or pamphlets. These texts are likewise seen lacking the aesthetics of features that make up queer popular culture globally. In sum, regional news, for example, seem far-fetched for journalism as we know it. In terms of mass consumption, these queer media acts missing could be the new *Queer Eye* (Lewis, 2007), but failed from the beginning.

Moreover, queer culture, as this all-or-nothing commodity cycle, can run yet very far from their target audience, despite recent changes. In journalism, there has been much speculation on how subjective and yet socially committed motivations can be reports coming from the margins (e.g., Schapals et al., 2019). It is also true that cultural journalism will inevitably put queer actors in cross-national dialogue (Kristensen & From, 2015; Kersten & Janssen, 2016). In this case, it is not rejecting journalism as a play with commodities but questioning whether journalism can perfectly encase *queer* on a global scale while limiting itself to the same queer cultural environments since decades ago (Edelman, 1998). News or facts dwell at the crossroads between culture and commodification, but journalistic reports can prioritise cosmopolitan publics, which creates a sort of false dialectics.

In regions such as Latin America, where popular culture has been instrumental in gathering support against authoritarian regimes and inequality, queer movements have not always conformed to a national tradition (Shaw, 2013). In many other cases, the reporting on several initiatives of local popular culture came to inspire a mindset of social change that has gone across the border to create a climate of regional solidarity (Palomino, 2020). This intense scenario of queer involvement in social affairs does not arrive, arguably, to the so-called queer news. Local, non-Western, or 'ethnic' queer fails to reach into journalism that circulates in the Global North, as much as their leaders and participants fail to be recognized on the *local* level. In the next section, I debunk the challenges of retrieving, comparing, and analysing queer news from a global and local perspective. The main idea of this chapter's research was to establish some criteria to track and observe queer mentions in several news media markets. It should ultimately create conditions to perceive whether digital journalism leans towards globalized queerness or whether there are other prioritizations of topics, actors, or locations.

Quantifying queer cultural news across media markets

An under-explored aspect of queer presence in popular culture lies in how news reporting can amplify, reduce, or alter the globalization of queer media. There is still a barrage of ontological, epistemological, and cultural definitions that impinge on the kind of coverage that sexual and gender diversity receives. Given this book's focus on media and popular culture, this research preferred to approach news that touched upon culture and cultural industries as opposed to other political aspects or controversies surrounding queer affairs in the media. Media flows between West-based correspondents, and the vast universe of smaller outlets in languages other than English can provide researchers with a traceable corpus consisting of vocabulary that pays reference to queer individuals in different ways (headlines, text, cues). By scraping queer news from outlets in the world's ten largest markets per revenue (PWC, 2017, 2021), it was possible to target pieces that typically approach queer culture from a standpoint that reaches both mainstream and non-mainstream producers (Lipton, 2008). Coverage is defined herein as the narration or storytelling of facts or episodes about queer popular culture (artists, cultural products) on any platform.

This market cut is a sound measure to mirror the media power behind gross sales and reach a quantifiable sample. This type of ranking is also more appropriate to observe exchanges allowed by the most significant investments available in queer media and their consequent mirroring on the news. This sample of countries yet offers diversity enough to enquire about the main terms that confer publicity to queer culture, their emphases, and their actors' entry into the local markets. In many publications, it also becomes evident what Sedgwick (2008) and many others have argued about the mainstreaming of queer culture and its consequences on language. In brief, scholars have seen Western queer culture as the epitome of an 'epistemological pressure' to conform to vocabularies that attest to the grouping and unimaginable levels of axiomatic visibility of queer populations. These debates become even more visible when publications such as Vogue or Vanity Fair may or may not employ the same language repertoire as smaller outlets located in less mediated contexts, for example.

The crossroads between the use of queer terms in journalism, journalists' varying interest in global/local queer culture, and the relative importance of cultural coverage in countries with larger or smaller cultural industries are found in the literature on comparative cultural studies (Geertz, 2017). Scholars saw the *incorporation* (the adoption of global terms) or the *excorporation* of such repertoire (adopting global culture but incorporating their elements). For example, how can one characterize the nationality of dubbed editions of *RuPaul's Drag Race*? How can one qualify the version initially performed in English and others enacted by local characters? Where do they stand in the global/local binary? The role of journalism in covering these exchanges remains, at best mysterious. This research has taken on new portraits that can encase some of these global or local appropriations in a permanent relationship.

Therefore, computational methods served this research at quantifying the mentions and qualifying the structure of these global and local or hybrid references found in each country and concerning English-language mentions. Simple but crucial questions helped locate the salience of terms related to queer media and artistry in journalistic reporting, in which the analysis followed the repetition or absence of this vocabulary: [RQ1] How do countries' news outlets compare in terms of the number of articles published on queer popular culture? [RQ2] To what extent do themes vary in the coverage of queer culture? [RQ3] What countries are more present or absent from the news published locally or internationally? [RQ4] What are the possible assumptions based on the number of references to every country's queer scene? These questions are not aimed at going deeper than topical references to queer culture, as most news articles do not generally allow for any ontological complexity. As said earlier, the purpose was to gain an initial insight into the dialogue between journalistic reporting and cultural boundaries surrounding the understanding of queer culture worldwide.

This research invited data ranging from distinct periods between January 2018 and ending in July 2022. The data aimed to map pre- and post-Covid-19 scenarios. One must remember the enormous impact the pandemic has posed on cultural life all around the world. Crucially, it has affected queer popular culture unprecedentedly because of the suspension of many countries' nightlife and crowded events. The situation also halted art exhibitions, online talks and concerts, book launches, and cultural discussions. Even so, the research found references to such events based on textual cues collected via a news API, an amalgamating tool based on a Python application. The software's main scope was to centre on news pieces gathered on Google News, Bing News, and Yandex News. This approach advances many opportunities (vast catalogue of different, multiple-sized outlets practising journalism and available in many languages), as well as limitations (platform's algorithm, gatekeeping, conformity with each operator's guidelines). Some of these limitations could be circumvented by adding up additional APIs, which could get hold of other sources, such as the Associated Press and Reuters news wires. The advantages also consisted of being able to trace content used on mainstream media, as well as in blogs, social media commenting on websites, and personal pages, all part of the digital news landscape. This approach was also helpful for favouring press articles as opposed to the unstructured content from social media and present in all countries included in this research (RQ1).

Using Latent Dirichlet Allocation (Blei et al., 2003) allows for identifying top-performing words with an unsupervised algorithm in which unigrams and bigrams were identified to determine the main topics contained in the sample (RQ2). The election of keywords in English and respective translations (n=11), namely, *queer, gay, lesbian, trans, transgender, LGBT, LGBTQ, LGBTQ+*, placed alone and in conjunction with one of the words, *culture, artist, art, celebrity*, and *influencer*, in English. These words happened following what Dorsey and Detlefsen (2010) argued about the need to follow the guidance regarding terms used to describe queer culture while taking a snapshot of standard terms that would enable a practical crawling on websites. The words were placed both in English and in each of the official languages of the countries/markets involved in this survey: the US, Japan, China (Simplified Chinese), Germany, the United Kingdom, France, Brazil, South Korea, Canada, and Italy.

Most of the articles were first obtained in their local languages and translated with the aid of the Google Translate software into English to form a full *lingua franca* dataset. Manual verification to ensure consistency between translation and common usage of words by the press was performed with a sample (n=330). Pre-processing techniques (e.g., Gunther et al., 2018) included textual fragments, hashtags, punctuation, and stop-words (e.g., ad pieces, repeated occurrences). Eventually, 5,624 articles matched the sampling criteria, including articles, headlines, content, and date. From which repetitions, unrelated articles (e.g., ad pieces, non-relative to queer culture), and tags were removed for better visibility of article content. Words such as *exhibit* were standardised as *exhibition*, or *homos*, as *homosexual*. Only articles strictly featuring queer artists or events, or those referring to them directly, their discourses, or productions were selected. The final sample comprised 3,236 unique articles published in the ten countries analysed. References of countries were also mapped and compared using clustering to track where they come from (RQ3). Furthermore, a random sample extracted from the full range of numbers (n=323) was coded and analysed to pull examples of stories and draw qualitative assumptions that could answer the latter question (RQ4).

To simplify the discussion and presentation of the outcomes, the results are calculated through a Qualitative Comparative Analysis solution based on Stayner (2014) (Chaudhary, 2001), in which he saw the use of a simple matrix to contrast occurrences in a small-sized n dataset. Each country was assigned an index (0–1) on their coverage of queer artists or media producers based on their mention of one of the keywords at stake. This method's aims allow for scenarios in which the comparative stance dwells on casual complexity based on how queer culture can be covered following specific flows or being juxtaposed or used for other purposes instead of suggesting a scenario of permanent influence from one country or culture over the other.

Direct mentions to queer artists around the world

The initial step was to obtain absolute results that could be a testament to the kinds of news occurrences about queer culture worldwide (RQ1). There was a need for different results between topical references and those representing queer culture through lengthy portraits of queer artists or characters. The data allows for a few correlations between the news pieces published in anglophone countries, such as the UK and the US. Unsurprisingly, many more mentions of 'queer' artists and the feature of queer artists or personalities are based on these countries. The opposite is true in Asian countries, such as China and Japan, where references to queer artists and performers appear vague and harder to trace. This table helps to balance the expectations about the employment and universality of the coverage of queer artists based on the keywords searched. On a closer look, these articles may refer to visual arts, public events, and non-LGBTQ artists that may voice support for gays, lesbians, or transgender causes or stir debate on sexuality.

To a lesser extent, some news may look queer because of a mention, statement or assumption from headlines, interviewees, or speculation. For example, articles reporting on controversies, such as when heterosexual actresses Scarlett Johansson or Halle Berry have withdrawn

Table 1 Countries with the highest number of topical references to queer popular culture and mentions to queer artists in news media articles

	Total (n)	Articles with references (n)	Direct mentions to queer culture (%)
Brazil	396	335	85
US	342	322	94
South Korea	373	237	64
Italy	333	255	77
Germany	250	222	89
Japan	367	298	81
France	375	228	61
Canada	335	287	86
China	295	108	37
UK	218	196	90
All stories	3236	2355	73

from productions for not being transgender or Lesbian as their characters (Moviepilot.de – 16.07.2018/Lfm.ch – 07/07/2020) or the 'gay' version of Disney's *Ariel, the Little Mermaid*, which had inspired articles published in Brazil, Japan, and many other countries. In brief, this sample of articles has adopted *queer* terms but did not discuss the queer culture based on queer protagonists. Reporters are somewhat preoccupied with assumptions or speculations that feed the discussion but do not advance specific queer cultural initiatives.

The literature on *queerbaiting* is still much hesitating to determine what are the *canonical* queer narratives that are attestations of a genuine interest in the community, if any, or those that can bear little interest in queer readers or only an illusion of this interest (Ng, 2017). Based on approaches that see queerbaiting as a cosmetic treatment of a text to appear queer but does not deliver on its facts (e.g., Sheehan, 2015), news in Italian and Japanese have invited global politics, non-queer celebrities, and media productions that are not necessarily about homosexuals to queer-headlined pieces. It entails the so-called denials which have prompted editors or journalists to publish it in queer sections. 'Lara Fabian: Her amazing kiss the Eva Longoria' (Public.fr – 17/05/2020) is the type of article that brands the kiss between two heterosexual female artists as a queer article and consequently will appear as queer or labelled as such for the broader audience. This kind of uncertainty regarding news *about* queer culture or those which touch upon its dilemmas and controversies remains a significant obstacle to quantifying queer news on many levels. Therefore, a more productive turn is to use the data that emerge from the association between terms, topics, and individuals, which have proved more resonant.

Main topics covered

This survey into topics (Table 2) allows for a further description of themes (RQ2) that, in turn, inform on the boundaries that surround the journalistic coverage of queer culture. The weight of American-based culture is latent in topics 1, 3, 5, 6, 7, and 9, which englobe conversations related to the history of American LGBTQ movements and the power of their televised or streamed shows. Not least associated icons such as the rainbow flag, but the highlight of local performers embedded in productions such as *Queer Eye* and the association of American celebrities with gay or lesbian causes, as shown below.

Table 2 Topic description

Topic	Description	Top terms	Example	n > 0.5
1	Features about queer artists generally on a global basis	Artist, queer, gay, art, transgender,	'15 queer art shows you can virtually tour now' (NBC News)	260
2	The social and legal situation of the queer community, not necessarily in the arts	LGBT, LGBTQ, LGBTQIA, people, world	'Seeking LGBT asylum in China: Similar experiences and different endings' (Deutsche Welle)	80
3	Acts, comments, or circumstances involving a particular artist or personality (e.g., coming out)	Singer, come, fight, comment, denounce	'Filipino genius singer Charis, who also appeared in Glee, is coming out as Lesbian' (TVGroove.com)	55
4	News related to Pride marches around the world	Pride, month, celebrate, event, power	'Europride 2023 will happen in Malta' (Tageskarte)	39
5	Artistic highlights of local artists, performer, or series	Popular, hot, why, who, performance	'Kiko Kizuhara appears on the popular reality show Queer Eye' (Elle.com Japan)	21
6	Film productions with queer characters or celebrities associated to it	Movie, star, release, scene, couple, gender	'Demi Lovato says Watching This Movie Helped Her Realize She Was Queer' (Billboard.com)	38
7	News about drag queens and transgender artists	Drag, drag queen, son, show, race	'Netflix's Brazilian reality show offers self-help for drag queens' (Folha.com)	37
8	Developments focusing on a particular queer community	Community, black, trans, corona, celebrate	'Blood Orange 1 Brain Dead releases charity t-shirt to support black and LGBTQ community' (Hyperbeast)	
9	History of a particular LGBTQ population	History, archive, generation, first, life	'Spotlighting Lesbian artists as central players in California's Queer History' (Hyperallergic.com)	26
10	Gathering support for queer individuals around the world	Support, complain, rainbow, power	'I support LGBTQ festival' embassies in Korea with rainbow' (Hari.co.kr)	23

Notes: LDA with $k = 11$, $\alpha = 0.05$, sampling method = Gibbs

Indeed, suppose one weighs American presence off the list. In that case, it is still possible to perceive much exchange between countries characterized by references to prominent American queer shows, such as *RuPaul's Drag Race*. In other words, irrespective of the language in which these articles have appeared, the leading assumption here posits subtle references to American repertoire (topic 9), including the history of civil rights and moments such as the 1969 Stonewall riots, whose 50th anniversary was commemorated during the period of this research.

Beyond America, globalized queer media topics also stand for international events (topic 1) that travelled the world. For example, China (to what concerns Hong Kong) republished much of the material imported from the Western press. The art exhibition *Hundred Years of Homosexuality*, organized by Tate Britain in London, was widely reported. There were short articles about LGBT, Google's *doodle* honouring Marsha P. Johnson and news about gay pride parades worldwide. 2019 and 2020 were particularly fruitful for queer popular culture, as cinemas received the Lesbian award-winning film *Portrait of a Lady* from France, which became news worldwide. Beyond cultural stories, data from the URLs retrieved also inform a distinct set of sections in which these topics were published originally (Figure 4).

This detail matters because of the variations in approach to queer culture across the globe. It is expectedly framed as arts and culture for the most part, but it also gets through in sections of *politics, society, cinema*, and *gender* or crime. In effect, the meaning of queer reporting cuts across the *direct referencing* already discussed to pursue other societal implications. Of course, queer culture can sprawl over the economy, fashion, and television, but its understanding as an invaluable topic for journalists stems from the location and the actor at stake.

People and characters

References to globetrotter queer photographers such as Wolfgang Tillmans or Sunil Gupta, and actors such as Ian McKellen, or Hollywood star Kirsten Stewart, show how queer presence in many markets is rooted in power, mainstream media promotion (topic 6). It springs from the same group of corporations that take non-queer stories to the cover of magazines and viral memes on social media. In this category, older references such as *Queer Eye* or Andy Warhol appear continuous times in countries such as China, as far as contemporary art names such as Cindy Sherman are featured in France. Still from outside of the US,

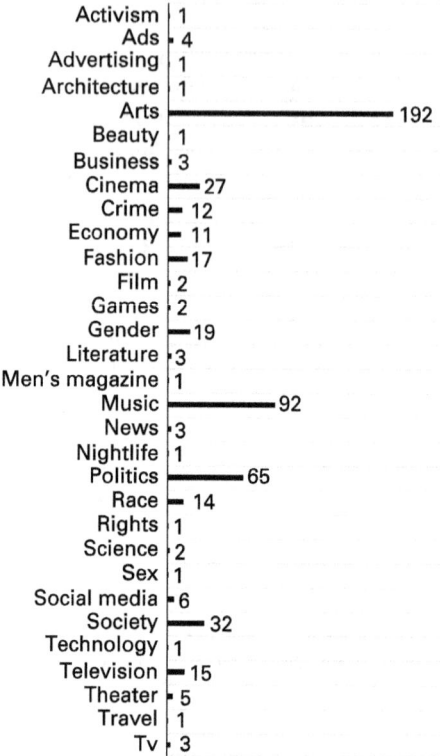

Figure 4 Count of sections that hosted the news about queer popular culture (including the US).

productions such as *Girl in Red*, featuring the Norwegian teen queer star Marie Ulven based the news in Canada, Japan, Germany, and many other countries. The *Tom of Finland* movie featured in articles from Japan, France, and Canada. Lastly, it is the case of Yayoi Kusama or Paris Jackson, who stem from the same mainstream sources, the former as the iconic Japanese visual artist and the latter as the daughter of Michael Jackson. She performed as a Lesbian Jesus in a movie. The continuous personalization of queer culture around players from this vast mainstream amalgam of subjects deserves a further look. Whether because it hosts a broad number of arts and non-sexualized queer debates or because there is a cut in time that seems somewhat elusive. For example, figures from the Renaissance, such as Leonardo Da Vinci or Michelangelo, appear more than artists who could better represent queer arts in a much more politicized fashion.

The presence of manga artist Mariko Tamaki in Japanese media, whose art is known in the US as much as in Japan, illustrates the less coverage of more minor acts, such as make-up artists, performers, dancers, and drag artists that have acted as spokespeople for the queer community in these places. The ascendence of transgender artistry has pushed many names, but these names often emerge under the spectrum of controversy. It was the case of Phia Ménard, a French transgender choreographer, which saw herself allegedly being deprogrammed from a festival to benefit singer Kanye West in 2020. This event pushed most of the mentions to a transgender artist for an extended period.

Regarding other parts of the world, there is the French case, which invites a few postcolonial undertones. Many French media outlets have covered the queer scene of the Maghreb, with several articles spearheaded by Moroccan writer *Abdellah Taïa*, who denounced the violence against *zamels*, or queers, in Morocco. The frequent call-ins of third countries with similar cultural traits are a specific product of the similar language between them, as also happens with French-speaking Canada. These relationships mix queer contexts with other issues among countries that share cultural or tongue ties as others do not. It is the case of Italy or Japan, where consistent global coverage of their artists is detected more than acts of their own. The exact process is observed in South Korea, even though 166 articles from this country represented a solid coverage of local Korean queer actors.

In reporting challenges in repressive countries, this relation of dependence from one country to another for producing the news has yet opened space to further visibility of issues involving queer or trans activists. The suicide of Egyptian trans activist Sara Hegazy was a headline in many countries. Similarly, the Japanese report about Liniker, a trans musician from Brazil and France reported about Houari Manar, from Algeria. By writing *bixa travesty* in big letters, the French newspaper *Le Monde* highlighted it as a very controversial slang used in Brazil, which served to feature *Linn da Quebrada*, another prominent artist born in the latter country's poor periphery. Regardless of the commercial interests involved or the advertising strategies employed, these examples touch upon complex realities of queer activists who are also artists. In contrast, their stories appear as anecdotes of oppression and small successes to far-away audiences.

As singer Apple from France mentioned in an interview: 'If I am a Lesbian, this is going to be the headline.' Transnational queer news has dramatically raised public awareness about festivals, art projects, music contests, and travel itineraries sponsored by artists. In Brazil, derogatory words such as *sapatão*, or 'big shoe woman' have seen journalists accommodating it in headlines and making it visible to conservative audiences. That said, the interest in celebrity comes-outs is still much in vogue. At the same time, more advanced approaches have levelled much criticism at society, as far as smaller queer communities have gained some highlight. Lesbian *visibility* has appeared rarely, whereby the queer representation of women is handed over to influential pop artists such as Madonna or Lady Gaga. Portraits of transgender women by Amanda Picotte in France and the extensive coverage of the queer section of the *Berlinale* are exceptions to this scenario.

The fact that queer news becomes newsworthy because of controversies makes it essentially global, as spread by American or European news agencies, ensuring repercussions exist. In that sense, Chinese news agencies have also built controversies of their own, such as *Sina*, a Chinese agency, has reported: 'A male teacher in Qingdao was expelled from the school and appealed to the court' (29/08/2018). Quickly, this case became viral on networks. Internet celebrity Han Ruixi suffered an assault, and the patient also got vast repercussions on the news. The attack was probably motivated by his being a homosexual, the report says. Contrary to what one could expect, these controversies get traction in Asian countries such as Japan, as in some cases, the backlash managed to get a fair amount of the press' attention, as Hayley Kiyoko, was quoted as saying: 'Queer is my greatest strength', visibly responding to a question that addressed victimhood. The next point addresses the issue of location in queer news.

Locations

The predominant presence of the United States in queer news has notoriously influenced epistemological and cultural references in many other national contexts, as seen above. Besides the US, there has been an opportunity to explore other highlights or the relationship between cultural scenes that can seem alien to each other. The second and third countries with the most citations by different countries are the UK and Canada. Other English-speaking countries somewhat echo developments and commentary from Europe and southern neighbours. In the periphery of this cycle of traded visibility among Western countries, one finds countries that have not received much coverage in non-queer news. Looking at samples from Brazil and Russia, the fact that (before the war in Ukraine) Russia is far less cited and its queer scene less reported than any

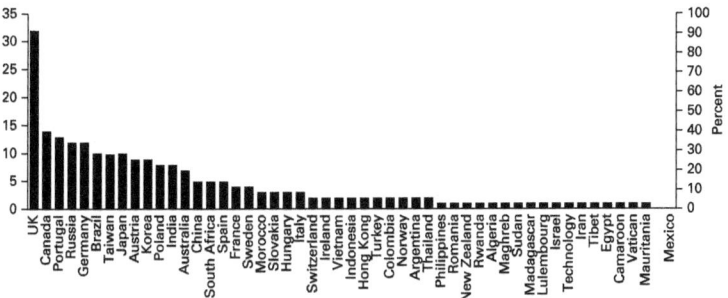

Figure 5 Countries cited in news reports about queer culture – except the US (n).

other country. Southern European countries, which instead have vibrant queer life, also receive less attention from the global media in English. Events such as *Queer Lisboa*, a gay-themed festival in Portugal, hit the news during a brief period of this analysis. Still, soon a stream of negative stories involving activists, murders, protests, repression, and homophobia could not allow this same agenda to flourish.

Two tiers separate coverage according to their coverage. The first one consists of large media markets that report about countries pursuing a similar political agenda. E.g., gay marriage, transgender debates, and homosexual adoption. Countries will mention each other accountable for the potential of following or not these agendas. The second tier consists of countries which inspire stories for its hosting of queer culture from abroad: they invest and invite queer actors – namely, Germany, Japan, Portugal, and Australia. Despite not boasting a lot of stories about their local scenes, these countries appear as *tour* destinations for queer artists or whereby they end up setting up temporary residences. The third tier consists of countries which are less cited due to their queer local scenes but end up offering the world a few names of their own, whether writers, actors, or names of migrating actors that publicize their careers locally – often, these names consist of political characters and refugees.

The overrepresentation of European countries in the news, led by the UK, contrasts with the underrepresentation of South America and the Caribbean. Even though Brazil was included here as one of the ten biggest media markets, South American queer artists are underrepresented overall. African countries are French references to the Maghreb, with thriving scenes in Morocco and Algeria extensively brought to light by successful French writers. In Oceania, Australian

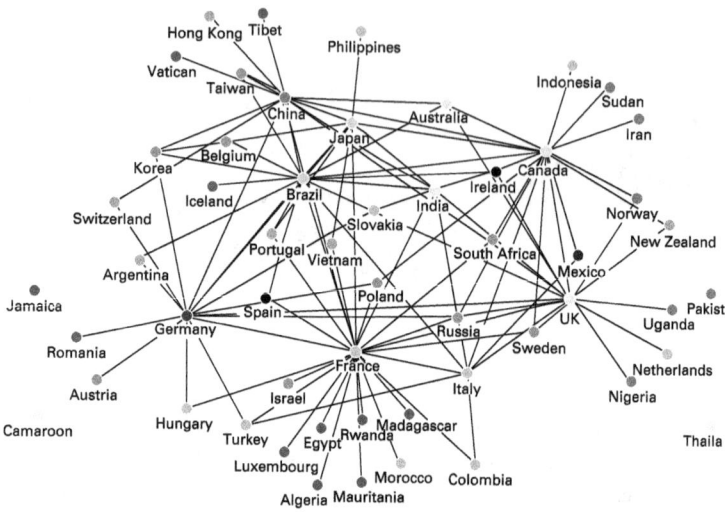

Figure 6 Citation and cross-citation of countries in queer news topics – including the US.

news brings to the fore local artists, sometimes in dialogue with British artists, and the American scene. Israel pushes the Middle East, the Emirates, and Iran, as these countries' artists come up as dissidents or emigres in the West. Once the US is removed from the sample, the count to Mexico and Canada totals 1.9% of the references.

There are elements to be weighed in here. First, the fact that distinct countries cannot mention what the book conceives as queer culture. Many of them have described queer individuals in a situation of persecution, but not their self-expression. The case of Brazil, the most cited country among the most critical markets, epitomizes this duality. It is a country with several references to queer culture, which offers term variations from north to south, but many are not cited elsewhere. All these could and should be leveraged as queer popular culture and news. However, to the extent that it involves the coverage of events and the agenda of news outlets, the attention to its queer media and arts appears reduced to homogenized plans or names that could be found in Brazil, France, or anywhere else. The second location issue here is the breadth of topics. The US has had the broadest coverage of queer artists and producers, but not necessarily American artists. Brazil, France, and South Korea have a substantially high number of queer coverages in their environment. In sum, location matters to understand global queer coverage because of the confluence between language and historical affinities, as well as other side aspects such as diasporic communities, religion, and context of oppression against queer communities.

The topics are relevant because queer actors appear to transcend the issue of being local or global when affairs are based in another country at a particular moment. The fact that the *arts* section allows many of these actors to be in the news as queers reveal contradictory avenues to explore. The phenomenon of importing global stories as local queer events was chiefly seen in Japan, where native queer artists or producers seem to miss in their news, which is the opposite of what happens in Brazil. In all cases, the occurrence of queer popular culture in the information follows two basic standards. Firstly, the topical coverage of exhibitions, project launches, interviews with artists, and other forms of artistic expression, such as music releases, the second highest number of mentions. Secondly, the mention of queer popular culture within the section on politics is also symptomatic of how journalists articulate queer popular culture to their audiences. The artist has become the spokesperson for the community, frequently a notion extended over a whole country or region of the world.

Within the realm of arts, the advent of the transnational queer artist contributes to this embracing of social causes. For example, Rima Sawayama and Wolfgang Tillmans are two prominent queer artists from Japan and Germany, respectively. Sawayama was born in Japan but lived in Britain. As a recent talent, she sings lyrics addressing identity, consumerism, and queer liberation. Her videos mock the fashion industry and old TV programmes. Tillmans is a notorious German photographer featured in an extensive solo exhibition at Tate Modern in London. He has received a lot of appraisals for his work in documenting his own life, his partners, and his friends. Both received in the news a reading that certainly addresses the originality of their work. Still, journalists are not subtly hiding the fact that both self-identify as queers and embody an amalgam of marginal communities that would seek a similar kind of expression if they could.

Wolfgang Tillmans supports the queer scene in New York.
Mannschaft Magazine, Germany, 15 June 2019

About racism, minority, and music by Rima Sawayama, a Japanese singer acclaimed by Elton John.
Yahoo! News Japan, 07 July 2020

To what concerns this research's interests, what seemed like a free flow of news in a global market has its emphases and absences. To the degree of mirroring local and global characteristics, this research has found three patterns of citation of queer artists by international media outlets, as far as other countries' scenes remain under-reported. Whether at the service of social justice causes, queer affirmation, or queer trends in different countries, these numbers have shown that location, mobility, and political affinity inform a selected view of queer artistry across the globe. On the other side, queer popular culture mingles with online culture and other subcultures, which have received less attention in this research. The Internet has undoubtedly disrupted the conventional routine of journalists and online outlets concerning the discovery and circulation of queer art from around the world. In this process, each country's soft power, media hegemony, and potential to acquire media products from other markets brokered the salience of queer media producers among markets and relegate part of them to obscurity.

Conclusion

This chapter has visited the chief levels of interaction between queer arts and culture and the news from a global perspective. Based on a survey that quantified headlines and article mentions to queer artists and media producers, it has presented results from a study that lined up the main kinds of interests that headlines have revealed. Through the influence of the mainstream media, social justice causes, activism, and political agendas, there is evidence that distinct interests base queer presence in news reports. It is argued that queer popular culture appears according to these specific interests, as many countries may import queer media without producing much content about those acting in their territory. On a global level, queer popular culture emerges as much embedded in global media flows that position Anglo-American artists on top of other guests of news stories and local scenes much limited to events.

On a local level, there is a range of countries with vibrant locations, including Brazil, and France, which retain their local terms and debates, as well as a strong interest in globalized queer culture. For this book's purposes, digital journalism appears as a driving force for globalized queerness as it establishes a series of conditions that permeate queer artists' presence in the news media. While it was not possible to deepen in factors such as the Internet and the charisma of artists individually, nor the financial aspect and profitability of queer culture on a global level, a pattern of queer branding according to global and local conditions is well perceived, in which the news helps to consolidate and sell certain acts. In the next chapter, I continue the discussion on queer appearances in popular culture by exploring legacy or new acts according to theories of cosmopolitanism and the nation.

References

Barnhurst, K. G. (2003). Queer political news: Election-year coverage of the lesbian and gay communities on National Public Radio, 1992–2000. *Journalism, 4*(1), 5–28.

Beaujon, A. (2013). BuzzFeed plans to approach LGBT coverage with same kind of intensity as politics. *Poynter.* 27 September 2013.

Bersani, L. (1995). *Homos.* Harvard University Press.

Bendix, T. (2019). The past, present, and precarious future of LGBT media. Buzzfeed News. 25 January 2019.

Betancourt, M. (2020). L2 Latinx LGBTQ TV characters who made us feel seen. ET online. Available at https://www.etonline.com/12-latinx-lgbtq-tv-characters-who-made-us-feel-seen-154398 Access 11 October 2020.

Blei, D. M., Ng, A. Y., & Jordan, M. I. (2003). Latent dirichlet allocation. *Journal of Machine Learning Research, 3*(Jan), 993–1022.

Bodó, Balázs, et al. (2019). Interested in diversity: The role of user attitudes, algorithmic feedback loops, and policy in news personalization. *Digital Journalism, 7*(2), 206–229.

Buckledee, S. (2020). From 'Zip Me Up Before You Go Go' to 'Boring Old Gits to Wed': The tabloids and celebrities. In S. Buckledee (Ed.). *Tabloiding the Truth* (pp. 131–150). Palgrave Macmillan, Cham.

Burgess, J., & Hurcombe, E. (2021). Digital journalism as symptom, response, and agent of change in the platformed media environment. In S. A. Eldridge II, K. Hess, E. Tandoc, Jr, & O. Westlund (Eds.). *Definitions of Digital Journalism (Studies)* (pp. 46–54). Routledge.

Chaudhary, A. G. (2001). A comparative content analytical study of negative news in western and third world newspapers. *Asian Journal of Communication, 11*(1), 25–50.

Cleland, J., Magrath, R., & Kian, E. (2018). The internet as a site of decreasing cultural homophobia in association football: An online response by fans to the coming out of Thomas Hitzlsperger. *Men and Masculinities, 21*(1), 91–111.

Copeland, S. (2018). Broadcasting queer feminisms: Lesbian and queer women programming in transnational, local, and community radio. *Journal of Radio & Audio Media, 25*(2), 209–223.

Dorsey, M. J., & Detlefsen, E. (2010, September). Vocabulary and taxonomy issues when searching lesbian, gay, bisexual and transgender (LGBT) health literature. In *International Conference on Dublin Core and Metadata Applications* (pp. 180–181).

Edelman, L. (1998). The future is kid stuff: Queer theory, disidentification, and the death drive. *Narrative*, 6(1), 18–30.

Fusco, M. (2020). *RuPaul's Drag Race en français: The influences of modern LGBTQ media translation on queer identity and visibility.* Master's thesis, Concordia University.

Geertz, C. (2017). *The interpretation of cultures.* United States: Basic Books.

Gilbert, H., & Gleghorn, C. (2014). *Introduction: Recasting commodity and spectacle in the indigenous Americas.* University of London.

Grossman, D. (2020). Sexuality and popular culture. In D. Grossman, (Ed.). *Companion to Sexuality Studies* (pp. 279–298). Wiley.

Günther, E., Buhl, F., & Quandt, T. (2018). Reconstructing the dynamics of the digital news ecosystem: A case study on news diffusion processes. In S. Eldridge II, & B. Franklin, (Eds.). *The Routledge handbook of developments in digital journalism studies* (pp. 118–131). Routledge.

Humprecht, E., & Esser, F. (2018). Mapping digital journalism: Comparing 48 news websites from six countries. *Journalism*, 19(4), 500–518.

Kerrigan, P., & Pramaggiore, M. (2021). Homoheroic or homophobic? Leo Varadkar, LGBTQ politics and contemporary news narratives. *Critical Studies in Media Communication*, 1–20.

Kersten, A., & Janssen, S. (2017). Trends in cultural journalism. *Journalism Practice*, 11(7), 840–856.

Kian, E. T. M. (2019). The success of LGBT athletes in the sports media. In R. Magrath, (Ed.). *LGBT athletes in the sports media* (pp. 253–275). Germany: Springer.

King, K. R. (2017). Three waves of gay male athlete coming out narratives. *Quarterly Journal of Speech*, 103(4), 372–394.

Kristensen, N. N., & From, U. (2015). Cultural journalism and cultural critique in a changing media landscape. *Journalism Practice*, 9(6), 760–772.

Leite, L. M. T. (2017). Let's get sickening!: O sucesso de RuPaul's drag race e a sua influência na cena drag brasileira. *Rascunho*, 9(16).

Lewis, M., Brynman, A. E., & Liao, T. F. (2003). *The Sage encyclopedia of social science research methods.* Sage Publications.

Lewis, T. (2007). 'He needs to face his fears with these five queers!' Queer Eye for the Straight Guy, makeover TV, and the lifestyle expert. *Television & New Media*, 8(4), 285–311.

Light, B., Fletcher, G., & Adam, A. (2008). Gay men, Gaydar and the commodification of difference. *Information Technology & People*, 21(3), 300–314.

Lipton, M. (2008). Queer readings of popular culture. *Queer youth culture*, 163–180.

Martel, F. (2019). *The Global Gay: How gay culture is changing the world*. Cambridge: MIT Press.

Moritz, M. (2009). Gay news narratives and changing cultural values. In A. Allan (Ed.) *The Routledge companion to news and journalism*, 1st edition, p. 320.

Motschenbacher, Heiko. (2019). Discursive shifts associated with coming out: A corpus-based analysis of news reports about Ricky Martin. *Journal of Sociolinguistics*, 23(3): 284–302.

Mowlabocus, S. (2017). Representing gay sexualities. In *The Routledge companion to media, sex and sexuality* (pp. 49–58). Routledge.

Nast, H. J. (2002). Queer patriarchies, queer racisms, international. *Antipode*, 34(5), 874–909.

Ng, E. (2017). Between text, paratext, and context: Queerbaiting and the contemporary media landscape. *Transformative Works and Cultures*, 24(0).

Palomino, P. (2020). *The invention of Latin America music*. Oxford: Oxford University Press.

Parahoo, R. (2020). *Exploring being queer and performing queerness in popular music* (Doctoral dissertation, The University of Western Ontario (Canada)).

PWC (2021). The PriceWaterHouseCoopers Media Insights. Largest media markets worldwide in 2017, ranking by revenue. Available at https://www.statista.com/statistics/260065/largest-media-markets-worldwide/ access 20 December 2019.

Radin, M. J., & Sunder, M. (2005). Foreword: The subject and object of commodification. In M. M. Ertman & J. C. Williams (Eds.), *Rethinking commodification: Cases and readings in law and culture* (Vol. 52). New York University Press.

Robinson, S., Lewis, S. S., & Carlson, M. (2019). Locating the 'digital' in digital journalism studies: Transformations in Research. *Digital Journalism*, 7(3), 368–377.

Savigliano, E. S. E. (2010). Notes on tango (as) queer (commodity). *Anthropological Notebooks*, 16(3).

Schapals, A., Maares, P., & Hanusch, F. (2019). Working on the margins: Comparative perspectives on the roles and motivations of peripheral actors in journalism. *Media and Communication,* 7(4), 19–30.

Sedgwick, E. K. (2008). *Epistemology of the closet*. Berkeley: University of California Press.

Shaw, L. (ed.) (2013). *Song and social change*. Lanham: Rowman & Littlefield.

Sheehan, C. (2015). Queerbaiting on the BBC's Sherlock: Addressing the invalidation of queer experience through online fan fiction communities. Available on http://scholarscompass.vcu.edu/cgi/viewcontent.cgi?article=1121&context=uresposters Access 16 November 2020.

Siebler, K. (2016). *Learning queer identity in the digital age*. Springer.

Stayner, M. L. (2014). *An investigation of the relationship between a computer-based method and academic performance* (Doctoral dissertation, University of Phoenix).

Stott, P. (2019). Traditional and contemporary methods of coming out in sport. In R. Magrath, (Ed.). *LGBT athletes in the sports media* (pp. 75–98). Germany: Springer.

Ula, D. (2019). Toward a local queer aesthetics: Nilbar Güreş's photography and female homoerotic intimacy. *GLQ: A Journal of Lesbian and Gay Studies, 25*(4), 513–543.

Wallace, L. R. (2020). *The view from somewhere: undoing the myth of journalistic objectivity*. University of Chicago Press.

Watson, L. J. (2019). 'Just like us'?: Investigating how LGBTQ Australians read celebrity media (Doctoral dissertation).

Zelizer, B. (2019). Why journalism is about more than digital technology. *Digital Journalism, 7*(3), 343–350.

Chapter 3

QUEER ARTISTS

Dame del tu amor poquito poquito, don't be shy, come on
— Cristiano Malgioglio, 'La Notte Perfetta'

In previous chapters, I discussed how globalized queerness emerges from the mingling between media industry opportunities, the global news, and the blur in artists' identities favouring homogenization and commodities. As in the evidence reviewed in Chapter 2, global queer affairs get most of its coverage from the West to become news in other parts of the world. While there is growing attention to queer artists or media producers almost everywhere, it is impossible to state that queer knowledge has received a translation into a fair spectrum of identities and realities elsewhere. The mainstream media pivots queer culture by exploiting a few topics it sees as authentically queer, particularly those artists who display forms of confession and sincerity or offer material or symbolic profitability. Even though 'the mainstream' hides a far more complex reality of media organizations and editorial boards that includes the news, the entertainment sector, the arts, and their operators, concerted actions create a bulwark against homophobia by globalizing queerness through terms, expressions, and movements.

In this chapter, I consciously veer towards a generic term, *artist*, to highlight performers or media producers belonging to an older order of queerness for a mass, pre-Internet audience. I juxtapose their trajectories to a newer kind of artist that belongs well in the Internet media spectrum. Both types of queer artistry have crossed paths in offline and online platforms, whereby they mix distinct forms of displaying their queerness. Whether coming from the TV universe or going back to the time of discos and live spectacles, the former kind of queer artistry is well embodied over the 20th century, especially after the '70s and '80s by US-based artists such as David Bowie or Madonna. More recently, though, queer artistry relates to the return to *camp* as seen in performers such as Lady Gaga in the 2000s (Horn, 2010). I take on this crossroads of pre- and post-digital queerness to observe connections with global or local queerness and the limits of one or the other. For example, what change in values has the Internet prompted in queer artistry over the years? To what extent has globalized queerness changed queer artistic endeavours by turning the formats and languages obsolete? How can the national queer artist, often a figure of extreme highlight and exoticism, co-exist with global talents on screen?

This chapter focuses on this latter kind of artistry as it appears from the late 2010s onwards. Let's think of artists as influencers, celebrities, and queer-baiters. These artists are those whose genesis springs directly from commodifying expectations of queerness. However, in times of more clarity on what LGBTQ stands for in terms of a public mission, is the case of a lack of self-criticism or one that will always push for more commodification and trivialization of queerness? I propose a sample of talents from different continents and languages to discuss these and other points. I include the likes of Brazilian singers Pabllo Vittar and Linn da Quebrada, Hong Konger weightlifter Siufung Law, South Korean pop artist Harisu, French performer Christine and the Queens, Italian performers Mahmood and songwriter Cristiano Malgioglio, South African visual artist Zanele Muholi, among others.

I agree that sampling queer artists will always represent limitations amidst an ever-growing list of prominent names or new ways of seeing prominence itself. Nonetheless, these names could offer the reader an adequate representation of global and local features or values that embody the change in career models and platforms. This discussion is interested in something other than the roots of their *success*, commercially speaking. I approach, instead, values of localness and globalization that permeate their appearances. The final goal was to perform a discourse and cultural analysis that identified the extent that these references are visible. If so, whether they are representative of specific national contexts or cultures reviewed here with the help of theories of queer cosmopolitanism.

The chapter draws extensively from first-hand accounts of these artists, the positions taken in their careers and choices of representation. To what degree can local identities still be enabled or impeded to a broader audience? To what degree can cosmopolitanism translate into globalization and remain faithful to queer politics? What are the mechanisms of insertion or de-escalation of local cultures or the urgency of these homeland connections, taking, for example, geography, language, and motivations? I start by problematizing the origin issue in queer artistry as seen through the lenses of modern popular culture and recent scholarship.

Queer artists and where they come from: a brief ontological overview

Before diving into the discussion of where queer art is heading amidst globalized queerness, it is essential to ask some basic questions on how close or far from the audience artists are and why the issue of location matters. As Doty (1993) and later authors noted, it is not the case of blindly checking queer artistry as if consulting a tag on a supermarket shelf but highlighting whether queer artists take some position about their relationship with popular culture. This negotiation of the meanings of belonging, the gender affinity at stake, and the influences posed on specific sectors of the audience, or the genres, hide fundamental questions for those wishing to follow them or not (Alfrey & Twine, 2017; Moore, 2019). Thus, to scrutinize queer art and production is to point out their stances about the audience collaterally. It is also to leverage the current expectations regarding that actor's availability to engage with queer politics. That being the case, the recent advent of self-styled *queer* or *gender-fluid* arts professionals denotes a set of attitudes that blend culture and critical discourse (Hines & Taylor, 2018).

Apart from the received wisdom of not setting in stone a definition for something that challenges definitions *par excellence*, one can narrow the queerness found in artists down to conversations initiated that touch upon issues regarding biological gender and an individual's right to redefine gender on its multiple façades in society (Scarcelli et al., 2020). To limit my focus and not create confusion over many possibilities of interpretation, the word *queer* has also amalgamated artistic transgender, transvestite, transexual or drag, though they do not point to the same act. These meanings are often extracted as these words appear in the media, as the latter plays an enormous part in the common perception of its many nuances and appropriation by many individuals (Attwood, 2017). Complementary to this book's purposes is the recent mainstreaming of gender fluidity *per se*, including speculations about the gender-fluidness of famous artists. For example, the public might ponder on whether they should treat these artists as individuals and respect their privacy or exploit these transitions as part of their artistic repertoire and, ultimately, raw material for encasing judgements of taste or acceptance.

Despite pop stars' numerous assistants, impresarios, and producers, there should be no question about the motivations of queer or gender-fluid artists as opposed to what is aired on right-wing tabloid media these days. Examples of these conversations were found when the issue of accepting flexible pronouns was first aired. Is Sam Smith posting on Twitter that his pronouns are *they/them because* of his early experiences in a small town in England or due to their position on the global stage? Are queer artists able to present themselves as such thanks to their status as international celebrities, or is this just the visible face of a process happening within all sectors? These are legitimate questions for most of the audience, who often aim to tackle a lot of their curiosity around personal affordances, openness, and the issue of publicity in dialogue with the novelty of globalized queerness. It is not hard to imagine that questions about attachment and detachment can erupt in a hyper-capitalized, simulacra-driven environment of record labels, film producers, and an artistic establishment used to project themselves as close while living miles away from the public.

This public self-assuming in the media vis-à-vis the limits of sincerity and authenticity is not so new. As discussed in this book's introduction, the mainstreaming of queerness breaks away from the ancient fear of being discovered as it trades what used to be a secret as an accessible thing. The advent of openness as a demarcation for queer artistry has demanded much more creativity to forge and entice audiences on what comes next. Whether or not this pressure to stand out results in new drag race competitions every season or celebrities rushing to join trendy discussions on gender identity, these are only a few possible cases of globalizing queerness through the mainstreaming of arts and culture. Let's take *RuPaul*, whom I discussed in past chapters. *RuPaul's Drag Race* echoes both sides of the divide between the sincere queer artist who transcended into the mainstream. His early memories revealed a formative process that shyly underscores a slow consciousness of gender identity to evolve into a self-conscious performance. As a son of an absent father, RuPaul Charles has told the press (Chakrabati, 2018) about this dilemma and the fact that he has embedded these early experiences in his drag persona:

> I recreated it until I was sick and tired of being sick and tired. I recreated the same scene. It's like, 'OK, here it is again. What's my lesson here in this?' And I recreated it in relationships, in my relationship to society. Being a black person in this country, we're always very sensitive about, 'Oh my goodness, is this going to be another put-down situation? Am I going to be rejected in this situation?' And I had to work through that, and I couldn't carry that hurt with me anymore. Until I did the work. And the work involved taking two steps back, figuratively speaking, and looking at the whole

scenario. And in regard to my father — my father was a damaged person. He was damaged by society, black rage, and so to key into my frequency of love and saying, 'I love you so much,' would force him to get in touch with his own feelings, which he couldn't.

To which challenge RuPaul has found the power to broker the later drag queen character:

> My therapist said, 'You know, the power that you feel in drag — or my Superman or Wonder Woman — you know, you can access that at any time.' I tell you, it had never occurred to me. Because, you put the outfit on, and immediately people see you differently, they treat you differently. But I have that same power out of drag, which is monumental.
>
> Chakrabati, 2018

This is not about comparing the experiences of well-known drag acts with that of other non-binary, transgender, and gender-fluid artists who, for several reasons, have taken a long time to disclose their gender status to the public. However, there is a question of *how* the advent of the queer statement has been put *into action* in ways that flow through from the mainstream to local instances and vice-versa. The so-called *power* while being in drag can perceptively be down to the dislocation that the clothes and make-up allow and other instruments one employs to accessorize one's queerness. It resonates with the distance created between performers and their origins. It appears as a vehicle to somewhere else safe and accepting. Arguably, this power of dislocating oneself from the rest deserves further investigation as this helps define the local (the pre-transformation) and the global (post-transformation) in a series of other queer acts.

More recently, this media ammunition has helped producers and artists protect themselves and forge an audience and ensure distance, security, dialogue, and access among queers and between them and society at large. Let us look at the audio-visual and the documenting of queer lives that have taken hold of mass media channels. Oppression, reaction, survival, and overall power to make choices; to name or rename oneself; existing under specific terms. The legal battle of Freddy McConnell, the 34-year-old journalist of the Guardian newspaper, who conceived his son by getting pregnant, was later denied by the UK Supreme Court the right to be legally named as the child's father. McConnell recorded all the steps of his trajectory, from his pregnancy to the courts. A 2020 BBC-distributed documentary called *The Seahorse: The Man Who Gave Birth* told his story. Cases like this have transformed queer media from an idea tied to spectacle and stages into an activist stance that thrives on its testamentary basis. Whether well-known or not, artists and media producers have envisioned the media as a vehicle for the reconstruction of themselves.

Like the above documentary and RuPaul Charles' awakening, many factors complicate today's queer sense of artistry as a cosmopolitan exercise. It comprises the cycle of searching to acknowledge difference, then representing difference, to reproduce it on a large scale. This chapter seeks to feed this discussion to the extent that it characterizes another aspect of *globalized* queerness. These episodes weave a more complex fabric for artistry as a kaleidoscopic set of media appearances, which consequently result in blurring local stories and dramas, which, in turn, become another stream of preferences and tastes in a menu of queer choices. Whether in fiction or real life, some of these conflicts help audiences to apprehend queerness on a large scale, as far as artists resort to strategies to amplify their *globalness* or *localness* according to what they see fitting. In the next section, I start to provide some of this chapter's grounds for analysis, in which ideas on cosmopolitanism become helpful to perceive globalness and localness as opposing elements in several tiers of artistic belonging.

Queer cosmopolitanism and the local artist

Over the last decades, the idea of the queer artist has fed an expectation of one being able to navigate global stages more than demonstrating a sense of roots. Based in California, New York City or other prominent Western capitals, queer stardom has signalled a kind of identity whose main objective was to run uncontested. At worst, there were aspects concealed from the masses. As in RuPaul's reconciliation case, *localness*, or the deliberate confession of belonging somewhere, geographically speaking, was to be made available to the audience only later in his life. Much before the likes of Sam Smith, George Michael, née Giorgios Kyriacos Panayiotou, went public as an English-named artistic persona. It is fair to say that the Cypriot origins of his father were mostly used as another piece of a homophobic heritage that one should get rid of (Carman, 2017). George Michael's fame streamlines Smith or Lil Nas X's emergence 40 years later. Nas X, née Montero Lamar Hill, adopted a rootless stage name but chose the scenes of his first video for the single,

Old Town Road, a Western backstage, a reference exploited in a few acts but which quickly disappeared from the artist's repertoire.

Queer cosmopolitanism is an overarching set of concepts that help understand these multiple pathways into transnational, transcultural queer relationships. Here in this brief exploration, the focus rests on one's cultural heritage as resisting or blending with external influences or yet the translation thereof into discourses. The first assumption is the extent to which queer cosmopolitanism bases this movement towards globalized queerness. Jon Binnie and Beverly Skeggs (2004) saw cosmopolitanism happening with competing dimensions that articulate race, sexuality, and class according to real or negotiated dimensions. The authors argued for the power of capitalism in creating these cosmopolitan experiences in a gay village in Manchester, for example. I would invite this argument to intersperse with the argument that artists articulate cosmopolitanism by revealing or concealing themselves in media appearances. Cosmopolitanism exists here to make queer artists or producers gauge steps towards an embrace of the mainstream.

By saying this, I mean that staging queerness can also erase local asymmetries, such as class or racial divides, in favour of well-accepted features or languages. Regarding the scenario of productions from the Global South airing in the West, for example, or smaller, rural locations being on screen, there is still a gap of being local without restrictions. Netflix, one of the world's biggest streaming platforms, has invited several 'LGBTQ' productions from elsewhere other than Europe and the US. The 2021's *Chandigarh Kare Aashiqui* – directly from Bollywood – or *Rosa Morena*, a story between Denmark and Brazil from 2010, are available in many markets. No matter how fitting these productions can be for the LGBTQ criteria established by Netflix and other streaming platforms, there is always the question of how the aesthetics, the language, and the audiences they reach correspond to the countries and cultures these productions represent.

It is increasingly difficult not to note the intention of building queerness on top of a discourse, but on whose realities? What is a positive effort of inclusion *or* a tokenization of queer stories and its participants? For example, many productions remain distant from telling queer stories based on early life difficulties. Experiences being brought up, religious traumas, and bullying do appear, but one should note their depth and complexity according to those who really suffered them. As a result, projections of these kinds arrive at the audience already marketed or obscured in semi-known tales that get many variations among the fandoms. These movements arguably converge to the heavy manufacturing of queer cosmopolitanism. In this way, the position of the cosmopolitan queer today vis-à-vis its local self de-escalates or even hide traits and values due to the gravitational camp that pulls one into cosmopolitanism as the final end of every story.

Fewer studies have come close to tracking these movements between cosmopolitanism and localism, especially when private life has been so much part of one's artistic presence. Scholars have asked this question based on queer cultural experience on online platforms, from using Grindr in disaster zones (Ong, 2017) to reflecting on the cosmopolitan preconception of gay scenes in countries as diverse as Lebanon, Russia, and China (Bao, 2011; Stella, 2013; Moussawi, 2018). Of course, the correlation between cosmopolitanism and tourism is evident in all these scenarios. It composes an experience that is much less possible for non-white queers in neoliberal, privatized cities (Rushbrook, 2002). Much like viral hashtags such as #lovealwayswins, is important not to overestimate cosmopolitanism as a life-changing event. Audiences can evade or submit to this reality according to evolving circumstances. In the case of modern media, queer cosmopolitanism finds paragon in the fluidity that springs from using technology constantly. Tracking technologies, for instance, renders the cosmopolitan *feeling* obligatory and unavoidable rather than casual or self-induced.

The bottom line of cosmopolitanism in conjunction with queer media lies in the degree to which it bridges or blocks localities, parlances, and territories that forge a single form of globalized queerness. In *The Globalization of Sexuality*, Jon Binnie (2004) warned against the transformation of sexuality into American sexuality in the context of modern cities. Essentially, the author saw how the constant orientation toward standards of consumption and the elevation of a 'consciousness' created a connection between the cultural, sexual, and economic factors surrounding queer individuals. What if queer individuals are *more* or *equally* attached to outside queer references than to early mirrors of sexuality or gender they encounter? In effect, the 'cosmopolitan self' for queer individuals based in the Global South (Schutte, 2018) has been much neglected in the literature, including those material aspirations uniquely tied to a move to the West (Levy, 2018).

Therefore, one must evade the binaries that view global values are upheld, superior or liberating and local values as prohibitive or homophobic. Overall, the problem of the literature on cosmopolitanism and queer culture is the straightforward determination that either capitalism will succeed in wiping out local cultures or queer culture is unlikely to thrive without leaving the local closet, otherwise seen as fundamentally oppressive. In this landscape, resisting or co-existing with the Americanization of queerness will not be possible. I attempted to balance these accounts while re-appraising artists' trajectories that succeeded by industry standards, making themselves household names in their original communities. This approach sees trajectories beyond resistance or colonization, the city vs the rural, and the global gay vs parochial versions.

Having discussed the upshot of commodified queer and the issue of authenticity in previous chapters, here, I interpreted results according to cultural analysis methods (Pickering, 2018, Snodgrass et al., 2020). This method broadly perceives aspects such as cultural change, consensus, lists, and networks that lead to a sense of cultural hegemony. Textual analysis maps cultural models (Polzer et al., 2020), offering less interpretative stances while allowing for the display of cultural actors' voices and the allocation of choices that can hold power or congregate large audiences. There has been the application of questionnaires and interviews to ensure precision in this method. Still, I adopted a simplified structural analysis by collecting and highlighting representative word choices or shared histories among these actors. In this way, I ordered 'sets of themes and shared knowledge, which helps members of groups reason about particular things, persons, and processes in the world.' (ibid.:23).

I started collecting these records based on press coverage, artists' interviews, and paratexts. I found more than cultural models, but a series of links, throwbacks to history, and issues that trespassed the territory of queer culture. Due to the globalized nature of these findings, meaning their prominence in the Global South and the particularities of these realities, I then decided to include more on how other authors have dealt with alternative queer realities. One inspiration was Quiroga's (2000) *Tropics of Desire*, in which queer culture receives a franker account of how artists have used their bodies and words to communicate with larger audiences. This politics is mainly cross-national but retains much local communicability. I aim to place global and regional arts emphases adjacent to one another and, in turn, problematize their role in the globalized queerness context by highlighting priorities and absences. One can thus appreciate the extent to which queer artists and media producers can seem over-susceptible or surrounded by globalization. Results appear according to these emphases, as the hierarchy of topics follows queer positions adopted at many levels, namely, the listing of queer artists as *national treasures*, queerness as a class divider, and, finally, the significant layer of queer artistry being invested in the cosmetics of transculturation.

The queer national treasure: Phia Ménard and Cristiano Malgioglio

One of the main cosmopolitan drivers in queer culture lies in the multiplication of queer celebrities of transnational fame. It has been long since Marlene Dietrich or Freddie Mercury, and the 'come-out' in showbiz has been a lifetime event. From reality show participants to sportspeople (Cashmore & Cleland, 2011), the multiplicity of queer public persons re-casts the expectations for queer young people, no longer needing websites such as *gaydar* or *Bigmuscle* to find a shape or presence that corresponded to their desires (Young, 2004). Celebrity culture has inspired some queers in the Global South, who have targeted especially white, anglophone celebrities at the forefront of taste (Schutte, 2018). As argued above, the extent to which cosmopolitanism opens or closes the universe of cultural references for queer individuals is down to a series of factors, including the distance to their local repertoire and the possibility of escaping hardship. Less knowledge exists, nonetheless, about the role of characters who are publicly queer but have remained under the gaze of the local public only.

These local actors, composers, writers, drag artists, performers, comedians, or influencers from the Internet age are still far from touting their gender or sexual preferences worldwide. Their treatment by the media has not grown as preternatural as queer relationships observed on American television, for example. Not long ago, American TV personalities such as Ellen DeGeneres and Rosie O'Donnell had to greatly ponder their coming out in the late 1990s and early 2000s. Still, soon as they did, they inspired generations abroad (Gever, 2012). When one looks at the Global South there are multiple examples of celebrities or personalities that had to hide their sexuality for sheer safety from punitive laws and an interested public until very recently. In South Africa, during apartheid, personalities and well-known figures had to fight accusations from the press in a time of illegal *sodomy* (Mbsi, 2021).

Brazil, a country with a deep-seated mediatization of gender binaries, has also popularized a string of local queer characters that have left a legacy. Aside from the tradition of heterosexual actors playing queer characters for mockery and heterosexual laughter, television offered a few exceptions. The late heterosexual comedian Chico Anysio (1931–2012) had in his *Professor Raimundo's School* (*Escolinha do Professor Raimundo*), written in the '90s, a string of gay or lesbian characters. Even if stereotypical, they were not fully out of the closet.

Figure 7 Clodovil Hernandes arrives at the Brazilian Congress in 2009. Photo: Jose Cruz, Agencia Brasil.

For example, *Seu Peru*, played by the late Orlando Drummond (1919–1921), and *Dona Catifunda*, by Zilda Cardoso (1936–1919), who was probably lesbian. The show represented the archetypical classroom attended by grown-ups, where gay and lesbian parts appeared pretty integrated with the rest. Coming from the 1970s, *clothing* designer Clodovil Hernandes (1937–2009) was one of the earliest celebrities living under the shadow of his gayness in a mix of public fascination and loathing. He lived to be the first openly gay congressman in the country (Bonham, 2014).

Cases like these expose the unbalanced knowledge of queer cultural history, partly because of the flaws of queer cosmopolitanism. By looking at the press in countries other than the US, an enormous body of contributions make queer appearances locally conditioned to hundreds of factors. These artists' bios and trajectory always come up mixed with excellent artistic skills, but likewise, their private lives are a target of journalists, commentators, and even their fans, due to unresolved prejudices or actual homophobia in distinct levels. In the context of globalized queerness, one watches in contemporaneity the formation of an antithetical image in that respect. No longer *persona non grata*, queer celebrities are emphasized in the same recognition framework that spans different countries simultaneously. What I call here the *queer national treasure* is a provocation to this inherited status inscribed into the artists of the past, but who, at their peak time, were not as celebrated as revivalists would want today. And yet, queer cosmopolitanism has ensured that part of this celebration happens in today's moral standards because of these artists' ambitions to be bigger than their local media wanted them to be. Magazine covers, award winners, reality show competitors, master chefs, storytellers, journalists: the media creates winners today, but it has not always been like that.

Whenever we look at the national contexts, it is harder to fathom the full extent of the making of queer national treasures. Either how they emerge in some media conglomerates and not others or why some moments and not others. To illustrate this section, I picked up two of the most cited celebrities in the news reports surveyed in Chapter 2. Still, there could be many others if I went on to invite regional realities in countries such as Spain and Ireland, or even smaller countries, such as Bulgaria or Thailand. Italy and France emerged as locations where robust scenes of queer artistry have generated two queer national treasures that have become crystalized at the heart of the national culture, coming from local forging. There is no shortage of pieces highlighting their experience, trajectory, and perception of themselves. Anchored in the survey's results, it is possible to locate a cultural model where many media texts help to give a critical perspective on their appearance and have cemented their reputation as visible queer artists for decades. Massively popular or not, they have achieved seniority while being the face of queerness in their languages.

The case of Phia Ménard, born in 1971 in Nantes, France, remains unique. Ménard founded her juggling company in 1998. Since then, she has invested in new languages for contemporary art. The artist has appeared in various media outlets as one of the few transgender practitioners to reach national prominence. Ménard has been far too elusive to qualify as a mass phenomenon or a conventional unanimity among her peers. Featured in a 2018 piece in the *New York Times* (Cappelle, 2018), she described the challenges behind her success in France. Growing up in proletarian Brittany, she wore her mother's clothes and 'thought herself crazy.' In another part of the interview, Ménard recognizes that her work owes a lot to grants from the French government while facing the suspicion of theatre counterparts.

In another interview, given in 2011 (QuaiTV, 2011), Ménard presented her work *L'après-midi D'un Foehn* with a soundtrack by Claude Debussy. In the play staged in Caen, she choreographs colourful plastic bags that dance according to the air infused in them. She appears in many videos on YouTube assembling these delicate pieces and blowing them away with the aid of fans, seemingly performing to the sounds played on stage. Ménard's work may lie miles away from the expectation of globalization or commodification discussed in this book, but her trajectory, as a transgender artist in deep Catholic France, is remarkable. Where social class intertwines with the impediments faced by transgender individuals in Western societies, her place in the small circuit and short budgets of avant-garde artistic production is undoubtedly well known.

These two facets of her trajectory: on the one hand, overcoming of doubts about the feasibility of her work and career to finally make it – partially because of public money and the relatively viable artistic conditions in France. On the other hand, showcasing of her national standing in the laudable avant-garde artistic circuit – both aspects lay bare the few exceptions of a queer artist somewhat thriving from the grassroots while not depending on social media networks and artificial ways of promotion. Her debt to her early days is apparent in her poetic, as she describes it:

> [the work] is made like when we are children (…) it is like returning to our first memories (…) where one can build everything, one can construct everything.
>
> QuaiTV, 2011

In other opportunities, she situates her work as part of a broader response to France's macho culture, where patriarchy is a driving force. In the *New York Times* piece, Ménard clarifies the degree of self-awareness that being a transgender artist had brought to her, especially in terms of the spatial presence to which she must be conscious and reactive:

> I lived on the side of power for 30 years (…). I was invisible then: I could walk into any street at night, and the chances that something would happen to me were very slim. Now it's absolutely impossible. I've lost the right to invisibility. It's a reminder that suddenly, I no longer own space — I'm just a tenant.

For the occasion of another spectacle in 2018, Ménard explains her interests:

> The issue of the transformation of the body, the transformation of identity, at the same time, the transformation of the matter.

The attention to her identity change and how it affected so much the shape of her work dialogues with other French transgender avant-garde artists, such as Claude Cahun (1894–1954), née Lucy Renee Mathilde Schwob, who worked during the French resistance as a photographer and had a productive life doing self-portrait (Shaw, 2017). Like Cahun, Ménard is prolifically interested in challenging the need to fit in at society but also in calling off older representations of herself. In Cahun's case, the argument came in her autobiographic book, *Disavowals, or Cancelled Confessions*, initially published in 1930. Both artists re-elaborate their discourse towards constantly reassessing their position as fluid artists. Through names, artworks, materials, or artistic research, these conversations indeed make a cultural model of their own, at least in contemporary queer European pop culture. That would be the place of artists such as Christine and the Queens. Born in Nantes as Heloïse Adelaide Letissier, the artist has undergone numerous name changes since debuting her album *Chaleur Humaine* in 2014. More recently, Letissier has changed pronouns to *he* and adopted the stage name of *Redcar*.

In 2020, the controversy that surrounded Ménard being deprogrammed 24 hours before performing at a French festival to benefit the appearance of the American pop star Kanye West took the headlines (Huffpost, 2020). Ménard is quoted as saying: 'I am an artist, a trans woman, a company director. I refuse denial and contempt for our team.' In fact, for the first time, the French press was positioning such a query from a transgender artist. Was it a small victory against the evils of cosmopolitanism? It is perhaps too little to declare the Ménard's victory in the face of the American blockbuster. And yet, the fact that she has rebuked the situation by stating her *transness* and received such a roaring reaction from the public is an attestation of her prevailing, to say the least, standing as a respected French artist. The respect from the establishment was not a problem for Cristiano Malgioglio, another artist invited to this discussion.

Malgioglio's extensive work spans roles as a singer, composer, and later as a TV personality. The mainstream media has cast Malgioglio as one of the best-known artists in modern Italy. From a shadow songwriter for popstar Mina in the 1970s, Malgioglio may have achieved the status of a national treasure long ago. Nonetheless, his blooming as a gender-fluid star comes much later. After decades of posing as a cis man with *exotic* taste in music, his public affiliation to queer causes, his openness about homosexual desire, and later performing as a cross-dresser in video clips have only dated from the last decade. In a recent interview, he admits that his taste in men corresponds to the archetype of old-style Italian icons like Marcello Mastroianni. Currently, though, 'his eyes were on the American actor Channing Tatum' (RAI, 2018).

In a 2019 music video called *Notte Perfetta*, or the 'perfect night,' Malgioglio sings along with the band The J.E.K., a video that instantly garnered millions of visualizations on YouTube. Malgioglio performs as a countryside Sicilian woman with a veil over her face as the camera cuts to show only his face and a woman's body dressed in a polka dot pattern and a long skirt. He/she is supposedly flirting with muscular Italian boys as he scrambles through the cobblestone streets of southern Sicily, with echoes of Madonna's *Take a Bow*. Indeed, he/she seems to point to many international artists when asked about his favourite singers, as he told in the same interview (RAI, 2018):

> Tony Bennett absolutely, and then Diana Ross. Among the youngsters, [I would say] Lady Gaga and Beyoncé, also I love Riccardo Cocciante, because he is very intense.

Having lived in Latin America, Malgioglio has also written songs in Portuguese, such as the 2017 hit, which could be roughly translated as 'I am in love with your husband,' boasting enormous success. All these interfaces between Malgioglio, international singers, and his androgynous and frequent appearances on Italian TV programmes position him in such an emblematic space in and out of queer cosmopolitanism. He is an artist who achieves to amalgamate himself in mainstream or as a local artist in scenes from across the globe.

At the same time, Malgioglio's many interviews with the Italian press are characterized by him speaking of close friendships with other Italian artists, fights, reconciliations, artistic partnerships, and his complete attachment to the local scene. With a distinctive white flack on top of abundant black hair and colourful sunglasses, Malgioglio crowns his legacy and fame in his native country. In one opportunity, he disappears amid a sea of references to global music stars who surround every interview (F.Q. Magazine, 2019). These tricks and ticks Malgioglio shows on TV may relate to what Mancini et al. (2011) have mentioned about 'queering' the audience or creating the conditions for a temporary suspension of homophobia from the audience – or at least the expectation of it.

The above description of Malgioglio's recent appearances channels this intersection between real and purely entertaining realities of cosmopolitan queerness. I want to liken Malgioglio's presence as a mediator between the cosmopolitanism of his queer impersonation and the adoration he receives from the Italian crowd. After many stints abroad, he resurfaced in Italy much due to this mix of old and new references and the love of the vintage that includes the perpetual revival of old TV acts as the *cool guest*. In March 2020, when the Covid-19 crisis was raging in the country and leading to numerous deaths, he attacked global stars Madonna and Lady Gaga for not issuing any message to Italy in its darkest hours:

'She [Lady Gaga] was worried because she could not perform in Paris, instead of sending a message of solidarity. I did not expect this from her,' he asserted.

Bocca, 2020

By the call of 'betrayers!' as if he was, according to him, an old acquaintance of both global artists and reaffirming his pseudo-global status, he also criticizes 'fellow' celebrities. By doing so, Malgioglio sums up this dialogue between the world and his village. Of course, these are small interventions to the public debate and said in the context of a man who is a *Big Brother* commentator. However, if conjugated with the decades of his juxtapositions to the image of global celebrities and his profound attachment to Italy, Malgioglio's opinions lead us to a proto-cosmopolitan presence. It is detached from Italy, simultaneously sitting on a cosmopolitan rendering of a patriotic queer.

Like Ménard, Malgioglio also keeps his reservations about his home country. It is not infrequently that he goes out to announce plans for a final departure, thanks to his friendships with other international stars. The publicity generated around the *grande addio*, or the grand farewell, gives us many insights into the permanent look abroad that local queer artistry demands as means to justify or legitimate itself before cosmopolitan connections. In this small excerpt, there are nuggets of detachment that hint at this interplay inside/outside, close/distant, subject to criticism or persecution/larger than national interests:

Cristiano Malgioglio, an emigrant artist, could soon leave Italy: fresh from the success of 'Volverte a ver', the Spanish version (broadcast on Telecinco) of 'There is mail for you', the Italian artist could see his arms wide open from Spain and dreams of working in Madrid, where he has received numerous proposals. But, he specifies to Adnkronos, [himself appears] 'as an artist', not as a columnist. At 'Volverte a ver', he says, 'I surprised Mónica Naranjo, one of the most famous singers in Spain, who was then told by all the most important Spanish newspapers.

Corriere Adriatico, 2019

Unlike Ménard, Malgioglio makes the most of his international prominence as a self-styled national treasure. While both artists remain distinct in many other ways, both have showcased an exciting dialogue between global and local influences, whether to counteract what they perceive as local limitations to their artistry, cases of homophobia or for the opportunity to educate and elevate the public to promote an international oversight. Part of a cultural model centred in the nation, these queer personalities do not resort to the cosmopolitan discourse of the 'scene' to carve out their space. They somehow live off their art or attract the new public. Their solid backing from the national mainstream media, loyal fanbase and record of intelligently planned interventions in the media.

Other countries have fed a shared sense of their queer national treasures: the series of celebrations around the 100th anniversary of Pierpaolo Pasolini's birth in Italy in 2022, and the strong attachment to Almodóvar in Spain and vice-versa, are among many other examples of Western popular culture. If that is the case, it is possible to extrapolate some of the aspects seen herein to assess how modes of reviving old and new queer artists are in their legacy. More focus or less focus on their queerness? Is the un-queering possible as subversive figures, such as Pasolini, grow into historical images? Queerness, formerly an intricated place to be, finds redemption and popularization, but will their queerness trigger the same kind of sympathy and admiration in future generations? Disease, disaster, problems with the police, or drug abuse have marked personalities such as Freddie Mercury, George Michael, and Anne Heche, to say a few famous names in the anglophone world, but does the oppressive context around them also matter in their revival? In the next section, I visit the case of emerging queer artists questioning class, race, and gender obstacles in the local or global landscape.

From the periphery to the nation: Pabllo Vittar and Linn da Quebrada

The elevation of a few queer artists to the national pantheon does not invalidate the current issues of race, poverty, homophobia, and transphobia that keep other hundreds or thousands of names away from any public recognition. Above, we saw how cosmopolitanism as a cultural model had assisted queer artists in growing in the public eye by relativizing their national landscape in the face of international prominence. In this section, the same values also liberate new artists from struggles associated with their background to get them further distinction and national respect. I start with the case of Brazilian queer stars Pabllo Vittar and Linn da Quebrada because they are outstanding in many ways. Both queer artists have, in the late 2010s, opened new avenues amid the harsh circumstances of their upbringing. Both are seen as brown and black in Brazil, raised in poverty and rising to prominence in the country's mainstream media, situated in the whiter Southeast.

Brazil remains one of the most dangerous countries in the world for LGBTQ+ populations by many counts of death rates and street violence (Mendes & Silva, 2020). To represent its over-populated urban peripheries have meant embodying the possibility of surviving these high violence rates, unemployment, and prejudice from the white middle classes. When looking at violence against women, the numbers are not encouraging either. The United Nations says that 16.7 per cent of females over 16 years old have experienced physical violence or threats in the country (UN Women, 2016). As the nation remains systematically and institutionally racist and misogynist, to inherit black traits, to embody female appearance, being from the periphery is to expose oneself to even further risks (Levy, 2018). Before these artists thrived as nationally and internationally recognized performers, their main success was one of rising from this scenario of extreme exclusion, besides physical or psychological annihilation.

The case of Vittar tells the story of a young northeastern gay man who saw himself wishing for fame and recognition. The northeast is one of the poorest and less developed areas of the country. With its vast populations of black and Indigenous groups and their descendants, it suffers chronically from a lack of public services and a competent education system for the disadvantaged. It is not unlikely that local artists remain confined to their regions, being victimized by patriarchal structures and patrons. Unexpected, the national fame that Pabllo Vittar has accumulated paradigm breaks. His prominence on national television, the biggest chain being owned by a white wealthy family who have thrived on top of the unequal Rio de Janeiro state, violates some of the class, race, and gender logic that have been perpetuated for decades on who gets media attention or not. In a country whose famous white-centric, heteronormative and, often, homophobic *telenovelas*, Vittar's overwhelming attendance of TV shows and ad campaigns contradicted a class-driven representation. His presence, first and foremost, goes against the trend of having northeastern artists always playing the domestic employees in the air or the representation of black or brown individuals as a stubborn image of everyday life (Pinho, 2015).

As a gender-fluid artist still gauging the first chapters of media notoriety, Vittar has unprecedentedly enjoyed international prominence and has had the chance to record their music in languages other than Portuguese. The successful launch of his/her image to multiple social channels was encased by American outlets such as *Vogue*, which undoubtedly occupies the spaces of heterosexual stars. Vittar's transcendence from the queer niche to the mainstream has surprised many Brazilian scholars. Brazil's queer presence in popular culture has traditionally reserved for queer characters a minimal space of the limelight, championed mainly by the then-hegemonic Globo TV. The latter, alas, come slowly re-building its positioning as homo-friendly despite the long-standing reputation of not allowing gay characters in the *telenovelas*. When so, gays and lesbians have hitherto played only small parts, otherwise shown as funny and shouty. For years, LGBTQ folks were seen as reporters for late-night coverage of carnival ballrooms. In soap operas, gay characters died at the start of seasons until broadcasters decided to air a few *gay kisses* to epitomize liberation and acceptance in the late 2010s (Baggio, 2013). Otherwise, gay comedians have enjoyed more in this share of the audience, but yet limited and charismatic. Parts such as *Seu Peru*, lived by late actor Orlando Drummond, is one of these notorious roles. More recently, actors such as the late Paulo Gustavo and the *Big Brother* winner Gil do Vigor have fulfilled and continued this gay-cum-funny guy portrait of homosexuals on TV.

These are the grounds that shelter Vittar's success. However, it is possible to say that past *transvestites* have enjoyed some public popularity but faced the harsher constraints of their time. *Vera Verão* was one of these characters. Embodied by Jorge Lafond (1952–2003), the late black comedian who had enormous success through the '80s and '90s, he managed to do something similar. Any topics or characters that have instead flirted with the homosexual rights agenda have traditionally triggered reactionary reactions (Romancini, 2018). In this conservative environment, Vittar receives wary responses, even in academia. Vittar is part of a 'trans tessitura' whose voice, like another Brazilian queer artist Ney Matogrosso, refuses to conform to existent classifications in popular music or genre (Da Silva, 2019). Vittar also aids in dislocating drag queen scenes that used to exist on risky public squares of countryside Brazil to social networks and mass media (Neto, 2018).

One thing that Vittar has not denied is that he/she is Brazilian. For example, Vittar has embraced many of the country's issues as a queer voice. In August 2020, as the country still battled the enormous toll that Covid-19 has inflicted in deaths and economic havoc, Vittar refused to perform in drive-ins as many other artists, which he argued: 'Who could afford to own a car in Brazil?' (UOL, 2020). The same patriotic verve Vittar demonstrated when reminding that he had shouted: 'Not him' (Barbosa, 2020), a protest chant against the homophobic president, Jair Bolsonaro. On Bolsonaro's election, Vittar challenged the climate of fear that took over in Brazil by declaring during a broadcast interview:

> Guys, check my face and see if I am putting up a scared face. If you have any doubt, it is over now. Darlings, I am not going to leave Brazil.

Vittar reinforced:

> Not a single black person will go back to the *senzala* (colonial slave inhabitation), neither women will go back to the kitchen, neither do gay men go to the closet.
>
> Notícias da TV, 2018

This defying tone shapes many other Vittar statements on social media or gossip websites. A few scholars have taken note of Vittar's activist stances (e.g., França, 2020). Close to this book's discussions, some have acknowledged Vittar's openness to cosmopolitan instances while politically and artistically embracing his roots. During a music festival in 2019, Vittar stated: 'Nothing changes if you haste the flag but do not defend LGBT causes.' (Fortuna & Rosa, 2019). In 2018, Vittar spoke fluently about his views on Brazil during another televised interview:

> [The country] is much homophobic, prejudicial, transphobic, racist. I see that every day (...) I want to take information [to other people in Brazil]. I want to show we are capable. (...) we have a strong

personality; we can work, and we should have the same rights [than heterosexual people] and we can do whatever we want.

Brenner, 2018

Vittar's discourse develops a cultural model based on work ethics, strong moral sense, and beauty standards that may blur with Brazilians' conservatism and white-centric landscape. For this research's purposes, these excerpts reveal a deep concern with the country and its ways toward gender-fluid people. As far as Vittar comes from a such underprivileged background, their views are wide enough to evidence unprecedented queer political contention. Vittar does so by employing terms from regional Brazil in his/her songs that can be, arguably, despised amongst the southern urban classes. That is Vittar's way of demonstrating queer sarcasm. For example, the song *Rajadão* is entirely based on Brazilian slang that means *a big strike* or *a big noise*, an expression that, while having sexual connotations, is not clear to the metropolitan elites. Titles like these are frequent in Vittar's lyrics, whether or not he collaborates with international artists. The same interface happened when Vittar joined the Brazilian rapper Jerry Smith to sing his release singing a *forró*, a dance style from rural Brazil, as they dressed in streetwear (Ferreira, 2020).

I want to argue that in Vittar's case, one of remixing music styles, aesthetics, and rhythms reverses the cosmopolitan tendency to elitism as it flirts with new models for queer popular culture. This unruly behaviour is not so much a move to break market categorizations or capitalism as it conforms with them. The bottom line is the opportunity to do so by seizing deep-seated prejudices and reversing race and class-based cultural hegemony: stealing from white Brazil and giving it to the rest. These series of dual references: urban/countryside, poor/rich, white/African Brazil would be only a list of appropriations if they did not cut across rigid divides in a country that often sees itself as only one. Popular culture has provenly provided Brazilians with political positions and a repertoire that has fed into democracy (Raphael, 1981). Whether carrying this strange fusion to the European Music Awards or collaborating with Latin American artists such as *Thalía* or British singer *Charlie XCX*, Vittar ignores, perhaps willfully, Brazil's divides, even if not consciously political all the time. If only, Vittar's cosmopolitanism de-homogenizes and hybridizes what one ultimately expects from the show of a drag artist.

Less unruly and chaotic than Vittar, other trans artists make other fixtures in the landscape. The singer and actor Linn da Quebrada has quickly established herself as another emerging artist of recent Brazil. She has not yet reached the same international projection as the latter with their various partnerships, but *Linn da Quebrada*, or Lina Pereira dos Santos, whose surname is slang for 'from the suburbs,' shares many of Vittar's biography. Born in 1990, she is black, born and raised in a *favela*. Distinct from Vittar, Linn grew up in São Paulo, in the industrialized southeast. Concerning her arts, Linn da Quebrada has engaged observers in a more critical way than Vittar has ever done. She has named her albums after typical indigenous names, such as *Pajubá*, and has made a career that has mixed rap, popular Brazilian music (MPB), and acting roles. More recently, she was a guest on *Big Brother*. Linn da Quebrada appears here in dialogue with Vittar's recent legacy due to the richness of their aims as transgender musicians who otherwise offer a take on being local and yet invites cosmopolitan features, even if not quoting these hints directly.

The 30-year-old has starred in her first long-length movie, called *Bixa Travesty*, or *Tranny Fag* in English. This title adds to the earlier discussion on how local terms can mediate the experience of queer artists and bridge queer realities to mainstream societies. Until recently, words such as *bicha* had an equivalent derogatory meaning of *fag* or *queer* in English. A similar meaning applies to *travesty*, or *transvestite*, as she often coins it, which is a word that Linn da Quebrada has reclaimed for herself. While it seems a subtle name change, a tweak, apparently, the use of words bases formal interactions between Linn and the media. Her steps as an artist, the intentions behind lyrics, and the positions taken, much like Pabllo Vittar, emulate this mix between political positions, moderate activism, and media fluency. During a trip to the Berlin Cinema Festival in 2020, wherein a documentary about her life directed by Brazilian filmmakers Kiko Goifman and Claudia Priscila received the Teddy Awards, she commented about the meaning of the trip:

> I feel like I am contributing to the European culture and thought. People value my production of knowledge. I always make it very clear that what I am going to do over there is to share and ask them for a historical reparation. [One] understands that Europe is one of the responsible [agents] for our colonisation.
>
> Balsemão, 2019

This level of political awareness and a critical stance of herself during a trip to Europe, still a dream for millions in her country, reveals the degree to which Linn da Quebrada embodies in her brand a permanent critique of Brazilian society and decolonial issues, often with elaborated language. She complements her thoughts about being overseas for the very first time: '[I will continue being] this black and transvestite body which occupies spaces through a discourse, which is, somehow, unexpected.' (ibid., 2019). What resonates in Linn da Quebrada based on her critical cosmopolitanism lies in this recurrent self-framing as temporary, exceptional, and 'unexpected.' Unlike Vittar, whose performance engages with a range of popular and critical issues, Linn da Quebrada does not seem to believe that her notoriety as an artist should extend across the borders, at least to what rests in embracing a total commercial stance. Her recent transition into having feminine features has probably problematized even more this critical distance on which she has built her name and audience. As a 2022 *Big Brother* participant who bears a tattoo of a crown of thorns on her forehead, she strikes a relationship with mainstream fame as far as her being trans continues to take the headlines in the Brazilian press.

As a cultural model, Vittar's unusual name and Linn's ambiguous reservation and openness to the world reveal an outstanding savviness in using media resources in their favour. Linn's *quebrada*, the obscure suburb, is permanently in crisis. She was not only the topic of an award-winning documentary but got a role in Globo TV, finally showing signs of modernization from its usual conservative values (Silva, 2022). Linn da Quebrada, furthermore, adds other accomplishments to her mainstream presence, such as a big record label and the affordance to buy a property, where she rests with her boyfriend on many Instagram posts (Guaraná, 2019). At this point, we return to interrupted cosmopolitanism, as visited in other stances. On the one hand, there is the paradox of success and mainstreaming Brazil's own cultural vernacular. On the other, there is an evident effort to become *big* nationally that does not necessarily conform to the commercial or profit side as it used to be. It occupies hegemonic media by being misunderstood and misrepresented rather than adjusting or whitewashing. These artists are hellbent on spreading a repertoire that assembles indigenous themes with international solidarity. In a nutshell, this advance became crystal clear when Linn da Quebrada offered public support during the commemorations of Marsha P. Johnson and Stonewall Day (Wakabara, 2020), fortifying these intercommunicating queer spheres of influence.

The cultural model that spells permanent exchange between local, global, and hybrid aspects underpins critical cosmopolitanism as a familiar repertoire of many others. One should also take note of *Liniker*, another black transgender artist with an emerging media presence in Brazil, with a similar life story. These artists represent a blind spot in Western ideas of queer cosmopolitanism theories because of the enormous social constraints they have gone through in life. Still, their flirt and ultimate embrace of the mainstream have not made them abandon causes of class, gender, and social inequalities. It is not to say that these artists' attachment to their local conditions, vocabularies, and early experiences in life are meant to signify a particular agenda. Still, their discourses concatenate with the media and advertising industry, which, in turn, does not break with the context of inequality in Brazil. Media industries continue to sway while hailing from the country's prosperous southeast, directed by a white majority.

Another example of these ongoing disparities lies in these artists' need to conform to an image of feminine, sexy, and silent in their appearance. Theirs is still a weak position to hold upon mainstream Brazilian society, which seems more interested in glamorizing the hardship they have faced in life rather than elevating other trans individuals or creating laws to protect them, as Linn recognizes later in an interview:

> I don't even like to think that I'm an icon. Icons are flat images, two-dimensional, static images. I'm alive, I'm on the move. I think it's important that we have new references, new images. What I am doing is a dispute. It is a power struggle, a language dispute. It is mainly the dispute within a social imagination, a dispute for new ones to be imagined.
>
> Stropasolas, 2020

This cultural model sees less connection with queer performers in other parts of the country, especially gay comedians, transexual or transvestites, and drag artists based in the hinterlands or the Amazon. Looking back on history, the new trans celebrity also misses a vital reminder of historical misunderstandings and endemic prejudice.

The case of Roberta Close, or Roberta Gambine Moreira, who was the first trans woman in Brazil to undergo gender reassignment surgery at the end of the '80s. Despite her ground-breaking battles to have her name corrected on a birth certificate, which paved the way for legal changes later, she was more famous in her time because of her move to Switzerland, romantic exploits, and wealth (Smith, 2015). Less prominent, though, is Jeison Mendes da Silva, or *Jeison Wallace*, a comedian from Recife that alternated in several transgender roles in the

1990s. His most famous was *Cinderela, the Story that Your Mother Hasn't Told You*, a play about a maid who speaks in foul language while working for a lower-middle-class household in Recife's poor periphery. Later, Wallace came to have his band named *Pão com Ovo*, or 'bread and fried eggs', a local slang for the food eaten by the poor. The band and the theatre plays have consolidated Wallace's presence alongside his multiple TV shows broadcast locally. While Wallace's case is one of thriving, his success has never been understood as global, and he could not count on the same attention given to Vittar and their counterparts, for example.

The cultural model around trans artistry in Brazil has transcended harsh prejudices and blindness from the mainstream media. On the other hand, it still seems ahistorical. It needs further contextualization with the country's past struggles, as the model is still centralized on who reaches the country's southeast creative industries. Success as a queer artist comes through establishing this specific framework that rewards artists with more cosmopolitanism, such as financial success, collaborations with the outside, and reproducibility. Leaving Brazil, one can also perceive this communication between the periphery and the centre in other contexts.

This discussion also pertains to other realities. Authored by British journalist Tom Rasmussen, *The Diaries of Crystal Rasmussen* was released in 2020 by Penguin as an innovative chronicle of a drag queen. It consists of journal entries by Crystal, ranging from memories from when the author lived in the north of England to global media topics such as Celine Dion. The book came out not only from a publishing powerhouse as it carries the endorsement of queer celebrities, such as Sam Smith, and reviews on publications, such as the *Gay Times*. Rasmussen was featured by the *New Yorker* and *The Guardian* and gave several interviews. Using 'northern, working-class' stories, Rasmussen's testimony reveals abreaction for what has been lost from their homeland. The personal ties and friendships remain consonant with who now writes from a completely distinct position. The same process of memorializing in drag happens with Wanda Gastrica, a drag queen from Florence, Italy. There is a similar effort to assemble a tapestry of archaic memories and embed their performance in nativist tones, as an interview with the latter tells:

> La Wanda Gastrica is a homage to Wanda Osiris, an actress, singer, and showgirl who worked between the 1930s and the '90s. She was a woman dressed in a very flamboyant, glamorous way, always dripping

with jewels and lots of feathers. She was really one of the first Italian divas (...) I like to be a bit like Lady Diana, the princess of the people. By that, I mean that I like to be a 'national treasure' among my people, making them laugh but also moving them. (...) There's no space in Tuscany for a drag artist, and no one is willing to risk giving us that forum. The only work is in the few gay venues that we have here.

Farrel, 2019

The acts reviewed above authorize a metamorphosis from drag or trans performance into a permanent character self-contained in many notes about displacement, the ideal homeland, and their new globalized self. Rasmussen is, in this sense, an exception for being able to quit their job as an assistant in the New York City fashion industry and sign up a deal with a big publishing house. If one looks at the earlier cases of Vittar, Linn da Quebrada, and other Brazilian artists, all circumstances weighed, they strongly make the case of a struggle between queers and their transcendence from their hometowns and villages to join the cosmopolitan cultural industries, even if bringing along a series of repertoires and images from who they were.

This section sought to discuss the life and opinions of queer artists entrenched in global and local references. By highlighting both Western and non-Western contexts, their different affordances and localities broker new insights into a cultural model existing within the national circumstances. It carries innate material values and the limitations of social inequality and constraints to their voice. I also observed how this relationship with heartlands does not change completely but receives a globalizing treatment to fit the new demands of the industry, the fans, and their self-awareness based on new realities. I review trans vocabularies online in Chapter 4. In this chapter's final section, I debate the degree to which concepts such as *mestizaje* help to make sense of another queer cultural model that transcends origin, race, and ethnicity, as well as re-establish layers of affiliation in mainstream society. I approximate this concept to problematize the sense of foreignness that has shaped the careers of queer artists who gained prominence over the years.

The cosmetics of transculturation: Harisu, Siufung Law, Zanele Muholi, and Mahmood

After stressing questions of location and how the place of one's birth matters to both the *national* treasure and the *peripheral* queer, it is also possible to see globalized queerness causing a series of contrasts beyond the local or national boundaries and even transcending cosmopolitanism. In sum, I have exposed two main situations: Queer artists who have chased contacts and careers abroad by sticking to local names and references or performers who have neutralized local homophobia by situating themselves beyond the national mindset. The two previous sections have stayed in artists' trajectories that have negotiated their self-image based on these exchanges. Here, I flesh out an opposite situation: one of the international attachments whose localness is based on holistic elements such as behaviours, public statements, language, or aesthetic resources borrowed to critique their upbringing. I invite theories on *mestizaje* and transculturation to illustrate subtle inherited references that blended and magnified queer artistry. I believe that decolonial approaches are necessary to perceive contradictions between local or global constructions of queerness.

Mestizaje aids us by taking us back to when a few societies invested in a new profile of human beings, the *mestizo*, a purposeful hybrid person. While I do not intend to dwell on this concept and its anthropological or sociological ramifications focused on race, I take it on its discursive roots. Academics have seen *mestizaje* as centred on the context of Hispanic Latin America. It has fostered an aesthetic that lies in the intersection between race, ethnicity, religion, and culture (Samora, 1996). It echoes the population of Mexicans or their descendants in the early 20th century and later in the United States, often merged with the idea of *Chicano* (Stavans, 2013). Scholars have looked very critically at *mestizaje* as a kind of religious utopia that has not forged a sustainable form of political power at local and national levels (Miller, 2009). It is not needed to delve into the validity or contemporaneity of *mestizaje* to perceive its forging of, or attempt at, a nationally oriented idea of race and culture to transcend external categorizations, then particularly tied to colonization. Queerness, alike, is borne out with the same impetus of transcendence, in which one is or can be or will be, but possibilities are never entirely closed.

If one takes *mestizaje* beyond its nationalist ambitions and injects it into queer theory, one sees its recent leveraging as a unifying form of affection and transcendence of the racialized archetypes. Gender-related ideas can be mirrored on *mestizaje* because of the imperatives that tie societal position to gender performance as much as racial categorization does to one's social status. A helpful case study lands in Cuzco, Peru, where *mestizaje* has inspired the claims of racial authenticity from the patriarchal elite. In search of asserting its masculine power over the local community, the masculine *mestizo* would be thus entitled to determine what the *Indians* are to, as some were fated to be agriculturalists because of their ancestry, i.e., the idea of *old vs new Inca* (De la Cadena, 2000).

Of course, scholarship has yet to conjugate further queer implications of *mestizaje*. What one can see from this analysis is how queer performance emerges as a sort of dividend from the patriarchal mestizo culture, which assigns identities to those within or outside their locality. Queerness, thus, appears as blurring the masculine aspect of this idea of mestizo. Firstly, *mestizaje* came into sight as an ethnic or racial hybridization in cultural identities, first imagined by Homi K. Bhabha (1985). It has also flirted with ideas of transculturation, as Fernando Ortiz saw it back in the 1940s (Rojas, 2008): transculturation is the threefold process of acquisition, loss and reinvention of a new culture based on foreign materials. For instance, Alicia Arrizón (2006:46) took on *Chicana* lesbianism to imagine *mestizaje* as a transcultural process that applied to gender and Latino performances in the United States. Arrizón perceived it as a 'juxtaposition' in which 'queer' and 'Latinidad' require the effects of representation not only through its materials: 'The performance of identity practices the configuration of discursive spaces.' That is, the knowledge of reconfiguring a self-referential discursive space based on the dynamics between queer globalization and cosmopolitanism: the interplay between distinct spheres of knowledge of other queer scenes, law advances, and new aesthetics or styles.

I settle this discussion between mestizaje, transculturation, and queer performance by highlighting the extent to which a few artists stand at this crossroads. Fully invested in commodified media identities, they have also relied on the effects of their representation rather than only on being themselves. For example, Cristiano Malgioglio remains an Italian artist, as Pabllo Vittar continues to embed vocabulary from his native northeast Brazil in their lyrics. Whatever Vittar's global aspirations or Malgioglio's celebrity name-dropping in TV shows, there is a trade-off that, while staying locally, reflects their being ambassadors of queer globalized emancipation. These and other artists have broadened up the public discernment of what they can do, where they can do it and with whom in such a competitive global mediascape. As discussed earlier, the cultural 'juxtaposition' happens between their standing in native languages and the global English-language queer repertoire, which is part of an arsenal of discourses employed during frequent media appearances. These shows hint at their hybridity, whose queerness relies on these superpowers of self-representation in the media.

Here, I add other non-Latino, non-Western scenarios to pinpoint a similar tension between fluidity, performance, and cultural rooting. For example, the case of Hong Kong weightlifter Siufung Law who described themselves as a genderqueer weightlifter (Amnesty International, 2017). Law has debuted on the public radar as a lesbian influencer, then as genderqueer. Law's interventions as a speaker or influencer are based mainly on their experience in China, a country with very limited or restricted legal rights provisions to cover its LGBTQ+ population. Law was born a female but has lived mainly as a trans man while competing in female competitions. 'Muscles have no gender,' they said to the press (Tsui 2018). Based in the US, Law's interventions have addressed the issue of dressing in bras or bikinis as a woman weightlifter while not completely opposing the requirement. Their position is one of being able to add new outfits to their practice. In sum, their message highlights the burden over those who struggle with specific compulsory patterns of femininity or masculinity (ibid., 2018).

Also from Asia, there is the case of Harisu, the stage name of Lee Kyung-Eun, a prominent transgender pop star in South Korea. Harisu assumedly underwent gender reassignment in 1995 and, since then, has appeared in several media pieces. Either baited by news put out by her social media or triggered by public curiosity, the press repeatedly reported on her verging on the bizarre to the point of claiming she had organ transplantations in her whole body. An article speculated about her transplanting a uterus to conceive children or plastic surgeries to conform to a certain kind of beauty standard. In a viral article published in 2019, columnist Lee Jae-Ik (2019) argued that the prejudice the artist suffered stemmed from the 'deep-seated Confucian values that lie at the heart of the South Korean society.' He argued against the values that Harisu embodies by remembering his trajectory. The author, a gay man, had been jailed for being homosexual decades ago on charges of citing Oscar Wilde, similar to the treatment the Irish author suffered himself in Britain back in the 19th century.

Both cases are miles away from the original settings of the debate on *mestizaje* and transculturation. However, both characters perfectly encased the idea of queer *mestizos* in times of queer globalization. Firstly, Law and Harisu have transcended national identities by temporarily taking visual or discursive assets from the global queer culture and transplanting them into the heart of their national context. The former is the gender-driven Chinese policies, and the latter is the body politics that involve going against heteronormativity in South Korea. Secondly, their making as public personae borrows from the native imagery and repertoire (male vs female, pure body vs transplanted body). Still, they continue to communicate directly with the local public and their priorities. Third, in the case of Harisu and Siufung, their non-conforming gender identity clashes directly with impediments born within the borders of the nation, and so lies their motivations. Their gender fluidity does not intend to leave the nation or be projected elsewhere, even if they no longer reside in their countries. These facts matter to reconfigure discursive spaces from the outset. Therefore, as the new *mestizo*, their bodies and adopted culture evoke global connections and self-design to emerge as genderqueer or transgender versions that no longer have to correspond to categories assigned in their beginnings.

On another note, a new generation of queer artists is coming to the fore by incorporating features of tradition and queerness while criticizing the former. It is perhaps the case of understanding the *local* influence not as an antithesis of the international but as an outward and necessary stance to stand creatively and politically. This response from the inside of the national boundaries in a fluid, queer way invites the further understanding of *mestizaje* and *transcultural* responses as this dashboard of distinct archetypes, all of which are pressed at any point through an arsenal of local or global discourses. Alongside this generation of Asian queer personalities, two other artists stir this remix of cultures to another level of publicity.

The first is a photographer and self-identified visual activist (Human Rights Watch, 2013), Zanele Muholi. They are perhaps the most celebrated visual artist from South Africa in the West over the last decades. Featured in a major retrospective at London's Tate Modern in 2020, Muholi has excelled in brokering difficult questions about the South African situation regarding queer folks. In a series of interviews with prestigious photography publications, such as *Aperture*, Muholi has underlined their vision as an artist by providing very enlightening statements on where their South African presence starts or ends vis-à-vis the strategies used so that their work gets the recognition it deserves. Firstly, the most prominent part of their photographic work is made of self-portraits in highly contrasted white and black tones dramatically reinforced. The poses adorned South African props and hairdos embedded with local meanings (Saner, 2017). In brief, their work is inheritably attached to their life story, and so it is the narration of life as a black lesbian in Africa:

I just realized that as black South Africans, especially lesbians, we don't have much visual history that speaks to pressing issues, both current and also in the past. South Africa has the best constitution on the African continent and, dare I say, world—when it comes to recognizing LGBTI (Lesbian, Gay, Bisexual, Transgender, Intersex) persons and other sexual minorities. It is the only country on the continent that legalized same-sex marriage in 2006. I thought to myself that if you have remarkable women in America and around the globe, you equally have remarkable lesbian women in South Africa.

Aperture, 2015

Muholi later came out as non-binary (O'Hagan, 2020). Over the cycle of five interviews analysed for this chapter, their prominence grew significantly in the West. Muholi has been the recipient of France's Knighthood of the Order Arts and Letters as well as several bursaries and awards in Europe, to which they add:

They might be exciting, there might be entertainment attached to them, but in true honesty, all of these awards, trophies, and honors are political (...) Honestly even my communicating or conversing with you is political, in which I have a choice to say I'm taking this job or I'm taking this honor or I don't.

Willis, 2019

But what is transcultural or *mestizo* about Muholi's body of work? Here, I located the transculturation and *mestizaje* as part of their constant referring to the experience in Europe vs life in South Africa. There have been episodes of aggression in their team and robberies in South Africa (O'Hagan, 2020), but the sense of moving up and down, the gaze launched in Muholi's work returns to challenge the European gaze over their work. Overall, the main take extracted from these first-hand accounts lies in the Black, queer experience as this purposeful *other* created, whether in South Africa or other places. As powerful as the representation found in Muholi's cosmetics can be for representing South African affairs, it is the design of this everlasting other that stands out as the new hybrid being presented to the audience. The communication of this other's characteristics is fully lived up to when the transcultural aspect reaches other audiences, as Muholi admitted:

> I was thinking as you cross borders, the racial profiling that happens, which has to do with who you are, the colour of your skin, the questions you're asked and the comments you get.
>
> Saner, 2017

This aspect of black queer communicability was even more salient when Muholi acknowledged the interviewer in the *Aperture* (2015) conversation, who happened to be a Black American transwoman. As Muholi commented:

> And I appreciate that I'm speaking to a person who probably feels like me, a person of color or a Black person – whether in America or in Africa – because you know for sure where you're seated, that this is not a position of comfort. This seat is hot, therefore we cannot dare to be callous.
>
> Aperture, 2015

This process of transculturation of their presence starts once the photographs can be read, as Muholi emphasized, as a piece of *resistance* (O'Hagan, 2020) which can happen everywhere given that the state of queer oppression in South Africa reflects that of other parts of the globe. In line with the cultural model discussed here, Muholi embodies an integration between works found in different contexts in the West and many countries of the Global South. The same is true for Jeremy Greer and Ajamu X, black queer photographers active in New York and London, respectively. Muholi's series pin down South Africa as another binding site of tension for queer individuals. Their facing the viewer introduces an elaborated cosmetic that shines a light on a generation of minoritized artists that, finally, air their grievances against decades of exclusion and mistreatment from mainstream society.

Before ending the section, I would like to connect Muholi's political production to an otherwise recent pop act that has made its way through notoriety by trailing rather commercial avenues. Like Muholi, the life of Mahmood or Alessandro Mahmoud has been the object of some of his lyrics and a central piece for public curiosity in Italy. As a Milanese singer of Italian and Egyptian descent born in 1992, Mahmood won Italy's most prestigious music award in 2019, *Sanremo*. After a life in the suburb without his father, Mahmood's victory led to further recognition and thriving as the number one in the charts. His position here, nevertheless, has less to do with the charts and is equally relevant for the debate on the frontiers of queerness as a globalized feature of contemporary culture. His work has brought to Italy, a deeply ethnocentric country with a lot to answer about everyday racism, a hint of alternative cultural models. Mahmood, to this day, is best known for his song 'Soldi', a rap whose title roughly translates into 'money'. The award-winning song reads like a heartfelt letter to his father, who left him and his mother when he was five. The references to his father are all very much embedded in religious, migrant connotations juxtaposed with other references to pop culture, like in this excerpt of 'Soldi':

> It looked like love to you, but it was something else
> He drinks champagne during Ramadan
> On TV they are airing Jackie Chan

Once one reads into Mahmood's interviews, mostly conceded to Italian franchises of American outlets, such as *Rolling Stone* or *Vanity Fair*, there is a lot to be critical about what is not said due to his ascension to stardom. Whether frank accounts of a lived experience or media exaggerations to trigger the public's curiosity, his presence as such as luminary stressed the mainstream cultural realm in a time of growing right-wing populism. As a destination for thousands of refugees and migrants, Italy sees boats arriving almost daily. Immigration has been based on a backlash by far-right parties, including fascist-reminiscent entities such as *The League* and the *Brothers of Italy* party, which won the 2022 general election. Recently, politicians on the right have seen Mahmood's sudden popularity with suspicion. Matteo Salvini, perhaps the most prominent conservative politician and a fluent Twitter user, has personally discredited Mahmood's fame and the content of his lyrics (*Today*, 2019).

This scenario of backlash has undoubtedly helped Mahmood's prominence. But what does he have to say? In a handful of lengthy interviews conceded to Italian and English-speaking outlets, the singer has placed much effort to de-emphasize his homosexuality from his public persona.

> In reality, I like Italian music a lot, and I listen to it often. If you must write in Italian, it is important to get an ear to what you hear around you because here we have our way of describing things. But yes, I grew up with international music, and the mood is certainly that of the artists I love the most: Frank Ocean, Jazmine Sullivan, Travis Scott, Beyoncé, Rosalìa.
>
> Tripodi, 2018

His most frequent concern has been casting himself as a regular Italian bloke, catholic-inclined, Sardinian-fluent, which would not have surprised anyone whose mother was born on that island. While lamenting the loss of the Arabic language as his father left too early to teach him, he has branded his music as 'Moroccan pop' (Rocca, 2019), while flirting with elements of the Arab culture in music titles and quick expressions. Still, he did the same with Japanese titles in *Inuyasha* and Spanish in *Barrio*. Perhaps, the cosmetics of fluidity in Mahmood, namely this collating of names, aesthetics, and thoughtless importations from other countries' arts and crafts, is more part of his being Italian than his alleged foreignness. It is enough to remember how the considered masters in Italian cinema used to exoticize the racialized others, often by making white actors wear Asian or African costumes (De Franceschi, 2015), like in Michelangelo Antonioni's *La Notte*.

What does set Mahmood apart against this backdrop? Should Mahmood play the Arab card on louder terms at all? It is unknown if the politics of race, ethnicity, and gender will weigh on Mahmood's ambitions as a star. Engaging with the language, accents, and regional variations is the maximum expression of the *italianità*, the modes and ways of a very idiosyncratic nation. All these questions have accompanied Mahmood in his recent fame. It is worth noting that the Italian press has been very suspicious of his being from such a background. Most interviews have Italian journalists being especially inquisitive on whether he was able to display the *italianità* or a foreign culture, as if he should do one *or* the other, which prompted Mahmood to recurrently state things about his link to the country or otherwise:

> As a child, I was not attracted to that world, like when you refuse vegetables as a child. Then you grow up, and things change. Today I cultivate memories. And I live it in everyday life: my hairdresser is called Mustafa, and I eat kebab with friends.
>
> Rocca, 2019

In that sense, Mahmood places transcultural cues in his lyrics. Still, in his active life, as in his interviews, there is a sense of ordinariness to be conveyed that links back to the *cosmopolitan self*, which was mentioned earlier on. At the same time, his reticence goes on to also relativize his queerness. When asked about the importance of talking about his homosexuality to a broader audience if that was helpful or not, he said:

That's true, but I also think it's wrong, in a sense, to talk about these things. Declaring 'I'm gay' leads nowhere, if not to be talked about. Going on TV to Barbara D'Urso to tell about one's homosexuality seems embarrassing to me: so you go back 50 years.

Rocca, 2019

One of the main displays of globalized queerness has been this transit between big and small gestures to signal one's cultures or affinities, always in the flow and never settled for longer. Hence, by situating his presence in Italy but constantly going across borders, Mahmood exploits transcultural references all around. And yet, the artist's goal does not seem to be, necessarily, to profit from but to evade cultural duties that stem from the honours attributed to national treasures. As fellow Italian Cristiano Malgioglio does by name-dropping old names to justify his continuous relevance in the mainstream media, Mahmood does it via international references and clothing style.

When winning *Sanremo* for the second time in 2022, Mahmood and his fellow singer Blanco, a white Italian, followed the commercial lines of average romantic pop songs. However, the music video of *Brividi* had a shirtless Mahmood sharing intimate moments with a black man in a bathroom. Mahmood inhabits different scenes in the video, shot in a very dark sky of the Dutch winter. Directed by Italian director Attilio Cusani, the video hints at this different environment that casts Mahmood aside both visually, sexually, and nationally vis-à-vis his co-singer, who is instead shot on top of a piano inside a sort of institutional setting. Both ride small bicycles and meet outside at the end.

Under the perspective of transculturation, the video serves well to flag the unfitting recreated and assimilated under certain conditions. Mahmood meets other artists discussed in this section by displaying the fundamental elements of *mestizaje*. He lives off the exploits of his hybridity as an Italian and queer artist. Nonetheless, he does not necessarily support a deconstruction or a revisit of his ancestry, nor does he contribute to any sexual politics, which, in Italy, would undoubtedly play a positive role. In that case, globalized queerness characterizes this permanent loop between historical, cultural, and gender references that eventually become part of a repertoire to serve external forces, whether commercial, advertising, or conforming to the nation's limits while opening oneself to new images. Globalized queer artists think of themselves as diverse stands, but fewer are voiceful regarding bigger or small acts of resistance that can happen along the way. Next, I make sense of this chapter's three empirical sections in consonance with the book's aims.

Conclusion

This chapter extensively explored a broader scene of queer artistry based mainly on the West but with links in Asia, Africa, and South America. From France to Brazil, South Korea to the UK and Italy, these artists have gathered cultural models in their lyrics, interviews, and visual discourses that concatenate local or global references and serve the globalization of queerness. These cultural models have served to evolve from a scenario of open homophobia, ensured a leeway to reaffirm new gender identities, and engaged the public in conversations about queerness and oppression. As this exploration offered incursions in theories about queer cosmopolitanism, *mestizaje*, and transculturation, the idea was to show that these cultural models do not come from anywhere, but from different platforms, career experiences, and backgrounds, which continue previous strategies to develop acceptance and enter the local taste. To a large extent, the cultural models seen here are predicated on early experiences in life, notions of class, ethnicity, and itinerant stays in Europe and the Global South. All this wealth of evidence serves the book's purposes by showing globalized queerness as something beyond commercial traps and commodification. It fits artists' self-ideas of being part of the local landscape and gives them images to play into an idea of cosmopolitanism that does not always result in queer emancipation. The next chapter will turn to the other political aspects resulting from the current expansion of trans visibility online.

References

Alfrey, L., & Twine, F. W. (2017). Gender-fluid geek girls: Negotiating inequality regimes in the tech industry. *Gender & Society, 31*(1), 28–50.

Amnesty International (2017). Bodybuilding and bikinis: The Hong Kong athlete fighting for transgender equality. Available at https://hongkongfp.com/2017/12/26/bodybuilding-bikinis-hong-kong-athlete-fighting-transgender-equality/ Access 02 January 2020.

Aperture (2015). Zanele Muholi's Faces & Phases. *Aperture*. 21 April 2015. Available at https://aperture.org/editorial/magazine-zanele-muholis-faces-phases/ Access 22 January 2020.

Arrizón, A. (2006). Queering Mestizaje: Transculturation and Performance. United States: University of Michigan Press.
Attwood, F. (2017). *Sex media*. John Wiley & Sons.
Baggio, A. T. (2013). A temática homossexual na publicidade de massa para público gay e não-gay: conflito entre representação e estereótipos. *Revista uninter de Comunicação, 1*(1), 100–117.
Balsemão, R. (2019) 'Invento forças a partir do meu corpo e das minhas relações', diz Linn da Quebrada, que faz show em Porto Alegre no sábado. Gaúcha Zero Hora. Available at https://gauchazh.clicrbs.com.br/cultura-e-lazer/musica/noticia/2019/11/invento-forcas-a-partir-do-meu-corpo-e-das-minhas-relacoes-diz-linn-da-quebrada-que-faz-show-em-porto-alegre-no-sabado-ck3ho6whv00ep01rza7706eag.html Last accessed 11 December 2020.
Bao, H. (2011). Queering/querying cosmopolitanism: queer spaces in Shanghai. *Culture unbound: Journal of current cultural research, 4*(1), 97–120.
Barbosa, L. (2020). Pabllo Vittar relembra quando gritou 'ELE NÃO' em premiação: 'Estamos vendo o que custou'. Available at https://observatoriodemusica.uol.com.br/noticia/pabllo-vittar-relembra-quando-gritou-ele-nao-em-premiacao-estamos-vendo-o-que-custou Access 08 December 2020.
Bhabha, Homi K. (1985). Signs taken for wonders: Questions of ambivalence and authority under a tree outside Delhi, May 1817. In H. L. Gates (Ed.), *'Race', Writing and Difference*. Chicago: University of Chicago Press, 163–185.
Binnie, J. (2004). *The globalization of sexuality*. London: Sage.
Binnie, J., & Skeggs, B. (2004). Cosmopolitan knowledge and the production and consumption of sexualized space: Manchester's gay village. *The Sociological Review, 52*(1), 39–61.
Bocca, D. (2020). Cristiano Malgioglio furioso: 'Traditrici! Devogono solo vergognarsi'. *La Nostra TV*. 26 March 2020.
Bonham, M. S. (2014). *Champions: Biographies of global LGBTQ pioneers*. Canada: Bonham & Company.
Brenner, S. (2018). Pabllo Vittar desabafa sobre o Brasil: 'Muito homofóbico e racista'. Metrópoles. Available at https://www.metropoles.com/celebridades/pabllo-vittar-desabafa-sobre-o-brasil-muito-homofobico-e-racista Access 09 December 2020.
Cappelle, L. (2018). A transgender director who defies genres (to France's confusion). *New York Times*. July 8.
Carman, C. (2017). George Michael made it big. *The Gay & Lesbian Review Worldwide, 24*(2), 29–31.
Cashmore, E., & Cleland, J. (2011). Glasswing butterflies: Gay professional football players and their culture. *Journal of Sport and Social Issues, 35*(4), 420–436.

Chakrabati, M. (2018). RuPaul on childhood, the power of drag and the tenacity of the human spirit. WBUR. Online. Available at https://www.wbur.org/onpoint/2018/10/22/rupaul-drag-race-guru Access 05 December 2020.

Corriere Adriatico (2019). Cristiano Malgioglio emigra: «Dopo il Gf lascio l'Italia, ho tante offerte». Available at https://www.corriereadriatico.it/spettacoli/cristiano_malgioglio_gf_addio_ecco_dove_va-4405827.html Access 08 December 2020.

Da Silva, R. P. (2020). *Ney Matogrosso . . . Para Além do Bustiê: Performances da Contraviolência na Obra Bandido (1976–1977)*. São Paulo: Editora Appris.

De Franceschi, L. (2015). Spaghetti blackface. Pratiche performative al di là della linea del colore. *Iperstoria*, (6).

De la Cadena, M. (2006). ¿ Son los mestizos híbridos? Las políticas conceptuales de las identidades andinas. *Universitas humanística*, 61, 51–84

Doty, A. (1993). *Making things perfectly queer: Interpreting mass culture.* United States: University of Minnesota Press.

Farrell, J. (2019). La Wanda Gastrica and the art of the drag queen. *The Florentine.* 04 July 2019. Available on https://www.theflorentine.net/2019/07/04/drag-wanda-gastrica/ Access 07 April 2023.

F.Q. Magazine (2019). Grande Fratello 2019, Cristiano intervista Malgioglio: 'Adoro la mia pelle burrosa come Sharon Stone. Il mio portafortuna? Me l'hanno sequestrato' 27 May 2019. Available at https://www.ilfattoquotidiano.it/2019/05/27/grande-fratello-2019-cristiano-intervista-malgioglio-adoro-la-mia-pelle-burrosa-come-sharon-stone-il-mio-portafortuna-me-lhanno-sequestrato/5211429/ Access 08 December 2020.

Ferreira, M. (2020). Pabllo Vittar dá pisadinha no forró com Jerry Smith em Clima Quente. G1. https://g1.globo.com/pop-arte/musica/blog/mauro-ferreira/post/2020/02/20/pabllo-vittar-da-pisadinha-no-forro-com-jerry-smith-em-clima-quente.ghtml Access 08 December 2020.

Fortuna, M; Rosa, B. (2019). Pabllo Vittar vai à Cidade do Rock: 'Não adianta levantar a Bandeira e não defender LGBT'. O Globo. 29 September 2019.

França, N. W. I. L. (2020). In the line of fire: Sex(uality) and gender ideology in Brazil. *Fermina*, 1, 139.

Gever, M. (2012). *Entertaining lesbians: Celebrity, sexuality, and self-invention.* United States: Taylor & Francis.

Guaraná, I (2019). Linn da Quebrada, atriz trans da série Segunda Chamada, compra fazenda e mostra marido. Blog NE10. Available at https://blogs.ne10.uol.com.br/social1/2019/12/28/linn-da-quebrada-atriz-trans-da-serie-segunda-chamada-compra-fazenda-e-mostra-marido/ Last accessed 10 December 2020.

Hines, S., & Taylor, M. (2018). *Is gender fluid? A primer for the 21st century.* Thames & Hudson.

Horn, K. (2010). Camping with the stars: Queer performativity, pop intertextuality, and camp in the pop art of Lady Gaga. *Current Objectives of Postgraduate American Studies, 11*.

Human Rights Watch (2013). Zanele Muholi: Visual activist. 25 November 2013. Available at https://www.hrw.org/video-photos/video/2013/11/22/zanele-muholi-visual-activist Access 20 January 2020.

Jae-Ik, L. (2019). Harisu, a transgender singer that has never lost her disgust. Hani. Available at http://m.hani.co.kr/arti/culture/culture_general/896174.html Last accessed 13 December 2020.

Levy, H. (2018). *The internet, politics, and inequality in contemporary Brazil: Peripheral media*. Rowman & Littlefield. Chapter 3.

Malici, L., Downing, L., & Gillett, R. (2011). Queer in Italy: Italian televisibility and the 'queerable' audience. *Queer in Europe: Contemporary case studies*, 113–128.

Mbsi, T. (2021). Being LGB in South Africa. In L. Gerber (Ed.), *Worldwide perspectives on lesbians, gays, and bisexuals* [3 volumes]. United States: ABC-CLIO.

Mendes, W. G., & Silva, C. M. F. P. D. (2020). Homicide of lesbians, gays, bisexuals, travestis, transexuals, and transgender people (LGBT) in Brazil: a spatial analysis. *Ciência & Saúde Coletiva, 25*, 1709–1722.

Miller, B. (2009). Between the revisionist and the frontier state: regional variations in state war-propensity. *Review of International Studies, 35*(S1), 85–119.

Moore, A. (2019). 'The term "all genders" would be more appropriate': Reflections on teaching trauma literature to a gender fluid youth. *Language and Literacy, 21*(1), 57–74.

Moussawi, G. (2018). Queer exceptionalism and exclusion: Cosmopolitanism and inequalities in 'gay-friendly' Beirut. *The Sociological Review, 66*(1), 174–190.

Neto, R. M. (2018). Da Praça Aos Palcos: Trânsitos e redes de jovens drag queens de Campinas-SP. Universidade de Campinas.

Notícias da TV (2018). 'Não vou sair do Brasil', diz Pabllo Vittar após eleição de Jair Bolsonaro. Available at https://noticiasdatv.uol.com.br/noticia/televisao/nao-vou-sair-do-brasil-diz-pabllo-vittar-apos-eleicao-de-jair-bolsonaro-23388 Access 09 December 2020.

O'Hagan, S. (2020). Zanele Muholi's queer South Africa: 'I do not dare shoot at night. It is not safe'. *The Guardian*. 2 Nov 2020.

Ong, J. C. (2017). Queer cosmopolitanism in the disaster zone: 'My Grindr became the United Nations'. *International Communication Gazette, 79*(6–7), 656–673.

Pickering, M. (Ed.). (2008). *Research methods for cultural studies*. Edinburgh University Press.

Pinho, P. D. S. (2015). The dirty body that cleans: Representations of domestic workers in Brazilian common sense. *Meridians, 13*(1), 103–128.

Polzer, E. R., Snodgrass, J. G., Dengah II, H. F., & Nixon, W. C. (2020). *Systematic methods for analyzing culture: A practical guide*. United Kingdom: Taylor & Francis.
QuaiTV (2011). Interview de Phia Ménard. Available at https://www.youtube.com/watch?v=f-mEOl68LvM Access 03 December 2020.
RAI (2018). Cristiano Malgioglio: 'Tuo marito' è Channing Tatum – La Vita in Diretta. Available at https://www.youtube.com/watch?v=-w_pjwrt9TQ&ab_channel=Rai
Raphael, A. (1981). *Samba and social control: popular culture and racial democracy in Rio de Janeiro*. Columbia University.
Rasmussen, C. (2020). *The diary of a drag queen*. London: Penguin. Available at https://www.penguin.co.uk/books/111/1116332/diary-of-a-drag-queen/9781785039508.html Last accessed 14 December 2020.
Rocca, F. (2019). Mahmood: «Vi piace cantautore» Moroccan pop? *Vanity Fair Italia*. 1 February 2019.
Rojas, R. (Ed.). (2008). Fernando Ortiz: Transculturation and nationalism. In *Essays in Cuban Intellectual History* (pp. 43–64). Palgrave Macmillan, New York.
Romancini, R. (2018). From 'gay kit' to 'indoctrination monitor': Conservative reaction in Brazil. *Contracampo*, 37(2), 1–22.
Rushbrook, D. (2002). Cities, queer space, and the cosmopolitan tourist. *GLQ: A Journal of Lesbian and Gay Studies*, 8(1), 183–206.
Samora, J. (1996). *Mestizaje: The formation of Chicanos* (Vol. 7). Stanford Center for Chicano Research.
Saner, E. (2017). 'I'm scared. But this work needs to be shown': Zanele Muholi's 365 protest photographs. *The Guardian*. 14 July 2017.
Scarcelli, C. M., Krijnen, T., & Nixon, P. (2020). Sexuality, gender, media. Identity articulations in the contemporary media landscape. *Information, Communication & Society*, 24(8), 1063–1072.
Schutte, J. (2018). *Third world cosmopolitanism in white spacetime: Intersectionality and mobility in sino-African encounters*. The University of Chicago.
Shaw, J. L. (2017). *Exist otherwise: The life and works of Claude Cahun*. Reaktion Books.
Silva, D. F. (2022). *Embodying Modernity: Race, Gender, and Fitness Culture in Brazil*. University of Pittsburgh Press.
Smith, P. J. (2015). *Close, Roberta (b. 1964)*. GLBT archive. Available at http://glbtqarchive.com/arts/close_r_A.pdf Access 01 Jan 2020.
Snodgrass, J. G., Nixon, W. C., Dengah II, H. F., Polzer, E. R. (2020). *Systematic methods for analyzing culture: A practical guide*. United Kingdom: Taylor & Francis.
Stella, F. (2013). Queer space, pride, and shame in Moscow. *Slavic Review*, 72(3), 458–480.
Stropasolas, P. (2020). Vídeo | Entrevista com Linn da Quebrada: 'A música salvou a minha vida' Brasil de Fato. Available at https://www.brasildefato.

com.br/2020/02/11/video-entrevista-com-linn-da-quebrada-a-musica-salvou-a-minha-vida Last accessed 11 December 2020.
Today (2019). 'A Sanremo vince Mahmood, sui social è 'scontro' tra Salvini e Elisa Isoardi'. *Today*. 10 Feb 2019.
Tripodi, M. B. (2018). La 'gioventù bruciata' di Mahmood. *Rolling Stone Italia*. 30 September 2018.
Tsui, S. (2018). 'Muscles are genderless': how bodybuilding has helped shape this Hongkonger's fluid identity. Available at https://www.scmp.com/news/hong-kong/health-environment/article/2172490/muscles-are-genderless-how-bodybuilding-has-helped Access 13 Jan 2020.
UOL (2020). Pabllo Vittar diz que não fará show drive-in: 'Quem tem carro no Brasil?' ... Available at https://entretenimento.uol.com.br/noticias/redacao/2020/08/11/pabllo-vittar-show-drive-in.htm?cmpid=copiaecola Access 08 December 2020.
Women, U. N. (2016). Global database on violence against women. *New York: UN Women*. nd.
Wakabara, J. (2020). Liniker e Linn da Quebrada no 'Marsha! Entra na Sala', festival online de apoio a mulheres trans. Available at https://www.lilianpacce.com.br/e-mais/liniker-e-linn-da-quebrada-no-marsha-entra-na-sala-festival-online-de-apoio-a-mulheres-trans/. Last accessed 10 December 2020.
Young, G. (2004). From broadcasting to narrowcasting to 'mycasting': A newfound celebrity in queer internet communities. *Continuum*, *18*(1), 43–62.
Willis, R. (2019). Zanele Muholi forever changed the image of Black queer South Africans. *Out*. 23 April 2019.

Chapter 4

TRANS CONTENT CREATORS

As a certain way of inverting the masculine and the feminine in oneself. Homosexuality appeared as one of the forms of sexuality when it was transposed from the practice of sodomy onto a kind of interior androgyny, a hermaphrodism of the soul.
— Foucault, *The Will to Knowledge*, 1971

The journey into understanding globalized queerness has hitherto involved traditional forms of popular culture and its vehicles and vernaculars, including the news and showbiz. The book's introduction has invited several theories to highlight the issue of distributing knowledge on queer life and unresolved dilemmas between *how* to bridge the experience of queer individuals and broader society. At best, knowledge has been commodified by modern media enterprises without due scrutiny from the LGBTQ+ public. At worst, knowledge is not entirely translated into media appearances due to the heavy weight of commercialization and the centralized nature of media industries in the West. Chapter 1 reviewed concepts of queer media commodification concerning ideas of authenticity and sincerity. Chapter 2 problematized news coverage as superficial and dependent on Western countries, particularly Britain and the US. Chapter 3 reviewed the prominence of several queer artists with varying levels of attachment or detachment to queer culture and national boundaries. The remaining chapters concentrate on the Internet as the central enabler of globalized queerness. New online self-representations have taken everyday queerness into other realms of discussion, including politics and an expectation of success that hold great sway on issues beyond gender and sexuality.

Here, I centre on the emerging universe of transgender influencers (henceforth, *trans*). The quickly shifting boundaries of trans representation deserve further attention, considering the recent boost in *content* borne out in user-generated content, social media posts, vlogs, and small-scale campaigns (Kaufmann, 2010; Raun, 2012; Horak, 2014; Miller, 2019). Some scholars have pointed to the activist potential of platforms such as YouTube as a site for critical narratives within the trans community (Tortajada et al., 2019). Such a popular online platform may help trans youth to create narratives of their own, including their fears and insecurities about the transition process (O'Neill, 2014; McInroy & Craig, 2015). As far as all these facts are undoubtedly positive, when an unprecedented number of trans people of many age groups are coming to the forefront in films, TV series, ad pieces, social media, and streaming platforms, it seems a rather precipitated conclusion to claim that this shift only concerns visibility and does not present any other form of impact on the trans community as it grows diverse (Berberick, 2018; Koch-Rein et al., 2020).

There are decades of trans invisibility or misrepresentation in the media that need addressing (Reitz, 2017). Some dilemmas sprout as more media is invited into trans lives. Fundamental processes for the trans person's well-being are today shown and exposed as never before: from the early stages of the transition to the full results of medical treatments, such as hormone taking and tests of *passing* as their confirmed gender on the streets. Even much-publicized come-outs such as Caitlyn Jenner on the 2015 cover of *Vanity Fair*, criticism of the mainstream media due to its transphobic bias can still apply (Humphrey, 2016; O'Shea, 2019). Social media may represent a window for self-expression, but hatred and abuse are common. There have been enormous efforts to deploy automated mechanisms for detecting homophobia and transphobia on social media (Chakravatti et al., 2022).

Perhaps, the biggest challenge remains identifying and debating 'internalized' models of transphobia that are less automatically detectable but equally offensive, dehumanizing. Also, the increase in trans dilemmas, questions related to civil rights, access to public facilities, and the equal treatment amongst other citizens of their gender are mostly exploited with sensationalist undertones (Rood et al., 2017). Cavalcante (2018) has debated at length the sense of 'everydayness' necessary for a good life, as expressed by trans groups. Trans individuals have been plagued for years by misconceptions and fantastic media stories. Even though it is still in the media that trans individuals seek resilience in oppressive times (Craig et al., 2015).

In the wake of mainstream media documentaries such as the 2017's *The Death and Life of Marsha P Johnson*, directed by David France, or *Disclosure*, by Sam Feder and award-winning trans actress Laverne Cox, many new productions came to the fore. Thirty-nine other releases were due in the US market for 2022, primarily favourable to trans causes. Despite the growth in the repertoire and inevitable globalization of trans narratives in cinema, TV, and streaming series, one can still grasp the need for vigilance against the dismantling of a fragile consensus around trans rights, mainly in the West. The same Internet that has given platforms for the lonely trans youth has eased the circulation of documentaries accused of transphobia, such as *What is a Woman* (2022), directed by Matt Walsh and sponsored by the right-wing website *The Daily Wire*. Even amidst trans celebrities, such as Elliot Page, there are episodes of calculated misgendering, 'deadnaming', and the failure to recognize fundamental rights such as gender reassignment and name changing (Hansford, 2022).

In search of trans themes on YouTube

Aware of all these debates involving trans rights, self-made narratives, and the popularization of a trans sphere, I employed the term *trans influencers* with much care. Even though there is no consensual definition of what an influencer is, the fluency through which trans individuals, especially the young, have taken over available online streaming channels to spread their stories authorizes a bolder look to see the glass half full. The role of trans influencers has symbolized both power and resilience, but also the necessary response against threats and vilification that one sees every day in the media. This chapter departs from a sense of allyship and solidarity with the trans community. It aims to portray a perspective of a viewer that can be ultimately influenced by trans self-made content, regardless of its purpose or target audience. Trans influencers have proven their ability to occupy mainstream platforms such as TikTok and YouTube, with communicators boasting over one million subscribers as some 'go viral' occasionally. In the case of *Dylan Mulvaney*, she crossed the mark of 10 million followers on TikTok. To this book's purposes, finding out the breadth of trans topics online sustains a broader discussion on what *global* or *local* values are like and how they can embed their production, both in terms of language and in the importing of themes into their reality.

The enormous variety of trans influencers is not entirely covered by literature due to its rapid change. Primarily if one focuses on the reproduction of similar titles and the replication of success formulae, it is possible to verify many trends that come and go very quickly. In preliminary research, similar titles populate YouTube in several languages: *How to start a transition, What is sex like with a trans guy*, or *15 days on Testosterone* (Raun, 2015). The popularity of some themes and not others does raise questions about a few complexities that cracked within the trans community after the advent of going online. Are their media productions part of a broader context of globalizing queerness in shaping non-trans, external expectations? How comparable is the mediatization of trans issues and the overall globalization of queerness? Are there specific discourses based on markets or local cultures? Does that inform a brand new way of seeing themselves?

The interest in trans topics springs from these replicating titles and styles across languages and countries. One finds not only the obvious issues such as transition, de-transition, and integration but some specificities that amalgamate across languages. There is an aspect of community and knowledge production that should not be underestimated (Raun, 2012). Together, big tech platforms such as YouTube have globalized transness to the extent that trans communicators can find and boost self-recognition by propping up their discussions, often reacting to each other or attacking each other due to political alignments. YouTube channels diametrically opposed on the ideological side, such as *Blaire White* and *ContraPoints* have accumulated millions of followers and sponsorship deals on the right-wing or left-wing parts of the spectrum, respectively. Even amid such diversity of opinions, the mainstreaming of all things trans does not stop these influencers from orbiting around the same topics, adopting the same aesthetics, and to a large extent, globalizing their understanding of the trans community, even to content producers inhabiting very distinct circumstances.

Studying a massive platform such as YouTube has its challenges and limitations. The website carries many issues of excessive commercialization, with some producers optimizing videos to boost views (Tafesse, 2020). The platform can also gather hubs of misinformation (Hussein et al., 2020) and be over-lenient when open homophobes achieve a large audience (Maurer, 2022). YouTube's algorithmic influence also enables the enactment of bias and polarization when political debates are at stake (Heuer et al., 2021; García Marín, 2021). The latter is especially problematic for this study because of the clear stances that split trans YouTubers into distinct political camps. In any case, it is also part of this book's purpose to contrast and bridge such differences vis-à-vis the broadening of trans expression. In such a sensitive area, one could argue that more dissent does more harm than good for a community whose complexities are still misunderstood by the majority.

Considering such kerbs, trans fluency on YouTube still offers a unique space to understanding differences and similarities that can help trans people to make sense of their visibility. To capture the themes of their discourse means to reveal local variations that trespass the platform's global design and proneness to capitalization and surveillance (Waugh et al., 2016). As controversial as some vlogs can be, they still reflect real-life dilemmas and come-outs which would be otherwise inaccessible. Not only that. One can reveal where subjectivity lies in shaping topics, conversations, and self-doubts into videos. Martino, Omercajic and Cumming-Potvin (2021) saw this as the 'desubjugation' of trans and non-binary youth. Identifying these themes allows for a greater appreciation of trans influencers under their terms and in opposition to values that local or global publics can associate or not with them. It is impossible to ignore the increasing expectations of developing careers or profits as content creators, even if these workers face a scenario of algorithmic unpredictability (Duffy & Meisner, 2022). The latter is by no means dissimilar among trans producers. In such a scenario, to engage with trans themes is also to inquire into productive vs subjective conditions in which trans content is found online.

The legitimate interest in the trans community from the broader society, either in politics, or culture, characterizes another aspect that needs further debunking. As Cavalcante (2018) has explored by employing focus groups, trans individuals do not live apart from recurrent societal concerns. As Swedish YouTube *Mia Mulder*, and British Natalie Wynn, in her *ContraPoints* channel, many producers have devoted their time to creating channels of random topics. In the latter's case, they were not *trans* channels but philosophy-directed channels. One should not see trans creativity as intermittently predicated on self-eulogies but as an attempt to delve into other affairs from a unique perspective. As perceived in the previous chapters, the interest in expressing queerness worldwide has inevitably led to a debate on the roots of the intersection between queerness and cosmopolitanism, economic affordances, migration, local languages and a global dialect that is not as homogenous as it seems. The trans mediatization on YouTube must not be oblivion to powerful forces that transplant genuine media initiatives and good ideas into memes and games at unprecedented speed. How the trans discourse on YouTube gets captured and analysed is discussed next.

Investing in trans topics

Aware of the diverse ecology of trans influencing, this chapter aims at those influencers with a recognized ability to communicate with an established audience. On YouTube, the level of following and real influence one can get is arguable (Perelli, 2022), and there is no correct number of subscribers to achieve brand deals and start making money out of the platform. Indeed, I deliberately focused on producers on the mark of over 5,000 followers. This determination meant that not only vlogs and single-handed testimonials were wanted for the analysis, but those which could manage to navigate YouTube's styles and idiosyncrasies, including its quick-paced language and avatar-making. This preference is necessary to perceive how trans communicators can consciously penetrate these globalized dictates of a highly capitalized platform. It can also reveal a potential showcase of crafted skills when speaking locally, in their language, and inviting local guests, for example. The art of influencing is still under close scholarly inspection, but there is no doubt that it demands skills and a solid determination to keep an updated backlog of videos. It also requires patience and resilience to keep talking to one's audience and replying to comments. In the case of trans influencers, this dialoguing sums up the risks of this exposure, not limited to bullying, abuse, and stalking.

YouTube-sourced sampling challenges anyone wishing to exhaust diversity in video production. To be on the platform demands a ritual that includes the quick absorption of global trends, self-teaching the tricks that guide algorithms, and self-assurance to speak in front of a camera. Surely, only a few producers can afford this routine for a long time. However, to the extent of the limited – albeit increasing – choices amongst the YouTubing trans community, it was possible to harvest communicators from distinct ethnic backgrounds and languages. Sampling reasoned both external aspects of popularity, such as the number of likes and visualizations, besides a trans-oriented relevance made of less followed trans influencers. Therefore, that should be enough to evade an algorithmic-based scope and meet the critical relevance necessary for this study. At the same time, I needed to advance voices that could represent competing interests or follow opposed political agendas. It was also convenient to bring names that have yet to become popular in other spheres, such as mass entertainment or TV or sign up for lucrative contracts. I had to choose producers still loyal to YouTube-focused content as a means to deliver a message as opposed to a hyper-strategic producer in whose personal agency loses to profit making. In the hope of some spontaneity and enthusiasm, this seemed to have been a choice that paid off, as this research's sampled characters mirrored notorious producers and innovative ones still on the rise.

To get to these names, a mixed approach of purposive and snowballing sampling methods (Konijn et al., 2013) was crucial to arrive at 20 names from five languages. Some producers have been identified thanks to a simple metadata search on YouTube (Malik & Tian, 2017). In contrast, others appeared after mentions in the press or by other YouTubers. The final sample counted influencers speaking English, Russian, Chinese-simplified, Portuguese, and Spanish. This choice was due to the potential of these languages to mirror complex realities, including postcolonial knowledge and outtakes from trans individuals located under distinct socioeconomic affordances. For example, Spanish can reflect Spain and trans stories and realities from Latin America, the same as Portuguese. Russian and Chinese give us insight into trans lives in countries where homophobia has been much more normalized. English is due to being the world's lingua franca, as well as its breadth of trans communicators speaking it in translation or a second language. A set of five influencers, two trans masculine and feminine, plus one non-binary trans person made it to the last sampling. The choice was for producers with at least five videos published and self-introduced as influencers as opposed to users who only posted videos but had no intention of creating an audience or selling products. All of them had five videos randomly selected, their spoken content transcribed and analysed uniquely to model the topics in their discussion.

The choice for a word cloud responds to the apparent variety of topics covered and the stress put into words. As discussed, trans communities worldwide seek to *own terms* that respond to their identification. Expressions such as *transvestite* are distinct from *travesti*, frequently used in Latin America, even though their translation may appear equivalent. In that case, the latter carries an enormous political weight due to the historical circumstances it has been applied with hateful or violent connotations. I used a word cloud method that designs maps with words sized according to their numerical repetition in a dataset. I furthered my interest by checking the embeddedness of words and their context (Xu et al., 2016). I followed other research akin to understanding gender-based parlance (e.g., Yeganeh et al., 2020) to problematize the use of certain words and not others and the timing of these words, observing aspects regarding sensitivity, history, and the local associations of words.

Furthermore, topic modelling appeared as a valuable resource to scope subjects from the vast amounts of information on Internet channels (e.g., Kee et al., 2019). For this research, a model tailor-based on Latent Dirichlet Allocation (LDA) to extract YouTube data aimed at thematic analysis (Daniel, 2019) was an asset for the debunking of trans narratives that span from such different places but also languages. While I did not pursue an entire debate on complexities behind all the indices possible to extract from an LDA, I consciously sought to queer those methods out of masculine assumptions of exactitude and correction. My commitment stands with presenting transparent data that allow a departure to imagine the subtleness and subjectivity that stem from these topics. Beyond debates of efficacy and predictability that lie in quantitative methods, one can also profit from an exploratory prompt first. From that, subsets of data containing each channel were merged to form a complete set of word data that would base both a longitudinal bank that cuts across time and several geographies.

At the same time, several cross-sectional attributes allow the perception of the same topic or event in words repeated by distinct producers and their lenses. Trans controversies and backlashes, new debates triggered by media coverage, and questions from the audience should pop up in videos produced in the same timeframe. All the content was transcribed, translated into English, and analysed using a Python application that calculated their latent topics via LDA. The analyses yielded scores based on word coherence, uniform distribution, and corpus distribution. These items offer no base for a more profound reflection on their statistical value except to anchor the discussion on the emphases found on trans YouTube and how the words hint at the connection between topics reflexive of shared interests among the media producers.

In the following sections, I debunk the results obtained from this series of word clouds and LDA analyses conducted on this transcribed text sample. The word sample (n=101,897) appears contextualized both from a global perspective, that is, the summative weight of all videos, but also offering space to discuss the local emphases and their relative differences to counterparts in other languages and countries. First, I present an analysis based on a straightforward account of word repetition, which gave place to word clouds that help us to visualize some of the stressed points and their weight to the context in each video. Secondly, I immerse myself in topic modelling analysis to discuss the position of these terms relative to others, their coherence and exclusivity. These sub-sections work on grasping the absences in this debate and how specific conversations appear in trans YouTube both from a global, English-speaking perspective and lesser-known, local contexts.

Vocabularies of trans YouTube

There is no surprise about the degree to which trans influencing has followed the trends of the broader YouTube scene. The recipe for the typical YouTube video includes the design of flashy avatars, catchy titles, and circling open questions to attract clicks. Content creation, overall, has been subdued to a general perception of algorithmic visibility and exposure, more than needing to be accurate or ethical (Duffy & Meisner, 2022). In that case, to find common words in such distinct realities, trans from many locations and cultures, is somewhat less unpredictable on the platform. It is expected that YouTubers look at each other's work constantly, get recommended to one another, and attract a similar audience that is likely to share comments on things that level up what is happening across the board. For example, clickbait remains one of the main challenges that prevent further engagement with YouTube text due to collective strategies that producers adapt to attract viewers (Varshney & Vishwakarma, 2021). In that way, all text from YouTube should be carefully seen as framed within the expectation of publicity that is either homogenously articulated in real time or replicated from time to time in waves that overlap any attempt at originality.

In trans YouTube, though, the scraped words point to the convergence of crucial areas of interest. Transition, hormones, transgender, and dysphoria are vital to understanding the main core of urgent topics for trans viewers. These topics form themes that are present in all languages researched. The final sample included *Jammidodger*, a trans man from Britain, and *CopsHateMoe*, a non-binary trans person also from Britain. I also counted on *Airy*, a trans woman from Taiwan, *Ander Martinez*, a trans man from Spain, *Rosa4*, a Black trans woman from Brazil, and *Stafaniya Bruin*, a trans woman from Russia. These channels have not only met an expectation of diversity in terms of finding producers from distinct languages but who struggle in various ways of local acceptance.

As shown in Figure 8, all the videos orbited around common themes and terms that posed dilemmas of changing bodies and problems with integrating into mainstream society. For example, *Airy* published *Ten Difficulties in Dressing Up as a Woman* as far as *Ander Martinez* published *My Physical Transformation as a Trans Boy*. Regarding problems, Rosa from Brazil titled her video *I Left Jail, Now What?* as far as Stafaniya Bruin approached *Escorts among Transgender*. Both featured interviews with trans folks who had gone through harrowing experiences in their life. The salience of random terms such as a *person, feel, everything, and much, here, being,* attest to testimonials and conversations in one's bedroom, where personal or collective impressions start from general points but move quickly to reveal the marks left by transphobia at different levels.

The Anglosphere of Trans YouTube has been relatively more focused on specific struggles and controversies surrounding social media and press coverage of trans affairs. The salience of *J. K. Rowling* and *transphobia* among the top terms signal how much the current media's further discussion on celebrities reflects onto these trans interlocutors. Conversely, a YouTube backlash goes unnoticed in the same mainstream media that triggers the debate. *The Evidence Transphobes Ignore, Transphobic Ad Asks 'What is a Woman'*: all these titles reveal what happens once English-speaking trans YouTubers start to debunk what they see as transphobic narratives. A new feature for publishing short videos on YouTube, an apparent response to the sharp, quick-paced interventions on TikTok, has allowed many of these trans fact-checking

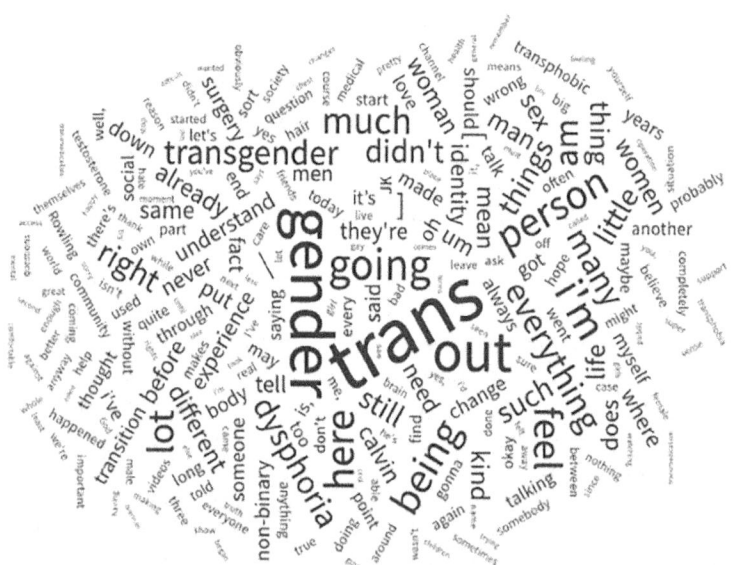

Figure 8 Most repeated terms in all trans YouTube videos sampled.

4. Trans Content Creators 143

Figure 9 Most repeated terms in trans YouTube in English.

or rebukes just after the headlines create viral posts on Twitter or other social media.

Non-binary channel *CopsHateMoe* has developed a mini-documentary titled *JK Rowling's History of Transphobia*. The same is true for other YouTubers seen as adversarial or enemies against trans-inclusive policies. Lesbian YouTuber *Arielle Scarcella* became another mention in these rebuttals due to her agenda against many of the so-called *progressive* trans, including the equal recognition of trans women as *women*. Her pursuit of antagonizing popular trans speakers is a step beyond the viewpoints associated with the Trans-exclusionary Radical Feminist (TERF). Scarcella has been accused of engaging in debates and battles aimed at delegitimizing and personalizing criticism of rival YouTubers such as *Noah Finnce*. Like these battles, many others are fought against trans influencers seen as transphobes or followers of a right-wing conception of gender and family. In the US, this segment of trans YouTube appears as Republican trans, gathering names such as Blaire White and Buck Angel.

The recurrence of terms connected to these online personalities is a common trait in both channels analysed in the English language. When YouTuber *Kalvin Garrah* 'fat-shamed' another YouTuber called *Brennen Beckwith*, that led to the latter going 'closeted', slang for her vanishing from the Internet. Beckwith only re-emerged online with videos three years later. These periods of absence and rebukes to attack, repeated in all channels, configured a broader space of discussion among trans YouTubers across the languages researched. Still, in its highly concentrated universe of English-speaking contents, political rivalries are mingled with arguments such as mental health and trans health in general. Hence the popularity of terms such as *blockers, hormones, healthcare, children, puberty, surgery*, and many co-related others.

I want to focus on this constant zoom-in and zoom-out of trans reality on YouTube. Regardless of the topic, a pattern observed here lies in wording situations according to local and global terms. Even if titles are meant to be catchy and aimed at click-baiting, emphasized or de-emphasized terms vary according to the narrator's feelings at the time they are producing the video. The pattern also concatenates other needs of communicating broader stances about topics that are dearer to the community, like in the case of the word *anxiety*. I have taken two excerpts from an English-speaker YouTuber's video to show how this term encapsulates many situations at once, leading to very personal situations and public awareness sessions:

> My anxiety also seems to have gotten a lot worse the other day, I saw this massive flying beetle crawl under my duvet as I was trying to get to sleep, and I got so scared that I've slept at my brother's room ever since and refused to go back outside (...)

> A diagnosis of gender dysphoria may be appropriate. The distress is typically a combination of anxiety, depression, and irritability gender dysphoria can often lead to thedevelopment of mental illnesses like anxiety, depression, and eating disorders. People with severe gender dysphoria may experience serious long-lasting symptoms.

That being the case, when one looks at other producers outside the anglosphere, zooming in or out becomes essential for correctly appreciating what one's very local issues look like for different audience segments. The extent to which central words are less focused is much indebted to the fact that these YouTubers are reasoning other stories and preoccupations rather than orbiting around the main agenda, often dictated by the mainstream media. For example, when analysing the *Ros4* channel in Portuguese, it becomes clear that *trans* and *transvestite* are not interchangeable but are a trigger for self-reflection. *LGBT, community, rights, country,* and *Brazil* enshrine immediate issues that concern that YouTuber. It does so by underlining readings that do not belong in English-speaking environments, for instance. The repetition of LGBT, a term as popularized as *queer*, reveals epistemological compliance that has an activist salience, even among those who do not share the same consumer or cultural space with folks based on the West.

One aspect that pops up when comparing all non-English speaking samples concerns the affordance of terms to participate in the trans debate on such a global platform. While aware of trending topics, the crux of YouTubers is to provide insight into their daily lives at the local level. They employ local vocabularies to mostly speak of social issues and the oppression of trans people. As in Portuguese, the Russian channel is fragmented and displays many less-recurrent terms such as *understand, church, transgender, and person*, but not related to specific trans debates initiated in mainstream society. As much as the Spanish channel dwells more on health care and transition topics, these channels share a great deal of preoccupation with how to frame trans issues from a local perspective. Therefore, less emphasis exists on showbiz in general. Most discussions approach media transphobia vis-à-vis issues that emerge from interviews and autobiographical stories.

Affording topics, zooming in and out on facts, and this dialogue with mainstream society can be less problematic in the Taiwanese channel *Allie Liao*. Most data appear as understatements related to trans issues. The topic of transition, for example, seems through more generic terms than those noticed in other languages. *Reassignment, surgery, what, why, own, maybe* express concerns about the transition process while not bringing any political dimension to this critical step. The YouTuber at stake is frequently filming travel blogs or live streaming. In the meantime, she skips a more political positioning than those brought up by YouTubers based in Russia or Brazil, for example. In the latter, these terms also suggest more legal and societal issues being aired than YouTubers engaging with media waves or memes. In Brazil, the YouTuber Rosa interviews another trans woman recently discharged from jail. In Russia, emphasis happened on ideas of transgender individuals being over-sexualized and seen as escorts.

This prioritization of local agendas in the Global South over viral or media backlash also happens with the Taiwan-based producer *Allie Liao, who* has actively covered annual rituals such as the Chinese New Year. She also brings up dressing aspects that become problematized from a trans person's viewpoint. As shown in Figure 10, words such as *reassignment, surgery, more, should, own,* and *can't* denote a frequent preoccupation with fitting into her immediate environment. Words such as *Taiwan, Taipei, and Taichung* confirm the channel's inclination to travel vlogging in local destinations. While touring places, Lao seems to correspond to her local audience in Chinese as the archetype of a successful trans person. She does so by calling up a normative sense of femininity and harmony instead of laying bare potential issues from the transition process, otherwise frequent in the English, Russian, Portuguese, and Spanish Trans YouTube. The lack of YouTube collaboration with other influencers is another aspect.

These varying emphases among YouTubers picture contexts that range from liberal and non-Western scenes in which trans influencers have revealed their vocabularies. As seen, YouTubers closely aligned to Western, anglophone media markets orbit around the same atmosphere of visibility and community as other producers. It also comprises competition, ripostes, and politics in which trans allyship or transphobia is always at stake. On the other hand, some YouTubers can occasionally engage in candid accounts of their surroundings. Most respect local limitations of repertoire or audience expectations to keep their language tied to localized terms or prudence where it fits. The latter scenario corresponds to the wording found in Brazil, Russia, and Taiwan. This perspective of opposite spheres in trans YouTube reflects each region's vernacular ways of referring to trans issues. However, it could also amount to the current media exposure of some debates, free time or other affordances that allow for more scenes to be about themselves as others have more urgent needs. Next, I explore the roots of these topics by allocating similar words to the topic by using Latent Dirichlet Allocation method (LDA). I specify conversations and speculate how they relate to one another more substantially.

Analysing trans topics in trans YouTube

As a more sophisticated method for text analysis, Latent Dirichlet Analysis (LDA) could find patterns in words as they are articulated in their natural form. In the last section, some stop-words, slang, and the concurrent use of vocabulary may have hindered more detailed explanations of how words appear for speakers and why they choose to employ them. Here, words are measured according to their distance from one of the other groups of words while establishing calculations for their appearance or uniqueness in a particular context. This technique has inspired multiple studies about finding topics amid the dominance of natural text, conversations, emojis, irony, and other metaphorical uses of language that can prove misleading for the researcher's perception (Towne et al., 2016). This categorization has probed many conversations on text-driven social media such as Twitter so that content quality can be seen against its veracity (Negara et al., 2019; Sheikha, 2020). Here, the topic allocation lists the words that assign a topic by common association of words among all trans YouTubers researched. Still, to ease the understanding of these topics and give it some qualitative sound, topic names were chosen according to the main keywords identified to ease and allow a more critical look at each topic.

As Table 3 demonstrates, subtle intersections between topics deserve further attention. Some of them may overlap, e.g., medical procedures and hormones. However, all these subjects are present in most of the trans channels on YouTube. The idea here is not leading to a generalization that *all* trans YouTube revolves around these conversations or these framings. Instead, the online dialogue between media producers and their audiences, despite all constraints from excessive commercialization or algorithmic censorship, leads to a mix of public service, identity-related discussions, or addressing dangers against the community. Of

Table 3 Topic names according to keywords found in LDA analysis

Number	Topic's name	Top keywords (sampling: Gibbs)
1	Transition	people, sex, transition, transgender, trans, different, dysphoria, social, often
2	General impressions	like, people, know, don't, ant, think, really, that's, one, time
3	Health issues	don't, good, ill, today, can't, save, talking, keep, start, public
4	Clashes within the trans community	video, calvin, sort, gonna, opinions, bad, yeah, non-binary, brennan, hate
5	Beliefs	it's, don't, yes, already, something, everything, I'm, say, life, God.
6	Hormones	trans, people, puberty, woman, kids, access, care, women, used, blockers
7	Medical procedures	operation, everything, surgery, didn't, vagina, sex, would, hospital, one, reassignment
8	Body changes	well, year, person, testosterone, hair, going, everything, super, put, change
9	Clashes outside the trans community	trans, people, Rowling, transphobic, tweet, women, sex, transgender, men, woman
10	Identities	non-binary, you're, they're, identity, coming, yeah, transphobic, guy, lesbians, love

course, the clashes we see above, herein split between those within and out of the trans community, also relate to these threats. Imminent or not, personal or not, these issues exist to various degrees of criticality and enrol multiple actors outside of the trans community. The fact that most of these topics belong directly to the range of trans interests, as seen in the previous section, is revelatory because of the varying priorities according to each trans YouTuber's location.

Let's take the coherence index, for instance, a high coherence index (<0) means the number of times a group of words appear together in a document (Röder, Both & Hinneburg, 2015). In the below case (Figure 11), the topic with the maximum score is *Clashes within the trans community*. To what concerns the nuances in trans expression, this index shows us how mentioning names such as *Brennan* and *Calvin*, protagonists of a controversy explained earlier, can happen in a distinct set of posts. The same goes for *identity*, another topic with an expressive coherence index that orbits around keywords such as *transphobic* or *lesbian*. It shows that a small range of words can base a whole set of

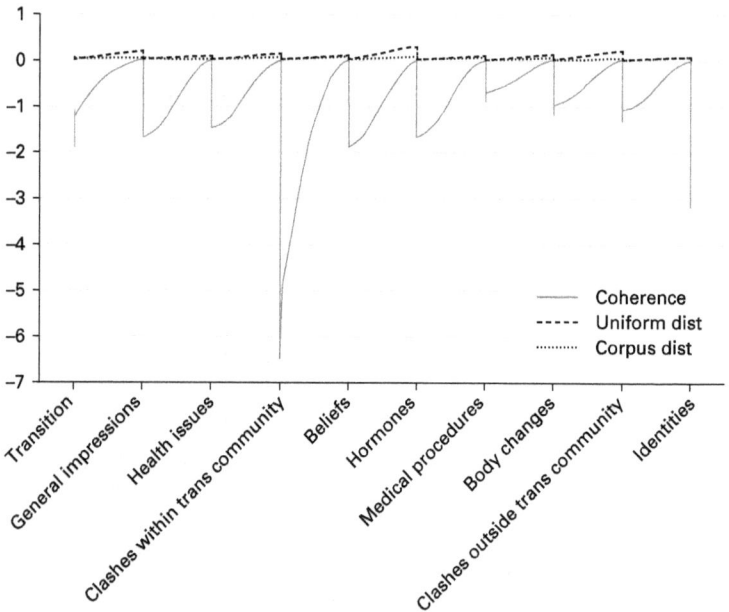

Figure 10 Relationship between topics and coherence, uniform distribution, and corpus distribution.

conversations that somewhat insist on the same facts or pieces of evidence about transphobic events, for example, or to contrast trans experience with that of other groups, such as the *lesbians*. A significant part of negative indices appear in coherence with one another. Words such as *hate, non-binary, brennan* (-0.65) belong in the same group, while in the *Identities* topic, it had the words *love* and *lesbians* (-0.35). This index reveals the great concentration of topics around issues that pertain to the politics of YouTube that affect trans relationships vis-à-vis the dispersion of words meaning other issues. Using only producers' names or keywords, one sees the propensity to brand these feelings after these people. To a large extent, the persistence of these words helps land the discussion among YouTubers that may even not know each other and be approximated only thanks to algorithms. It may also suggest a larger alienation of others who are not part of this debate or controversy.

In terms of similarity of corpus distribution (Figure 11), i.e., the extent to which the same words appear in more than one topic and the probability of that appearance, there are relevant outtakes regarding words that connect to distinct topics. For instance, one sees how *everything* is a word that appears in *Beliefs, Body changes,* and *Medical procedures*. One sees terms such as *transphobic* strike a relationship with *Identities* and *Clashes Outside Trans Community*. While not deepening the statistical properties of these scores' topic modelling, they can refer to a logic that may contradict human perception (Towne et al., 2016) as the similarity between how generic words appear in these distinct contexts may vary in meaning, urgency, and uniformity.

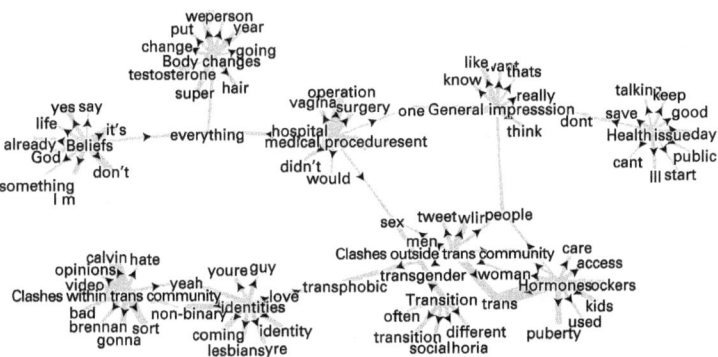

Figure 11 Most repeated terms according to corpus distribution (>0).

However, it is possible to establish a few assumptions in that regard. For example, trans YouTubers stress their impressions using evocative expressions such as *yeah*, *don't*, as they *trans* everything. The name *trans* becomes an accompanying adjective for all things related to everyday life, including public services, medication, and toiletries. This process happens with many topics. And yet, words with apparently banal meanings purposefully serve YouTubers to refer to gender confirmation operations, physical appearance, and body traits, as these excerpts from a few YouTubers show. I italicized passages that contain these terms:

> I came up with this word *everything*, which is cool and great [laughter]. There was a moment with a psychologist when I had a different personality. (...) There are some more channel drugs that block the production of testosterone, and they are very difficult for the body to give it a go. (...) From what time after the start of taking hormone replacement therapy, the chest begins to grow, and hair disappears for everyone. *Everything*, individually, *everything* depends on your age.

> I've ever seen so it will just depend on your body. Obviously, try to do *everything* that's within your power to try and minimise stretching and listen to what your surgeon recommends (...)

> You noticed when it was one year for the first year of testosterones like a rollercoaster, they change a lot of things, and you become a totally different person but when you are two years old well things are more stabilised if *everything* is more normal what happens.

> Well, the first year, I wanted to change everything. I used minoxidil so that it [hair] would grow faster, it let me wash them for a super long period of time. I decided to look masculine. I lost weight very fast to be better. I still did not want to have surgery on *everything*.

On the other hand, this research also tried to understand the occurrence of exclusive words (<1). The *identities* topic concentrates the highest concentration of unique words (Figure 12), with *transphobic*, *non-binary*, and *lesbians* ranking high in this criterion. Following this, one sees *Clashes outside the trans community* as the second topic carrying the most significant number of exclusive words such as a *tweet*,

Rowling, and *transphobic*. These terms denote a substantial preoccupation in reacting to and debating issues that arise from social media networks and its controversies, such as the contentious exchange with writer J. K. Rowling on Twitter about the extension of trans policies. Third, the *Body changes* topic accumulates exclusive words such as *testosterone*, *year*, *hair*, and *super* ranking high. These words attest to much material available documenting one's transition phases, as discussed earlier. The categories with less exclusive words appear as *Health issues*, *General impressions*, and *Transitions*.

While statistics relating to exclusivity here can indeed find limitations, as similar words can also appear in other topic categories, these repetitions show consistency in the intent of the conversations held under these particular topics. Topics that scored less in exclusivity, such as *Transition*, in which *dysphoria*, *transition*, and *different* figure as exclusive occurrences, signal the aim of narrating facts of life chronologically. Another possible interpretation of the three topics with the highest score of exclusive terms, namely, *Identities*, *Clashes within the trans community*, *Body changes*, and *Medical procedures*, relates to the lower score these topics received in the analysis. In other words, the terms seen here are more likely to appear in the former topics than in the latter. A hypothesis is that by closing ranks around these debates, by making them more specific and less subjective, trans YouTubers can articulate a joint discourse that purports to represent them to outsiders, while *Health issues*, *General impressions*, and *Transition*

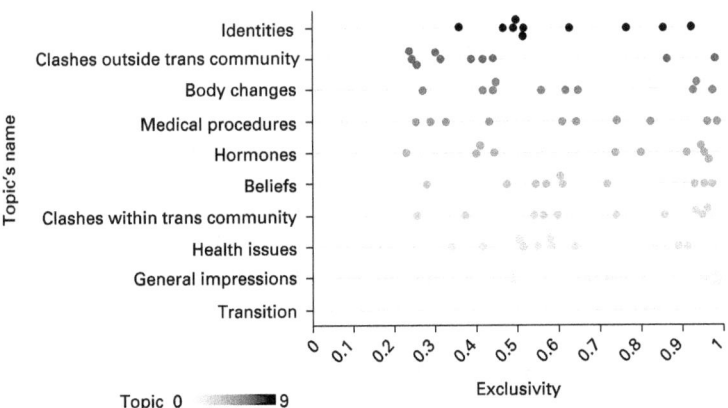

Figure 12 Trans YouTube topic as per exclusivity index.

reserve less of a defensive stance from them or words with less relatable potential are employed. In the latter's case, exclusive words such as *want*, *think*, and *know* are likely to feature in conversations with their viewers.

The main gain from understanding exclusivity in this scenario is fortifying the topic with more exclusive words that generate the most discursive power for the trans community. In effect, these words confer to the trans YouTube the ability to elect priorities and name what they sense as opponents to further conquests. By seeing highly exclusive words in *Hormones*, such as *kids*, *puberty*, and *blockers*, these YouTube channels anticipate much of the legal or societal challenges to movements that mainstream media channels are only about to perceive. For example, the issue of puberty blockers crowns a whole discussion that goes into *transmedicalism* that happened in at least three of the languages researched. Although an agenda that has been growing over the years (e.g., Preciado & Despentes, 2020), the manipulation of trans folks by pharmaceutical complexes remains a priority for trans producers, at least using these terms. Alas, one could hypothesize that the low exclusivity scores in *transition* are down to the lack of uniformity in how the debate happens in some scenes. Influencers have approached transition both from the side of a social transition and a medical transition, but the above analysis showed that this happens without regard to local contexts and follows a general way of perceiving it.

On the one hand, whether nearing consensus or not, one could argue that fracturing terms and the multidirectional nature of this debate nurture the community with groups of ideas as opposed to homogenizing their ideas at the expense of YouTube. It is a somewhat healthy relationship that surveyed trans producers could make sense of its terms, share knowledge, and, at worst, silo its counter-public sphere by echoing debates and controversies not allowed in non-trans spaces. On the other hand, one may want to recognize the importance of sharing this knowledge that cuts across local and global spaces and level the conversation up to contexts in which trans communities cannot count on other forms of dissemination. Next, I return to this book's topic concerning the possible findings extracted from each method demonstrated above and its relation to *globalized queerness*.

Local and global standards in trans YouTube

Both methods have allowed a deeper insight into the array of YouTube videos portraying trans life both in the West and non-Western contexts.

In my analysis, I have prioritized a distinct assortment of local conversations while focusing on a few matters of global importance. The main contribution to scholarly knowledge lies in understanding the constitution of singular spheres of trans debates online. As a global platform, YouTube has the architecture to design dialogue and shape the viewer-producer relationship to reward sameness and homophily as opposed to diversity and spontaneity. Significantly, many YouTubers have conformed to aesthetic choices and discursive standards that constrain their ability to innovate and generate unwanted discussions at the expense of getting trans stories more views and likes. However, aware of the enormous constraints that stopped decades of trans-created media debates, one should recognize the incredible networks of knowledge established by trans YouTubers. They have taken the task to document, share, and pave the way for all sorts of questions and answers concerning unique insights into the trans experience.

Both word cloud and LDA methods allowed me to track, in the forest of language, several trans articulations that pointed in many directions. As Raun (2016) has thoroughly investigated trans-self-representation on YouTube, there can be much expectation on the visual aspect of it, partly due to the trans legacy in being performative, partly due to the possibilities of vlogging. As the author points out, the delivery of multiple cues increases the perception of transness while informing the viewer about trans diversity. In this chapter, text appears as a powerful tool for trans expression because it accords for exchanging topics across cultures and languages. As seen in the section on trans vocabularies, the text unveils nuances and struggles through persuasive content that touch upon broader audiences by reversing the former derogatory use of some words (e.g., *travesti, bixa, transvestite*), and debunking the step-by-step of the trans experience. Textual repetitions have also revealed how affordances vary among YouTubers in wealthy countries such as the UK (e.g., affordance to discuss bodies at length, social media backlash) from those in poorer countries (e.g., affordances to thrive morally and economically, surviving jail).

The globalization of trans vocabularies on YouTube stems from the perception of unification in subjects and interests that flow across different repertoires and affordances. The evidence of budding local differences abounds, primarily because of the entrepreneurship demonstrated in cases such as Russia and Brazil. As far as past episodes of trans leadership have been evidenced in many interviews with pioneers such as Sylvia Rivera (Marcus, 2009), not limited to the 1969 Stonewall riots in New York City, there are many calls for new engagements in trans diversity, and political affinities. YouTube and online streaming may join these new avenues of acceptance, which should become part of multiple and permanent stances of liberation. In this way, globalized queerness comes through as this set of narratives of personal and collective stories that become a unified front. It insists on lenses to fix problematic mainstream media presentations. It poses a critique on the latter, but without giving trans influencers space or interface to create substantial versions of reality that could lead to palpable agreement and community rather than algorithm-prompted dissent.

The phenomenon noticed here as this zoom-in and zoom-out of the trans experience, intimate and real-world together, ends by globalizing inner struggles in the trans communities, gathering YouTubers across new lines of thought and ideology. Once similarities, coherence, and exclusivity of words are observed in the topics retrieved, one sees how transness becomes content due to YouTubers' diligent work online. Transphobic events and characters, clashes in and out of the trans community, and reactions to Internet memes are some of the tactics explored to produce content that invariably becomes very politicized. This dual agency leaves queerness as the intellectual struggle to end heteronormative templates for trans existence. It results in the creation of an aesthetic that joins mainstream debates through performative politics. Channels like *ContraPoints* have shown how trans media production can grow professionally, which may involve textual innovation and the excellent tailoring of costumes and theatre.

Concerning the broader context of globalized queerness seen in previous chapters, vernacular trans on YouTube seems way ahead in terms of its criticality and urgency. Instead of generic mainstream products, one finds dense and complex questions being asked all the time. If films like *A Fantastic Woman* (2017), directed by Chilean director Sebastian Lello, claimed to innovate by casting a trans actress in the leading role, here we have first-person accounts that can not only react but also foreshadow political and heteronormative challenges coming. One concludes that YouTube politics can merge with trans politics in the moment trans individuals approach characters and references detached from everyday societal concerns. The spread of vocabularies, the battle for the 'most accurate' understanding of gender, and the issue of the prevailing of non-binary genders vis-à-vis the recent obsession about confirmation surgeries are just some of these battles that create forms of media that is entirely participatory, as opposed to reductive portraits based on only one or two aspects of the trans experience.

The only question about the superiority in terms of politics and the veracity of the Internet regarding commodity queer is about the affordability of this model. By taking the topics and words investigated, one may wonder whether non-English speaking, non-Western channels can be more than just spectators of these conversations and become agenda-setters. The sample explored here shows deeply engaged actors in the Global South, Taiwan, and Russia. Still, there is much more to know about the universalization of these debates and affordability. These YouTubers have addressed fundamental issues such as access to medicines and health care but *knowing* more trans arguments should be part of many other media and formats existing in multiple realities and languages.

Furthermore, the affordability of holding specific conversations and evading binaries remains an excellent advantage for those who can do it. Essentially, the employed research methods permitted a deconstruction of an idea of trans sameness online, pointing to a positive picture regarding the speed at which topics expand and interlocutors grow their audience bases. On the lower side of this equation, the exchange of ideas and intelligent exploration of issues makes us leave the paradox of visibility and enter one of seeing the permanent flow of trans conversations, active dialoguing, and opposition. In the future, initiatives such as transactual.org.uk, a website gathering much information about trans rights and partnerships, can also partner with these YouTube projects to help the production of several online knowledge spheres. Producers should also try to promote ethnic, gender-normative, economic, or other intersectional cuts within these trans spheres to find out more about who can speak or still cannot do it. Future research must amalgamate other allies of trans communities to help alleviate these divides beyond the advent of an Internet platform that essentially fills the needs of its creators, but not much more outside it.

Conclusion

This chapter explored through quantitative methods ways to retrieve and analyse popular topics gathered from channels run by trans individuals. The quantitative analysis of words employed by trans producers aligned with a Latent Dirichlet Allocation (LDA) showed that the prioritization of personal experiences and the politicization of trans lives in a process called zoom-in and zoom-out of trans realities. On the flip side, the LDA application identified topics that had revealed a rich universe of trans interests that repeat across different landscapes.

Regardless of their native tongue, trans language on YouTube has revealed a positive aspect of globalizing their presence by emphasizing common topics of transition, de-transition, and reaction to recent controversies. As the last section has debated, analysing these video's texts gives us the privilege of knowing what kinds of affordances these producers have when creating their videos and speaking to their cameras without the resource of the image. As a conscious limitation, this method distracts us from the video's visuals and cues. On the other hand, identifying emphases and topics has revealed elements of reaction, defence, and trans creativity in occurrences often ending in politicized stances. However, the constitution of spheres of trans knowledge and debate remains underexplored to the extent that they can exist without being subordinated to mainstream media-brokered discussions. In the final chapter, I invite the universe of queer digital practitioners.

References

Berberick, S. N. (2018). The paradox of trans visibility: Interrogating the 'Year of Trans Visibility'. *Journal of Media Critiques*, 4(13), 123–144.

Cavalcante, A. (2018). *Struggling for ordinary: Media and transgender belonging in everyday life*. United States: NYU Press.

Chakravarthi, B. R., Priyadharshini, R., Durairaj, T., McCrae, J. P., Buitelaar, P., Kumaresan, P., & Ponnusamy, R. (2022, May). Overview of the shared task on homophobia and transphobia detection in social media comments. In Proceedings of the Second Workshop on Language Technology for Equality, Diversity and Inclusion (pp. 369–377).

Craig, S. L., McInroy, L., McCready, L. T., & Alaggia, R. (2015). Media: A catalyst for resilience in lesbian, gay, bisexual, transgender, and queer youth. *Journal of LGBT Youth*, 12(3), 254–275.

Daniel, C. (2019). Thematic exploration of YouTube data: A methodology for discovering latent topics. *Muma Business Review*, 1, 141–155.

Duffy, B. E., & Meisner, C. (2022). Platform governance at the margins: Social media creators' experiences with algorithmic (in) visibility. *Media, Culture & Society*, 45(2), 285–304.

Foucault, M. (1971, 2019). *The history of sexuality: 2: The use of pleasure*. United Kingdom: Penguin Books Limited.

García-Marín, J. (2021). YouTube and traditional media: Polarization in the Catalan political conflict. In M. Musiał-Karg & Ó. G. Luengo (Eds.), *Digitalization of democratic processes in Europe* (pp. 31–41). Springer.

Hansford, A. (2022). Twitter 'deletes' Jordan Peterson tweet deadnaming Elliot Page after he said he'd 'rather die'. Available at https://www.pinknews.co.uk/2022/07/02/jordan-peterson-elliot-page-twitter/ Access 25 August 2022.

Heuer, H., Hoch, H., Breiter, A., & Theocharis, Y. (2021). Auditing the biases enacted by YouTube for political topics in Germany. In S. Schneegass, B. Pfleging, & D. Kern (Eds.), *Proceedings of Mensch und Computer 2021*. ACM (pp. 456–468).

Horak, Laura. (2014) 'Trans on YouTube: Intimacy, visibility, temporality'. *Transgender Studies Quarterly*, *1*(4), 572–585.

Humphrey, R. (2016). 'I think journalists sometimes forget that we're just people': Analysing the effects of UK trans media representation on trans audiences. *Gender Forum: An Internet Journal for Gender* Studies, *56*, 23–43. University of Cologne English Department.

Hussein, E., Juneja, P., & Mitra, T. (2020). Measuring misinformation in video search platforms: An audit study on YouTube. Proceedings of the ACM on Human-Computer Interaction, 4(CSCW1), 1–27.

Kaufmann, J. (2010). Trans-representation. *Qualitative Inquiry*, *16*(2), 104–115.

Koch-Rein, A., Haschemi Yekani, E., & Verlinden, J. J. (2020). Representing trans: Visibility and its discontents. *European Journal of English Studies*, *24*(1), 1–12.

Konijn, E. A., Veldhuis, J., & Plaisier, X. S. (2013). YouTube as a research tool: three approaches. *Cyberpsychology, Behavior, and Social Networking*, *16*(9), 695–701.

Kee, Y. H., Li, C., Kong, L. C., Tang, C. J., & Chuang, K. L. (2019). Scoping review of mindfulness research: A topic modelling approach. *Mindfulness*, *10*(8), 1474–1488.

Malik, H., & Tian, Z. (2017). A framework for collecting YouTube meta-data. *Procedia Computer Science*, *113*, 194–201.

Marcus, E. (2009). *Making gay history: The half-century fight for lesbian and gay equal rights*. New York: Harper Collins.

Martino, W., Omercajic, K., & Cumming-Potvin, W. (2021). YouTube as a site of desubjugation for trans and nonbinary youth: pedagogical potentialities and the limits of whiteness. *Pedagogy, Culture & Society*, *29*(5), 753–772.

Maurer, L. G. (2022). Cyber-silencing the community: YouTube, Divino Group, and reimagining section 230. *Washington Journal of Law, Technology & Arts*, *17*(2), 172.

McInroy, L. B., & Craig, S. L. (2015). Transgender representation in offline and online media: LGBTQ youth perspectives. *Journal of Human Behavior in the Social Environment*, *25*(6), 606–617.

Miller, J. F. (2019). YouTube as a site of counternarratives to transnormativity. *Journal of Homosexuality*, *66*(6), 815–837.

Negara, E. S., Triadi, D., & Andryani, R. (2019, October). Topic modelling Twitter data with Latent Dirichlet allocation method. *2019 International Conference on Electrical Engineering and Computer Science* (ICECOS) (pp. 386–390). IEEE.

O'Shea, S. C. (2019). I am not that Caitlin: a critique of the transphobic media reaction to Caitlyn Jenner's Vanity Fair cover shoot and of passing. *Culture and Organization*, 25(3), 202–216.

O'Neill, M. G. (2014). Transgender youth and YouTube videos: Self-representation and five identifiable trans youth narratives. In C. Pullen (Ed.), *Queer youth and media cultures* (pp. 34–45). Springer.

Perelli, A. (2022). How many YouTube subscribers you need to start making money. *Business Insider*. 14 October 2022.

Preciado, P. B., & Despentes, V. (2020). *An apartment on Uranus*. London: Fitzcarraldo Editions.

Raun, T. (2012). DIY therapy: Exploring affective self-representations in trans video blogs on YouTube. In A. Karatzogianni & A. Kuntsman (Eds.), *Digital cultures and the politics of emotion* (pp. 165–180). Springer.

Raun, T. (2015). Archiving the wonders of testosterone via YouTube. *Transgender Studies Quarterly*, 2(4), 701–709.

Raun, T. (2016). *Out online: Trans self-representation and community building on YouTube*. United Kingdom: Taylor & Francis.

Reitz, N. (2017). The representation of trans women in film and television. *Cinesthesia*, 7(1), 2.

Röder, M., Both, A., & Hinneburg, A. (2015, February). Exploring the space of topic coherence measures. In Proceedings of the Eighth ACM International Conference on Web search and data mining (pp. 399–408).

Rood, B. A., Reisner, S. L., Puckett, J. A., Surace, F. I., Berman, A. K., & Pantalone, D. W. (2017). Internalized transphobia: Exploring perceptions of social messages in transgender and gender-nonconforming adults. *International Journal of transgenderism*, 18(4), 411–426.

Sheikha, H. (2020). Text mining Twitter social media for Covid-19: Comparing latent semantic analysis and Latent Dirichlet Allocation. University of Gavle. Doctoral Dissertation.

Tafesse, W. (2020). YouTube marketing: how marketers' video optimization practices influence video views. *Internet research*, 30(6), 1689–1707.

Tortajada, I., Caballero-Gálvez, A. A., & Willem, C. (2019). Contrapúblicos en YouTube: el caso del colectivo trans. *El profesional de la información (EPI)*, 28(6).

Tortajada, I., Willem, C., Platero Mendez, R. L., & Araüna, N. (2021). Lost in transition? Digital trans activism on YouTube. *Information, Communication & Society*, 24(8), 1091–1107.

Towne, W. B., Rosé, C. P., & Herbsleb, J. D. (2016). Measuring similarity similarly: LDA and human perception. *ACM Transactions on Intelligent Systems and Technology (TIST)*, 8(1), 1–28.

Varshney, D., & Vishwakarma, D. K. (2021). A unified approach for detection of Clickbait videos on YouTube using cognitive evidences. *Applied Intelligence*, 51(7), 4214–4235.

Xu, J., Tao, Y., & Lin, H. (2016, April). Semantic word cloud generation based on word embeddings. In *2016 IEEE Pacific Visualization Symposium (PacificVis)* (pp. 239–243). IEEE.

Yeganeh, L., Boyle, J. A., Gibson-Helm, M., Teede, H., & Vincent, A. J. (2020). Women's perspectives of early menopause: development of a word cloud. *Climacteric, 23*(4), 417–420.

Waugh, L. R., Catalano, T., Masaeed, K. A., Hong Do, T., & Renigar, P. G. (2016). Critical discourse analysis: Definition, approaches, relation to pragmatics, critique, and trends. In A. Capone & J. L. Mey (Eds.), *Interdisciplinary studies in pragmatics, culture and society* (pp. 71–135). Springer.

Chapter 5

GLOBAL PLATFORMS, LOCAL CHARACTERS

Any night you can watch genuine artists, intellectuals, and so forths boisterously protesting, or being loudly indifferent to such common social practices as sobriety and amiable conversation.
— Nan Allamida Boyd, *Wide Open Town: A History of Queer San Francisco to 1965*

The book's last chapter covers queer artists and media producers who actively use social media for their projects. Previous chapters expanded on globalized queerness as a phenomenon that creates homogenous modes of expression that can affect queer commodities negatively in the case of obfuscating local ways of being queer. But global queer discourses can also have an informative role, such as the advent of queer news that spread worldwide or the recent explosion of trans YouTube that has boosted further engagement and knowledge among trans communities worldwide. Insofar as globalized queerness stems mostly from global media industries that profit at the expense of these commodified aspects seen hitherto, it can yet design an architecture that shelters the minimum conversation about queerness at the local level. To what extent have local actors developed a consciousness of living in a time of globalized queerness? What is the process of learning global or local discourses? These are some outstanding questions that should be discussed in this chapter.

The talk of media industries is not complete until we mention social media platforms such as Facebook, Twitter or TikTok. The Internet has anchored not only spaces of discussion, but also self-styling, media production, professional network, fandom waves, and many other purposes that can be a lifeline for queer folks. Duguay (2016b), for instance, saw how selfies gathered celebrity endorsements, activism, and conversations on gender and sexuality without bending to heteronormative discourses. On the other way around, these platforms have acknowledged queer publics and shown support. By changing their logos for pride flags, they have embraced LGBTQ movements, while raising eyebrows on the right-wing spectrum, including Twitter's owner Elon Musk (Griffith, 2022). It is also true that most platforms' 'community guidelines', or the rules through which one can be blocked or banished from these spaces, have tried to punish those promoting homophobia and transphobia. TikTok and Facebook have reportedly been working with organizations such as GLAAD (Gay and Lesbian Alliance Against Defamation) to develop policies that can provide a better sense of safety for LGBTQ users.

However, there are many issues regarding the acceptance and thriving of LGBTQ audiences on social media. Queer media producers on YouTube, for example, may find that the Google-owned video and streaming service will still hit them with demonetization (videos do not confer their publishers any profit) and eventual suspension if content seen as legitimate for queer viewers but not for the heterosexual audience is published (Rodriguez, 2022). From a global perspective, this restriction or ambiguity on what can or cannot be published dearly affects how heterosexual users can possibly be integrated into a queer space of contention and dialogue. Moreover, one asks if there could ever be social media without judgement and fear (Middleton, 2021). Evidence has proved that LGBTQ use of social media is directly connected to increased surveillance. The case of queer refugees in Denmark in what Andreassen (2021) saw as social media being used to probe one's claims on being homosexual, a claim that was connected to one's claim for political asylum. This targeting of queer individuals online goes hand in hand with the continuous risks posed by content moderation, an activity often exercised in Westernized settings with no consideration of local variations of queerness, vocabularies, and challenges (Thiago et al., 2021).

These debates seek to problematize social media not as the haven one might have thought at its outset nor as a location of utter fear and panic. This chapter extends to open more holistic ways of approaching not platforms and their evidenced disadvantages but corners and moments LGBTQ populations may find, despite all the caveats. One might still believe in social media as a space for multiple languages and cultures, favouring communities, but without them giving in to its design and algorithms. The case of a French meme inspires new readings beyond the dominance of *queer* as an encompassing term. *Si Beau Ma Queen* has thrived among migrant queers in Francophone settings who were seeking to dodge negative stereotypes about them (Firmonasari, 2021). The latter has similarly served queers of Appalachian descent to reinforce their community (Watts, 2020). Social media has also softened up the queer coming out vis-à-vis old forms of gay come-outs, in which affect, politics, and performance intertwine (Cho, 2015; Johnson, 2020). Social media websites have encased networks of affection after the recovery from a traumatic event, as in the aftermath of the Orlando mass shooting in a gay disco back in 2016 (Jenkins et al., 2019).

This chapter, therefore, introduces globalized queerness to this complex living in social media. Seizing this appropriation of social media networks as an entrepreneurial activity demands that I mix various aspects already visited in this book. For instance, queer relationships with the media have entailed ideas of cosmopolitanism, affect, and media connections between countries and queer history. Here, digital fluency offers the perfect ingredients to savour queer repertoire across borders and check social media architecture against these new idioms and codes of behaviour. Furthermore, social media popularity can drive creative and financial independence. Can these digital queer selves clash with local ways of displaying queerness? To what extent does crafting a global standing as a queer actor online come down as a way of homogenizing and over-simplifying queer online existence? Can there be a sustainable way of globalizing queerness under algorithmic surveillance settings, which are global? I start answering these questions by discussing social media presence and the notion of prominence.

Navigating layers of queer prominence

To perform this study, I speculated how prominent social media actors self-identified as queers can remain true to their backgrounds and forms of affiliation outside social media. Most selected cohorts were based in Western Europe, the US, and South America. The aim was to discuss how their networking habits and knowledge sharing could lead to more or fewer local affiliations. This case study used interviews performed with 30 digital-focused artists and media producers. I also conducted ethnographic participant observation with five artists based in Spain, Italy, and the United Kingdom, from which I selected two profiles, one meant to represent global connections and the second one local forms of queer artistry. The central hypothesis is how information and context traded on social media websites have facilitated or constrained local forms of queerness or even brokered other ambitions or knowledges. At the same time, I wanted to observe those social media users who operated under the label queer as their identity of choice online. Therefore, I developed a framework to look at individuals who have had any expectation of queer digital *prominence* either voiced or signalled up on their social media profiles.

The notion of queer prominence was helpful, yet it offers many ambiguous expectations. It responds to the basic purpose of creating a social media profile that reveals personal information. Prominence in queer media studies may also respond to a long trail of controversy, danger, and societal pushback. It is enough to remember Oscar Wilde, one very prominent writer of his time. Wilde embodied many myths of queer artists and their flame of enchanting, entertaining but also shocking, and probing society's innermost fears. In the 21st century, queer prominence is assumed due to the unexpected popularity of queer popular culture across cleavages of heteronormative society. The mass reproduction of affirmative signs, such as the rainbow flag and its variations, from queer shows to openly gay celebrities, have driven the perception that *those* are prominent queer acts, while not speaking about one's gender or sexuality is to remain in obscurity. What some may see as queerbaiting, others may see as media and culture purporting to show queerness through genuine life trajectories, no matter how dramatized, reinvented or adapted they can be. Consequently, both *being* online or chasing the steps of the latter type of prominence have been seen as valid for this book's purpose.

On the Internet, prominence can still be leveraged in the quantified realm of social media likes or following. The case of Phillip Picardi tells us a story about the lifecycle of this kind of queer social media prominence today. Picardi started as an intern at Condé Nast group and quickly emerged to be promoted as an editor at the prominent publishing house, where he managed *Vogue Teen*. The quick transference between online and offline prominence can be seen as the epitome of queer success in competitive contexts like New York. Whether other factors should be considered, this tale exemplifies that digital prominence *may be enough* when other factors, such as job opportunities or peers' recognition, triangulate. US-based and educated, Picardi was profiled in the *New York Times* aged 26 in a piece headlined: 'Condé Nast's Man of the Moment' (Ember, 2018). Eloquent on Twitter and ubiquitous on Instagram, Picardi saw himself in hot water when he published a guide to anal sex, which did not bode well with parents preoccupied with the readers of a teen magazine. Fast forward to 2022, Picardi has left the magazine, edited another gay reference publication, *Out*, founded an outlet called *Them*, worked for Harvard Divinity

School and remained digitally prominent. In 2022, his Twitter bio indicated he was working at a Los Angeles LGBT Centre.

Picardi's short story encapsulates that queer prominence does not necessarily need stardom and millions of fans worldwide. The rise of queer stars such as Kim Petras and Troye Silvan, who are YouTube self-made stars, suggests that besides the fascination with pop culture or controversial appearances, there is much more in queer culture. While not an artist, Picardi's sojourn in the mainstream media sheds light on how queer media professionals, for example, can go in directions that are often creative roles but also prominent in their sense. They do not need such a notion of the legacy, and often heteronormative, aspect of fame. In *Phrases and Philosophies for the Use of the Young* (1894), Oscar Wilde (Wilde, 2022) famously said that 'One should either be a work of art or wear a work of art', in which the Irish poet placed queer fame in such binary terms to the degree of the unsustainable. Insomuch as the idea has not translated as necessarily false in times of massive brand following, Wilde's provocation has indirectly contributed to the same fascination of queerness as pure style with no substance, an 'aestheticisation', a 'style', as Sontag (2018) points out in *Notes on Camp*. Picardi's and so many unknown stories show other routes for queer prominence in and out of the artistic world, not least because of Internet projects but the intricacies of consuming and producing media for all.

Whether 'architects of taste' or not, as Sontag once put it, contemporary queer folks have nonetheless faced an increasingly tricky media environment. Surrounded by algorithms, queer digital use can be extremely elusive to users who fall prey to the suggestions offered to them and scholars who can value false trends replicated across borders. Perhaps, a truer purpose to the experience of most queers is to come back to the entrepreneurial side of queer digital presence on global and local levels. Digitally based, grassroots, and urban proletarian sources could perceptively strike a balance between the commodified queer self and a localized digital experience that connect to local peers. Therefore, prominence can stem from the observational role, i.e., being able to mock the habits of celebrities and lifestyles without displaying the genuine desire to acquire them. Prominence can be crafty activism and standing up for issues at the right time. Local prominence, if we want to call it that, consists of reversing the mainstream media's homogenizing force and dominance over queerness to re-discover it through rhizomatic forms of expression.

As we shall see, queer social media prominence responds to an immediate imperative for being visible with a purpose. It could entail being an activist, an editor, an artist, or an interlocutor if one wants to translate quick thoughts and projects. Below, I question producers about these affordances that involve being able to embody queer culture in the offline world while being digitally prominent. From practitioners of digital photography to those developing multimedia initiatives that grow into music, visual arts, and handcraft, I have seen a rich scene that corresponds to a mosaic of ages and locations, with a thriving contingent of people of colour and people with disabilities. I focused on the strategies they use to achieve a sense of *thriving* online and the motivations for continuing online despite the risks of being abused or *trolled*. Based on their responses, I approached queer prominence based on Goffman's theory of *facework*, which served to articulate these case studies according to layers of local prominence pursued in the chapter.

Searching for local characters on global platforms

The growing number of queer artists and aspirant personalities on social media is a testament to *prominence* not only as a concept but as a practice embedded in a myriad of other digital attitudes. Literature splits in treating queer digital culture on social media as a place where homosexual interests meet heterosexual mainstream media but get away with its characters, *hunks*, or *bitches*. In fact, it is not as simple as it seems. There is a whole sense of generating chats, likes, and virality. Hashtags anchor snippets of queer contention, disputes, and anger. Fan-led campaigns have rebuked portraits deemed unacceptable by the queer community for years. It was the case of queer characters that inevitably die in mainstream series. This predictable fate has stirred the #buryyourgays movement. This hashtag was aimed at scriptwriters and the way they frame queer characters. The 2022's torrent of disagreement about Harry Styles' queer status while being a straight man (Staples, 2022) and *RuPaul's Drag Race* presence of Maddy Morphosis (Draw, 2022) has invited the public to join and have their say on queer affairs. Despite the intense media coverage, studies have seen how these trends and campaigns fall short of more critical reflection in the longer run (Navar-Gill & Stanfill, 2018).

More than the politics of media reception, queers resorting to social media have also crowned efforts indeed directed at social justice. Successful campaigns, such as *#justiceforsheila*, managed to inform a new generation of issues connected to homophobia and backward laws. The hashtag drove the headlines about the murder of a non-binary lesbian in Nairobi on 17 April 2022 (Okech, 2022). The campaign followed #justiceforsharon, #justiceforjosh, and #justiceforericachandra as awareness hashtags about other murders involving queers, women, and sex workers. Even when happening miles away, these facts have forged new ties among queer folks worldwide. In 2022, #dontsaygay protested the Florida bill to prevent gender or sexual education through third grade. The hashtag followed #stopthestickers and #wewillnotbeerased to fight the bans on stickers and other materials displayed in classrooms that contradicted the law (The Associated Press, 2022).

These cyclical social media movements have followed a conversation thread between queer audiences and the public. But how about queer popularity on an individual level? Social networks are seen as modern piazzas for the young, where they may profit from several information sources. In this book, I aimed to conceive digital queer culture by watching the politics of visibility that play at the individual's level. The extent to which social media can personalize queerness around causes is well debated, but to look at individuals is to achieve a complete picture of how, simultaneously, those viral campaigns may or may not achieve any sort of impact on personal trajectories or viewpoints. Less than the individual struggles that inform one's opinion and influences, the susceptibility of everyone to join these social media movements also depends on their sense of self and belonging. At the local level, one confers publicity to queer developments that affect them or the world. Local attachment conveys a personal sense of ethics and values through these support systems. From fighting surveillance to a new Spring of trans activism online, this local sharing of information has inspired methods, results, and visions for the future (e.g., Burgess et al., 2016; Fischer et al., 2018).

In this way, the idea of prominence assisted me in observing characters that may seek prominence online and yet be disconnected from these global standards of queer participation. They may engage on the Internet by reacting to political or economic facts but republish celebrity quotes or activist messages in the next second. They may subscribe to pornographic acts online and hold progressive views about sex. The bifold nature of local prominence, participative and yet so individualist invites questions on what the quality of their social media project is, if any. This form of local fluency in digital media has users who have already engaged in online relationships but demonstrated against involuntary exposure to dating apps (e.g., Sousa et al., 2020). This framework opens a more holistic look into a local character who can embrace globalized queerness based on the predicaments of being prominent but maintaining their reservations. We can find the extent to which globalized queerness can affect individuals vis-à-vis their relationship with the Internet.

Social media, queerness, and facework

To research this topic with appropriate length and depth, I designed a purposive sampling strategy that could invest in this middle range of users who are neither entirely disconnected nor fully immersed in the possibilities of digital media. That layer of usage seems to host most of the public that can be equally exposed to global and local factors, languages, and repertoires. For example, the extent to which these actors have engaged in global cultures of activism and queer contention can be an interesting indicator to understand their motivations on the global level. On the local level, they can be creative individuals chasing local viewers or clients. They are dwellers of rural or urbanized settings with eyes on the labour market or trying to fit in or be outside local conventions. Both levels of participation are determinants of the degree of attachment or detachment to local or globalized queerness, especially if one is the artist or a creative individual looked at in this research.

Participants were recruited based on their ability to design their visibility according to the available resources on social media. *Prominence* is translated methodologically as the ability to project one's name and work as a content creator without being part of the mainstream media or getting enough featuring in mass media, for example. This criterion remains vague, as queer culture may not even be reported once in many contexts, nor all practising artists are on social media. To ensure that the sample was not biased by mainstream media prominence, I also prioritized producers under the radar of journalists and producers and those who were still to achieve more visibility for their work in these means. The search for these participants involved joining queer groups on Facebook, visiting several Twitter profiles, and developing a relationship that could allow closer observation of the individual's routines and expectations regarding their levels of recognition. Moreover, this contact would evolve into analysing one's local and global affiliations, culminating in a more critical perspective of their limitations and possibilities.

In the second phase of this research, I proceeded to interview artists or media producers with active social media profiles. I prioritized queer media producers whose profiles provided evidence of recent activity during the investigation. That is, those discussing online, sharing links, and creating bridges with other practitioners. On sampling, I profit from other studies that have used snowballing sampling methods with non-heterosexual populations, such as Browne (2005), which, for example, have served to see queer communities in their bonding and individuality. Recruiting participants from all parts of the LGBTQ spectrum is challenging, and on social media, the scope must be broadened to achieve success. The researcher's likelihood of receiving positive feedback on participation also varies according to the social networks. By recruiting on Twitter, Facebook, and Instagram, this research faced varying degrees of resistance from prospective participants that wanted to respond to an in-depth interview. Ultimately, 50 profiles have been mapped to fit these criteria of study concentrated on global and local interests. Of 50 social media profiles, 20 producers agreed to talk, initially recruiting from a sample of men, women and non-binary participants, among them white, black, Latino, and Asian participants, with no restriction of age. The remaining names served this study with the biographic information these pages contained, particularly self-descriptions.

These participants were initially recruited based on their interaction with two hashtags: #queerartist and #queerart. The selection of hashtags for a qualitative study can be controversial as there is no definitive list of them and many new ones pop up daily related to the same subject. Some artists may use many of them, others may use none. The choice of being straightforward by studying #queermedia, #queerartist and #queerart fulfilled the purpose of picking practitioners working on queer themes in several supports. In a preliminary search, these hashtags have attracted artists with a verve for handcrafts, paintings, and visual arts more than media making and commentators. The significance of these hashtags has varied among platforms. Twitter has yielded the most significant number of participants who wanted to speak. Instagram has provided the least number. The ideal scenario was to balance the purpose of these participants in the respective platforms and their association with this research topic. Only two male artists accepted the in-depth interviews, even though the initial plan was to shadow practitioners of more diverse backgrounds. 50 artists joined other interviews about their practice, most of whom were based in cities in Western Europe (15), the United States (20), and Brazil (5), and scattered in other cities of the Global South such as Argentina and Morocco (10). I preferred not to disclose further details of their identity to avoid any harm or personal identification.

Finally, once interviews were collected and data could be analysed, I invested in what Josselson (1996) defined as narrative analysis in the study of lives. The author has insisted on narrative analysis as the selection of facts or stories in people's lives that help researchers make sense of a broader context that surrounds them, of which they might not necessarily be aware. More importantly, it is how analysis of the 'embeddedness' of facts (ibid., 57) in the stories told, if seen in detail, can reveal other factors concealed in the daily experience of life. Besides, the author posits ethical commitments demanded from the method. Paying attention to participants' vulnerability and analysts' interpretive authority (ibid., 45) appears crucial in a context where participants may seek visibility. Still, they may also be submitted to a context of oppression and struggle for societal acceptance and media representation. In Nash (2016:171), we learn that the ethics of learning from queer lives also imply leaving the realm of bureaucracy and being bound to intimacy and affectivity that can effectively allow queer stories to flourish.

To respond to these preoccupations, I strictly discuss the participants' views, lives, and experiences according to their appearance online, and the terms were chosen to frame themselves. The attempt here was to make these quotes into data, instead of the opposite, without exploiting them or making them look sensationalist, for example. Concealing names or exchanging them for pseudonyms was necessary to protect these individuals' identities or prevent these portraits from creating any harm to their lives. While some level of detail regarding their present lives, jobs, and position in society is necessary to provide context, this information is given in a way that prevents personal identification or stereotypical impressions. It is, however, allowed in the research to promote what Nash (2016:181) titled as 'political intimacies', the possibility of voicing these views on the global and local sides of queerness without being penalized or placed in a situation of constraint due to these views.

The material discussed below, essentially these interviews and social media biographic information, will be reviewed according to Goffman's social interactionist ideas (Goffman, 1967; Scheff, 2005). It is known how Goffman's takes on symbolic interactionism have been widely adopted in media and communications studies (Littlejohn, 1977). This theory's use has gained new colours more recently, thanks to its interface with interactive rituals of everyday life, particularly in the context of fast, purely symbolic exchange (Hausmann et al., 2011). Scholars' immersion in symbolic interactionism as a tributary of gender studies has appeared as an alternative to revitalizing a set of ideas much crystalized in the 1920s (Carter & Fuller, 2016). In this research, I seized upon Goffman's take on symbolic interactionism without much ambition to advance the theory's application in the field but to project his ideas of performance through which one establishes queer 'actors' in the digital stage.

Goffman's (1967) take on 'actors', 'dramaturgy', and ultimately, 'performance', fits the emerging scenario of queer digital prominence because it matches the fluid roles and expectations deposited on queer characters. For example, the extent to which profiles and bios can correspond to real expectations that the individual bears in the off-line world. His departure from 'frames' to 'situations' expose the back and forth of online discourse as this constant opening and closure to global and local affordances that one could exhibit. As Goffman argued on the multi-layered aspect of theatrical performance, whereby he extrapolates to affirm that the presentation of self is a threefold aspect, the first one being our self-image, the image others make of us, and the image held by the audience (Goffman, 1967:10):

> In real life, the three parties are compressed into two, the part one individual plays is tailored to the parts played by the others present, and yet these others also constitute the audience.
>
> ibid., 10

The appropriateness of this framework has inspired a set of studies involving gender and sexuality. The vast Goffman's repertoire of symbolic interactionism has recognizably involved emotions, such as shame and embarrassment and similar feelings. More recently, the notion of dramaturgy has been basing reviews of gay introductions on dating and sex platforms (Hogan, 2010). The study of *stigma* has also probed gendered presentations by gay men as a form of 'stigma management' (Han, 2009). The latter takes to similar thoughts on the 'impression management' that entails the homosexual representation on social networking sites (Duguay, 2016a) or the stigma of being Muslim and queer (Javaid, 2020).

From Goffman's enormous body of work, I dwell on *facework* as a wise yet under-explored part of this theoretical work to understand gender relations. For Goffman (1967: 5), the *face* is 'the positive social value a person effectively claims for himself by the line others assume he has taken during a particular contact'. Goffman conceptualized facework as a threefold development, an avoidance gesture (to evade face-threatening episodes), a corrective process (to adjust one's face) and 'making points' (the aggressive use of facework). Although the upshot of Goffman's interactionist beliefs was applied to the political discourse, or at least this is how scholars have used it until now, it is possible to queer it up so that facework can also extend to *queerness* as a value in contemporary social media contention. In short, queerness is used as cues for fleeing persecution on the grounds of one's sexuality (avoidance), the transformation of one's face, like in come-outs (corrective), or as means to fight prejudice or bigotry online by reaffirming queerness (making points). These three points are analysed according to the global or local elements intertwined with this facework.

One example of such an approach lies in Hutson (2010), who discussed the 'fitting in' of gays and lesbians after coming out and the unique challenges that come after that. Unlike this approach, which stayed on the symbolic value of the 'coming out' deposited in visual cues that 'make' gays and lesbians in the aftermath of going public, the symbolic values analysed rest in other indices. In this case, queer presence is expressed using the word *queer* in consonance with global trends, memes, and the news. The connections made with other creative partners worldwide, one's personal framing of issues of acceptance and challenges, and one's embeddedness in queer history and global icons such as the rainbow flag or LGBTQ history month, give us some food for thought in that sense. I would argue that these appropriations could also signal the adherence to globalized queerness articulated through one or more of this threefold stages of facework. Next, I start the empirical discussion from the interviews conducted with several social media users and the shape-up of their impressions as queer creatives on social media.

'I haven't seen any local queer artists in mainstream media'

Recent collections containing case studies on queer digital cultures (e.g., Kataria, 2022) have listed digital queer cultures as a complex reality of actions and expectations spanning distinct regions of the world. Social media users studied can fit into 'activism, advocacy, education, empowerment, identity, protest, and self-expression' (ibid., 2022). Other users have revolved around diasporic expressions and other intersections, including 'race, disability, colonialism, sexuality, and gender'. To a large extent, the *reality* of digital queer communities appears in the interviews below, but in some interviews, it does not. The first limitation lies in this book's purposes, which has prioritized actions that showed queer users in situations of their everyday life rather than approaching them during Twitter storms or trendy hashtags. Secondly, much of the unsolicited control exerted by algorithms can affect the design and notions of agency, so much so that none of the interviewees seemed to be immersed in such a context of activism or political action. Moreover, the rigorous governance policies that censor and block users on platforms constrain or taint the sheer act of being queer online, leave alone LGBTQ activism in its radical facets.

Otherwise, most individuals who have responded to this research's query could be categorized as regularly subscribed to these networks, frequent posters, but with a low level of intensity. They have acquired some level of self-conscious independence to use platforms, but enough to boast thousands of followers. They have also maintained consistency in publishing on the same account for at least two years or more. By inquiring into how they self-represent and the weight they put on social media disclosure of *queerness*, whether as an umbrella of opportunities for de-normalizing one's identities or as simply another tag, many have responded that social media disclosure as *queer* does not live up to replacing other identities, such as *gay* or artistic-related affirmations, as this producer describes below:

> I am cis he/him. I identify as a gay man, but I like to consider myself politically queer. I think of the term 'queer' as a good way of being part of the broader community. But gay pretty much covers it. My Twitter account is a mix of sharing my art, political posting and opinions. This is mostly about LGBTQ+ rights and equality. I also share art posts that inspire me. My Instagram account is mainly just my work, with some personal updates or sharing of other artists' work in my Instagram stories.
>
> Interviewee 2

The above account illustrates how many self-identification statements confirm queerness as a political statement, as one producer said: 'I identify as a cis gay man. However, I do feel comfortable with every pronoun.' When looking at the data from users who were at least forty years old, they tended to refrain at first sight from adopting queer as their main identity demarcation. Younger users, differently, framed themselves as 'queer man', 'queer woman', or non-binary queer since their first statements. Others seize the question to reflect on gender hermeneutics, as this set of quotes shows:

You can call me [producer's first name], or [producer's initials]. I identify as a queer woman and use she/her pronouns.

Interviewee 8

I identify as non-binary (specifically, genderqueer), and in Italian, I use he/him pronouns just because it's easier and because I'm used to it.

Interviewee 9

I identify as a genderqueer individual in the sense that I do not identify on the spectrum of gender. In general, I do not have a preference for pronouns, I easily identify with masculine and feminine pronouns. However, if I had the "grammatical" opportunity to use gender-neutral pronouns, I would definitely use them. For me, the deconstruction and reconstruction of the way I perceive gender is a constant process in a society that is built within binary structures.

Interviewee 11

The issue of identification seems eased on social media, as most interviewees have voiced their queerness in their bios. And yet, when asked to reflect on the significance of gender from a local or global perspective and perceived in their work, interviewees were more careful in voicing such alignments. The historical element of *queer*, a term still perceived as a novelty among some participants, weighs in to moderate these alignments with global LGBTQ references. Interviewees do not necessarily embrace global terminology only if they are asked more than once whether queerness is a theme for their work vis-à-vis their lives regardless of terms:

In that way, I suppose my past sort of informs my work. In my youth, I would've been terrified of being caught drawing or even looking at images of a nude man. I lived in the country before the internet. I would get insights into queer history and culture on TV, but it might as well have been broadcast from Mars as it seemed so unattainable. (...) if I have much in the way of global cultural references in many of my pieces, there are more historical references which have a queer connection. For example, I'm inspired by the male 'beefcake' photography of the 1930s–60s, as well as Greek mythology and Hellenistic sculpture.

Interviewee 1

In that case, their *locality* is expressed in aspects connected to time and space: The extent to which one can own *queerness* as a recent or fashionable element but not at the expense of their ancestry, language, or country. Another interviewee voiced the links between queerness and the English language. To another degree, they said, living in cities makes queerness happen because of the sharing experiences with other artists:

> As someone whose first language is English, I do feel like I have more of a reach since it's the most common language in the world!
>
> Interviewee 3

> I see myself as a local artist, and, especially, [I] see myself as a London artist. I think this is because London represents more personal freedom – I feel I can explore my art thanks to a greater network of models and artists.
>
> Interviewee 5

When talking about media representation and outreach of queer folks, interviewees have unanimously agreed that queer presence, as opposed to *queerness*, in the mainstream media is, at best, underrated, at worst inexistent. I approach the possibility of being queer and local, whatever that assumption could mean for them. When making the question, I explicated those categories of *global, globalized* or *mainstream media* as content seen in prominent media outlets such as *The New York Times*, for example, or associated with symbols such as the *Stonewall* events in New York City or Gay Pride events. Artists who worked with creating their images, i.e., drawers, painters, and embroiders, were more vocal regarding the topic of being local but not appropriating cultures they do not own. Even if it is *queerness* is something up for grabs for many, and queer a nationless, blurry notion of identity, there was an effort not to step onto the territory of cultural appropriation. This sentiment was less voiced or less present among artists and media producers who were not based in the West.

> I may consider using elements of national dress or props that might reflect another culture, but I don't want to simply appropriate other cultures or their motifs. It would have to be appropriate to the model, and o would ask them how comfortable they felt with it.
>
> Interviewee 2

> Not particularly [focused on my local settings]. My posts almost never include direct references to my hometown or the culture of the place where I currently live.
>
> Interviewee 29

> I think my 'content' reflects what's around me or what inspires me for sure.
>
> Interviewee 12

> Some but not a heavy amount [of my work includes local references].
>
> Interviewee 15

I also explored in these interviews the weight of *globalized* queerness concerning the existence of cultural markers of specific towns or provinces within the same country. Among the American interviewees, that amounted to the extent that one can go in or out of queerness along with or without whiteness and heteronormative standards. Both concepts were frequently linked to exclusionary practices within the LGBTQ community. In other words, the intertwinement of these categories meant that localized queerness was likened to the ability to be queer and not being white, for example. Or being queer and non-binary.

In Brazil and Argentina, the locals revealed other kinds of national boundaries. There was frequent tension in showing regional parts of the queer discourse nationally, which often orbits references from the Global North but does not acknowledge regional cultures or queer folklore as needed or desired for an assumed national identity. In Italy, two interviewees voiced this reconnection with other regions of the country in its cultural tapestry, as the testimonials below assert:

> I mainly post using captions both in English and in Italian, [while] drawing from personal thoughts or lyrics from songs. In the past, I also used slang from my region in order to express my attachment to southern Italy. I feel a strong connection to the Neapolitan dialect, but I've never even thought about how this could hinder or enhance my followings on Instagram. My contents include many references to where I grew up, i.e., Naples and its surroundings ... areas that I immensely love. Moreover, having Russian origins, I try to include this part of me that, inevitably, is way less tangible and ends up being a predominantly ancestral bond with the land I was born in. Expressing my cultural belongings is fundamental to me, from my queerness to my 'Neapolitan-ness.' I think it's a way of getting to know myself better and letting others

know who I am. Gaining knowledge of the roots helps me understand little by little where I started my journey and where I am headed to.

Interviewee 10

I do not necessarily reference places/characteristics of my hometown's culture. However, it is also true that I sometimes use words from the Veronese dialect, as I mentioned before. For me, it is very important to let people know that I come from the Veneto region. This is not because I am very attached to this region, but because I want to make people realize that queer people do exist in Veneto, as this region is most of the times perceived as a place where this sort of raw masculinity characterizes men. To give you some context, Veneto is a region where a very rotted fascist culture still exists ... in Verona, specifically, right-wing parties have held the annual World Congress of Families.

Interviewee 9

A smaller portion of the interviewee group, particularly artists focused on selling products online or representing themselves to the local public, have interpreted the *global* or *local* binary on the grounds of their sheer objective of being online, that is, the extent to which they can sell and communicate with clients about their works. It was also possible to learn that artists, including handcrafters, did not fully connect with what sounded to them too intellectual or philosophical conversations about globalized queerness as opposed to the materiality of their being queer, e.g., the ability to live off their work. Rather, they have insisted on general impressions or dropping any expectations of being local or global, when asked what kind of queer representation they received in the media, if global, local or neither:

Absolutely not [no representation on the mainstream]. I think the only queer artists who receive any kind of attention from the mainstream media are ones that don't upset the majority. Anyone who questions the parameters established by heteronormative or cis culture is so often pushed out or silenced. This is why our trans and non-binary representation exists almost exclusively on the binary still.

Interviewee 21

Both? But also neither! Social media is a great opportunity, for me, to connect with other artists. That's the biggest value for me.

Interviewee 4

> Partly, I feel that there is a nascent globalisation in queer identity and struggle, but there could be much more. Solidarity and exchanging best practices and queer joy could be so much more. We live in hope. At the moment, I would say I am local and national. Maybe global is something for the future. But there is much to do in the local spaces, so let's get that sorted first.
>
> Interviewee 20

> Definitely local. Probably micro, to be honest. I have global followers and make sales and work for global commissions, but I don't have the bandwidth to work in that market without going to extreme measures. I feel very grassroots and any work I sell or make or the reach I have is purely through my persistence paired with the visibility that's awarded to me by being fit and white. A lot of my traction online comes from 'thirst trapping' that I use to build my following and then to try to sell art after. It feels very gross, but I have to make money somehow. Womp womp.
>
> Interviewee 22

Eventually, consensus lay in queerness as a detachable notion one uses according to personal circumstances, current context, and late political awakening. The *globalized* aspect of queerness appeared much less salient once one removed its vocabularies and episteme as identification conditions. For example, whenever one did not mention queerness at all, it was because one would instead get covered or accepted in essential spheres of existence (business, media, spectacle, handcrafts) according to their *localness*. Their immediate concerns or preoccupations, their ambitions to sell and to position themselves within their community, have yet to prompt the employment of global terms or mention of US-based, rainbow-like references. In sum, globalized queerness does not resist the test of contrasting its ideas and imagery with one's very personal challenges of everyday life. Next, I aim to collect more elements from queer artistry present on social media by presenting the results of an in-depth interview with two artists who inhabit distinct parts of Europe. Both have worked with their bodies as their primary subject matter, but in opposite ways.

'You get a boost after you appear naked'

Even if social media platform policies tend to suppress adult content, the multiplication of hashtags involving keywords such as twink, daddy, hairy, hung, and similar others attest to nudity, social self-exposure as synonymous with new standards of queer globalized self-presentation (Wang, 2021). I first met *Oliver* at Dalston Junction, East London. I had been receiving his Instagram updates two years before our meeting. His work as a photographer includes pictures of young men in suggestive poses. Most of them are entirely or semi-naked, as their genitals appear on Instagram censored so as not to breach platforms' anti-nudity guidelines. When we first met for an interview, in 2019, Tumblr was still the platform of choice for queer artists exploring the territory of frontal nudity and pornography. That liberty came later to face complete banishment from the website, a blow against the aspirational visual freedom enjoyed by the LGBTQ community worldwide (Bronstein, 2020). *Oliver* said he lived in Stratford in a seemingly rented place where part of his essays was shot. Another aspect of his photographs was their shooting on the streets, parking lots, and the Epping Forest, a traditional cruising spot in East London. His models were said to shoot unpaid or based on collaboration. Models were primarily young white men in their 20s, who often displayed a profound or mysterious mood, rarely sporting cheeky smiles and often making provocative gestures with their hands.

One of the first aspects of Oliver's work lies in the interplay between anonymity and publicity. The only known person in the photographs is the photographer, a handful of collaborator photographers, and porn actors, mainly from London and across the US. The slenderness or toned models' bodies, twink-looking, lying in bed, pulling down their trousers in public places, or simply staring at the viewer, only amplifies the mystery surrounding how he found them in the first place. I understand it is mainly through hook-up apps such as Grindr, but there is another side to convincing them to pose with the face in the picture. The anonymity aspect of it is limited to the names and real identities. Oliver tells me that he makes a calculation on whether he will be only a producer or another model for his shots. I inquired Oliver on the relationship between prominence on platforms such as Instagram, seemingly important for his work, and any expectation of privacy that he or one of his models could have:

> Yeah. those are the people who will likely message me and be likely I love to shoot, [but] no face. No tattoos. I'm like, okay. I did do a series only of anonymous folks, which was like two years ago. Every now and then, it comes back up just because too many people just don't want to do face and stuff. It's a comfort-level thing. So, the innominate

is always people who just don't want her face shown. Since the part is concerned and part of it is just simply, you're beautiful. Yeah, it's your boundary.

The issue of being prominent, becoming prominent, and expecting prominence from appearing in one of his photographs makes another topic in our conversation. From initially blogging on Tumblr, then Instagram, and Twitter most frequently, to the inevitable move into *Onlyfans*, I watched over the years the pre- and post-Covid-19 Oliver expanding toward a series of work and sex partners, including well-known porn producers, such as the Portuguese Antonio da Silva. I asked him what sets producers and performers together, whether it is this expectation of publicity and prominence or the selection according to the law of desire, on which he said:

I have never said no to anyone. I've definitely told people what you got. If there are too many boundaries, I won't probably go to do it. If they're like only patients where I'm like, okay [to shoot] face, whatever bits and pieces, it is what will happen. Most time, if that's all they want. You can't go off it. And also, if someone goes into it thinking they're just going to have sex with me. Because that is never that, that never really, that's never really been the case. Basically, the best part is this sort of ethics or something. That you think that, you know, not, not just distracting. I think if it's like a natural, good connection, which probably rates to honouring [the agreement]. I've always had, and I like surprises. I don't like everything being upfront. Okay, let's just let's move this supposed to...but if somebody was just [to focus on], 'I love your photographs. When you [are going to] fuck me'... I might. This is just one way or the other. If it is just too hot, this [double layered interest] blocks [the shoot] because of you, your workforce. Because of you as a person. You don't. Yeah. It's probably [a] combination [between attraction and work drive].

In another moment of the conversation, we approach the issue of platforms and globalizing oneself through being present on different social media websites. During our interview, Oliver confessed to constantly monitoring his number of followers and had an application to track recent unfollowers so he could unfollow them too. The first time we met, he boasted a couple of thousands of followers on Instagram and Twitter, now, in 2022, it is in the tens of thousands on both platforms. After being censored on Instagram multiple times, he even suggested that some jealous competitor or potential model, angered at being rejected, could do some sabotage by denouncing him to moderators. This part of our dialogue in this peaceful café makes me seize the opportunity to question what the notion of community is, in the face of the existence of contributors and conspirators online, to which he says:

> Those [who report] are not part of the community, because those who are, I mean it, really matter. Probably, in this mix [of those who report him], some are not comfortable with themselves. When you think about community, it's more about artists, they are okay people. They all have different voices and want reasons for what they're doing. I guess you always visualize the LGBT shoot as the one that fits better when you are also [LGBT person]. Yeah, that's a good definition because that's probably what I'm representing.

Those 'who are not comfortable' can also include potential models who later regret and could also report him according to 'community's guidelines', which leads to account suspension. On his Instagram account, he stated his bio: 'A life of censorship', which turns out to be much less used nowadays than it was when we first met. To this, handing his work over to social media platforms, he argued:

> The power of the capital is capitalized in your work, which is capitalism, but you also capitalize. How profitable is…Jesus…very tough on you. Because I heard something some masters of you in that sense, but do I think it's possible to bring the life out of it, though? Yeah, for sure. Is that possible? I feel like I'm definitely on an awkward road in that direction. So, I've been doing commissions for – like photographer commissions – good private shoots up into a lot of work recently, which is good. Do you know Q boy? I did some of the sketches for his next club night, which is coming out soon.

Oliver has also mentioned many partnerships he managed to set up through his publicity on social media and the growing number of followers over the years. Either as a photographer or filmmaker or even acting in porn productions. More recently, he developed an amalgam of partners and clients that make him a versatile sort of contributor in their shootings. Thanks to contacts in the US, he occasionally travels to the West Coast, where he meets with other potential models, photographers, and partners. One of whom was a frequent collaborator,

Derek, a white American man in his 20s who often shows up on social media. He appears as being a prolific *self-sucker* in live streaming sessions or seen riding his bike fully naked in Seattle. In this case, despite algorithmic power, Oliver discusses his nudity as an aspect that has propelled his number of followers and boosted the number of collaborators with likeminded exposers:

> Well, now I am showing myself or something, or it started to appear in. Then I collected a number of new followers or something. This year, after I started with Pierre [porn actor], I started to appear in [the footage], and then I got to reach 3000 [followers]. Then at Lori's [another porn actor], another boost. You get a boost after you appear naked versus when there is no nudity. I've been using this very pretty frequently, it was definitely. Yeah, it definitely helped me get more involved. And people connected with that because it's more intimate. Because that just lets us throw out and live versus having to control my purpose to live. Because we know that most people do not show themselves. I have a fair share of this beautiful work as opposed to trying in as a bloodless, gay man.

On the other end of the interview, Oliver refuted the thesis that his philosophy is only about garnering followers and accumulating as many nudes as possible. In opposition to the mechanics of algorithms and follower power, a sense of self-worth impinges on any attempt to make his craft look artificial or manufactured. When asked whether this appeal of his own body and life having been exposed as fuel for media prominence, if it does not corrupt his commitment to models or others next to him, his answers do suggest a degree of intimacy that has to be reached before one considers it a successful shoot or a beneficial collaboration with others, as he says:

> You know, [nobody is] forced to enjoy themselves and get some pleasure out of it. At the same time, I do think that there is another thing that you get from these people whom you get to do this. Most guys, I'd say, let's assume, almost all your public go through the website to that objective was just, you know, just wanking off. That's also a lie. In the process of shooting, it's never because I'm just like – you know, take your clothes off and get erections – it's not like that. I'm always like [to models]: be comfortable. It's all-natural, and they do it themselves as exhibitionists do anytime, if you force up, something is wrong.

Moving off to more local aspects of his practice, I bridge facts of his life, his background and his position regarding others, including his family, who might know about his work or recognize him elsewhere. Oliver refrains from questions about the profile of his models, primarily white, able, and fit to muscled bodies. He has also not mentioned his background as of Southeast Asian descent as a restriction or impediment to joining the gay porn business, which has long been accused of being white-focused and discriminatory to other body shapes. While fewer trans women appear in his work, he published some material with trans men, featuring full-body nudity and repeating the same eroticized gaze. Oliver says he holds nothing against shooting trans people, but this was a rarer situation. He credits it to his taste and his methods of finding models, often hanging on Grindr, a gay-centric application. Whether he inherits or not all prejudices existing on applications like the latter, often accused of incentivizing discriminatory practices due to its layout and appeal, this point remains critical and yet unanswered in this interview. Going back to his roots, I asked if his family knew his online profile and self-exposure on gay networks. To which responded:

> No but yeah, I'm really comfortable about nudity and sexuality, [about] being out there with my family. So [there are] lot of questions like I like, I love my family and they accept me, but I don't know. It kind of prevents me [from telling what I do]. The more I do this the more it's probably going to be a thing with them.

At this point, the answers I have from Oliver get more abstract and evasive. I understood that his family is unaware of this nude photography practice. Oliver might be a pseudonym to brand his content so as not to be traceable online through any ethnic-related name. His Southeast Asian background has received little mention during our conversation, despite Oliver having shown himself open to all kinds of partnership, given this mix of personal attraction and ethics of stripping off in front of the camera. As I shall discuss later, digital platforms have made self-entrepreneurial artists like Oliver more aware of their possibilities in terms of online prominence than the limitations, such as censorship. With the benefit of hindsight, having met himself in person, it is possible to know that there is some symbolical exchange. He conjugates the interest in shooting someone's nude essay with the desire to express oneself in the queer terms of unpredictability and freedom, i.e., stripping off in public places, by travelling around the world with an erection, by showing no local affiliation to any grassroots queer community. The following artist adds more local nuance as another practitioner of nude photography. He, instead, follows a home-based ideological orientation.

'Narcissism, vanity: That was initially a game'

I first met *Giuseppe* in Bologna, Italy. We gathered for a couple of hours in the Bolognina neighbourhood, very close to where I was staying. He is a short Italian man, smoking, sporting a fuzzy beard, who spoke very politely. His work was selected for this research due to its unique yet awkward approach to queer use of social networks. His posts interspersed shots of himself fully naked or semi-naked, especially rear shots, in unrelated snaps of his routine. At the time, he worked as a baker. Therefore, pictures of Italian candies and ovens and his bum and hairy body permeated notorious Instagram posts. I noticed that his account was named after himself but translated into several languages, resulting in names such as Yuzif von Karat, among similar transliterations that change from time to time. He was also adopting *Profezia Barimetrica* as a brand, alike other mentions of religious readings. As a Bologna dweller, he often attends the city's public library, where part of his Instagram shots take place. His Flickr profile seemed way more artistic and displayed frontal nudity, which is not allowed on Instagram. The dark scenario in his photos almost always portrayed what seemed to be his home. At times, he appeared alone or with another man in his 50s, his partner.

All the above assumptions were confirmed true by Giuseppe, who seemed rather shy as opposed to an eloquent Instagram influencer with 11 thousand followers. He refused to acknowledge himself as an artist, repeating that he was just a baker. Our interview flowed in different directions simultaneously, but he gave me an account of his start. He is originally from a tiny city near Bari, in the Puglia region, southern Italy. He moved to Bologna around 2009 to live with his artist boyfriend. Both seemed very arty, as the latter was also an AIDS activist whose work involved nudity and short films, albeit not entirely available on social media networks. To some extent, Giuseppe was *less* of an artist than his partner. Still, his participation on social media, being a prolific publisher of several shots a day, rendered his action less unintentional than he seemed to suggest and incredibly more popular:

> [To understand my publications], you must go back to myself to when I was 22, 23, then 18. [I was] insecure about myself, and,

therefore, social media is somewhat of a fill-in for that insecurity. That is, to seek confirmation from others that I was not ugly. As we say, this was born in me over time. I see the moment of that first photo as the key. After as much as 15 years later, what has changed is the true safety from that moment. Fifteen years have been so many [years for me]. I have studied so much that I have confronted many people [about the pictures]. Because thinking about those reactions [about pictures]: you liked or it did you well today. These emotions, these positive feelings, how you meet them in this sense. Then, I will have a different situation today that I did not have it yesterday, but I saw the photo, then it will stimulate feelings of pleasure in anyone.

When I ask again about the impact the pictures have and how they serve to feel prominent online, as opposed to just a baker from Bologna, he answers:

Even more [impact now]. You feed a narcissistic game and get off anything, that is, it is an action game from the virtual world that is beyond me. As far as I am concerned, the photos tell only the dumb [part] and then I add very complex speech. Well, it's nice despite that I don't talk to the viewer about it. As I see, what I like [to do] has changed a lot, that is, I needed like weeks [to produce a photo]. As it confirms how much of a social action is now for me, i.e. function is positive. Only now that [the platform] is a much more critical center.

In opposition to Oliver, the previous interviewee, there is a clear separation between Giuseppe's life, the local layer in his prominence, and the expectations of building an audience on a global platform. He acknowledges using Instagram more often than Facebook due to the proximity it strikes with family members and friends back in Puglia. Instagram, however, gives more exposure to his portraits. However, Giuseppe clarifies that even though he appears naked in many portraits, he does invite sexual reactions from commentators. I asked him to speak about the weight of platforms to what he does:

The worst thing about Instagram is the censorship of the platform. The subjects intersect. About five years ago, I had a little bit of Instagram followers. I had a full Flickr account without any problems. However, at this point, nobody ever explained to me I became a profile that was losing accounts. In other words, [on Instagram] I don't even have to tell [what] people [to communicate with], so communicating with others while exchanging opinions has become difficult elsewhere and, therefore, other platforms for me became a place of forgotten profiles [On Flickr]. Now I need to show it on Instagram. But how on Earth can I do this with censorship? I don't like it, nor sense that I find myself having to cut my photos. This is the price to pay in a sense. I do not interact [with commentators] because I put a photo that it is no different from me than a photo of the sea or naked. And the people immediately go with the comment 'what a nice cock and the ass.' I have no problems with these comments here, but, honestly, it bothers me that I am in the photo at the sea naked with my boyfriend with friends chatting I find that comment out of place. I put the naked photo here with some critical caption, then you write me that we should fuck. Because I'm throwing something that happens [on the everyday] to you, I don't spend a minute [to do it], and you already write me let's fuck. That is, that comment is out of place.

Giuseppe's speech revolves around patterns that address his domestic needs on top of queer needs of expression. By no means his photographic work, according to him, should allude to something sexual. In this platform discussion, he also mentioned *Vero*, a smaller network tailored to self-exposure, primarily mobile-based. He says his work is more about religious and deep philosophical thoughts than sex and exposure. Many of his posts come captioned with things like: 'In the name of the Father.' Therefore, his sense of giving more than one sees in the pictures stems from the context he claims to add in the visuals and his captions. He referred multiple times to adding some text to his photographs or making mentions that span the Byzantine empire, pagan Greece and Rome, and other historical episodes. I inquired into these references, and, for Giuseppe, they derive from the deliberate gesture of confusing his audience between connections that are not sexual or religious. He wants to complicate the equation of being a gay man in search of attention, as he explains:

The reference is the world where we are not the centre of society 24/7. The problem is that I am a conservative. I fell for the traditional values and so on. This is often at odds with the Internet spaces of today, that is, one must participate in sexual liberation. Because I am opposed to this order, the family of a father and a mother is not so strange to me. I am opposed to this contemporary vision of the society man.

5. Global Platforms, Local Characters 187

Giuseppe's statement of being a conservative may sound striking because of his past militancy among the so-called gay activists in Italy, most of whom are from the left. Giuseppe quit this LGBTQ activism scene before moving to Bologna. He admits that his work can be interpreted differently based on his insistence on framing it as a 'prophecy' or a religious-like body of work. Whatever that means, he prefers to concede that he would like to make people think against the absurd of the Internet and existing prohibitions rather than himself as a body that can be sexualized, as he says:

> This is a society where if one exists as male, there is a sort of earthquake in the current world. Any piece [of photography] exacerbates this problem. I'm trying to solve it in my way. Still, maybe when I get to 80 years old, I will realize that this piece of me, a photo reconstruction of a gay man with his naked boyfriend around like him, may also be a bit reactionary, if not ultraconservative, intensely religious, so there will be little contrast to this [with something else deemed as liberal or progressive]. Sometimes they attack me by calling me a fascist, but I feel bad. They put censorship on the photo because you will have to translate what an arse is.

The frustration about one's acceptance of his work or where the boundary of liberality lies is much down to the censorship in many platforms, even if he is not sexually provocative. To the extent that his work fits global or local standards, I would argue for the latter. His work showcases a continuous connection with traditions of the Italian labour resistance movement, more specifically, the *operaismo*. This method of resistance under repressive times employed irony and subjectivity as a way of dodging top-down orders (Roggero, 2010). The thorough look at how platforms treated his content, censored his practice, and still profited from his online presence takes Giuseppe to recognize that, despite the narcissistic inspirations, the platform life has captured his image. This hijacking does not mean he will change his message to get more likes or followers. In the global village, Giuseppe prefers to stick to references very dear to him. His partner, his suburban neighbourhood, and regards to immemorial times in Latin, Greek, Persian, and other invented ancient cultures. This latter collection of themes invokes the local aspect of his Instagram presence and, therefore, the rejection of the globalized aspects of queerness, a concept thrown out by his conservative leanings.

I have not looked at Giuseppe's Facebook presence to contrast his comments with this prominence in photographs nor to test how far his conservative profile goes. I have not done so because of the centring on his Instagram presence, the overall coherence in his focusing on each platform at a time, and the popularity on Instagram. All evidence he gave me is enough to attest to his *localness* and the rejection of the cosmopolitan values that characterizes globalized queerness. As opposed to other interviewees in this research, Giuseppe confirms that behind the façade of social media prominence, there lies a diverse spectrum of what *prominence* can bring to queer users beyond commodified ideas of notoriety and creative life. More recently, Giuseppe has taken a job as a security guard and has grown a moustache, which, on the one hand, intensifies a stereotype of a straight, married man and a conservative person. On the other hand, the naked pictures continued with less of his explorations into ancient cultures and wordsmithing. Next, I present the third part of this research by examining the evidence collected from young social media account holders and their expectations of queer prominence.

Global and local attachments: Avoidance, correction, and making points

As a fascinating part of Goffman's facework theory (1957), facework consists of three steps to emphasize distinct aspects of queerness: avoidance, correction, and making points. One well-known form of facework used to exemplify this concept is politeness and rudeness as its violation. In the case of the characters interviewed for this book, I wanted to verify how globalized queerness can emerge from concatenating any of these three moments while one is engaged with online queer media. One assumption was, for example, that displaying signs of queerness on social networks, such as hashtags or the rainbow pride flag, *corrects* representations most of the time because it avoids identification with heterosexual communities. Or one can *make points by* adding #queer to posts where sexuality was not at stake so one can challenge the status quo. That operation with queer signs is to perform facework online because one deals, at first glance, with language and performative stances.

This chapter's interviewees did not confirm the above assumption. The online coming out as queer is not to 'save one's face' or *avoid* the topic but a slow, political or artistic gesture that involves much awareness of its consequences, if any. As pointed out by Interviewee 1, the queer word is made to be part of the community, in which case *queerness* is used to make a point, to inform those doubting one's ability to do so. Also, as per Goffman (1967:7), to save face is to 'go to certain lengths to save the feelings and the face of others present. And he is willing to do this willingly and spontaneously because of emotional identification with others and their feelings'. According to the latter, most interviewees demonstrated this ability to coalesce into a form of queerness that, while a bit alien to some locations (Interviewees 10, 11), is a start for further integration with one's local culture. The main factor is the feeling of *making a point* while creating a *corrective* image. They can identify with queerness if that does not suggest they are beneficiaries of the increasingly globalized queer character that emerges in mainstream media.

The case of Oliver and Giuseppe set opposing scenarios according to this theory. Oliver can appear as having a work of making points with nudity. As Goffman (1967:19) defines it:

> When a person treats facework not as something he needed be prepared to perform, but rather as something that others can be counted on to perform or to accept, then an encounter or an undertaking becomes less a scene of mutual considerateness than an arena in which a contest or a match is held.

In that case, should the nude photographs be seen as the 'points scored' in the 'competition'? Is the inclusion of some models, but not others, the competition? The 'favourable or unfavourable facts' are those in which the models fit a certain standard or level of sexual performance. Here, the photographic work becomes facework to the extent that it can contest the prohibition of displaying gay pornographic material on social networks. To a lesser extent, it is the domination exerted by a queer of colour over a vast majority of white, lean guys with a European background. The making points is the scoring against heteronormative and white-centric standards of gay taste.

Regarding Giuseppe's lifework, the tone he gives to his photographs is always grave with mythological undertones, as he mentioned. His *correctional* stance is one of restoring queerness to a level in which it can dialogue with societal institutions, as he has said, in the shape of elements like the family and masculine identity, instead of blurring the lines. As per Goffman's (1967:14) on the corrective process:

> When the participants in an undertaking or encounter fail to prevent the occurrence of an event that. Is expressively incompatible with the

judgements of social worth that are being maintained, and when the event is one of a kind that is difficult to overlook (...).

In that case, Giuseppe's public body, a daily material in queer photography, serves as the proxy for criticism. It displays the same taste in queer exposure, often characterized by a lack of control, anarchy, and explicitness. Still, his corrective gesture offers seriousness and stability, contrary to the scenario of provocative and hypersexualized queerness on the Internet.

In both cases, one sees how facework helps to explain the complex system of scoring points and leading queerness to one place or the other in the dynamics of social media publicity. Facework is unhelpful in the circumstances controlled mainly by robots and social media algorithms. For example, hashtag-led trends can be primarily managed by an artificial degree of exposure which disturbs the personal agency of facework one deposits on social media. Otherwise, when getting to know the individual trajectories equally present on social media platforms, factors such as age, personal socioeconomic or historical affordances, and location of residence can contradict the belief that all is lost due to automation and digital advertisement. In turn, these conversations revealed that signs and values tied to globalized queerness are less repeated by those who are older, do not live in the west, and have grown less involved in times of mass media or farther from the Internet age.

After the above discussion, it is possible to conclude that prominence on social media has given queer actors aspirations of more communication and visibility over straightforward financial gratification. After weighing up values such as personal history, the local climate for homosexuals, and, lastly, the use of the body to express oneself, one can de-escalate expectations of social media as the ultimate stage for globalizing queerness. Conjugating this empirical wealth with Goffman's facework theory, evidence points to globalized queerness as means of *making points*. When not employing textual resources or images, actors focus on local conversations, patterns, or cultural heritage instead. Whether globalized queerness means the repetition of American-centred standards of queer communication or the compliance with exclusionary images or practices, the resistance to it exists whenever actors can develop self-consciousness and critically posit on their localness or roots. It does so where homosexuality has been concatenated with other guarantees, such as a thriving local community, a strong history of resilience to commodities. When nested in local settings, however, these publics are not necessarily safe from homophobia and other prejudices.

Next, I draw a few conclusions from this experiment of observing queer user engagement on global platforms while trying to assert limits to globalization and localness based on the facework theory.

Conclusion

This chapter inquired into the prominence of several queer artists and media producers with active profiles on social media platforms such as Twitter, Facebook, and Instagram. It proposed Goffman's theory of facework to analyse how queerness is juxtaposed on social media along with other factors while observing the relationship between global or local elements in these actors' opinions and values. Through in-depth and semi-structured interviews, I watched the contours of their social media prominence. In the first stage of the research, semi-structured interviews conducted with actors based in Western Europe, the United States and some located in South America and Northern Africa stated that their relationship with global aspects of queerness depended upon the level of their usage of social media either for networking or direct purposes such as product selling. In the second stage, in-depth interviews allowed for writing profiles of two prominent social media producers. They used their and others' naked bodies as themes for photographs that draw distinct possibilities for queer actors online One actor was more connected to globalized queerness and its signs and the other showcased more conservative tendencies and localized ways to queerness. Applying Goffman's facework theory framework, social media-based actors tended to reveal corrective, or making-points stances based on where they were found, their age, and their ethnic background. Globalized queerness remains a highly salient event, whereby social media prominence may also help to de-escalate these references and make actors reconnect with their localness if conditions allow, as explored in the following chapter. Next, I close the book's argument with a review of the main points visited in this research and some thoughts for the future.

References

Andreassen, R. (2021). Social media surveillance, LGBTQ refugees and asylum: How migration authorities use social media profiles to determine refugees as 'genuine' or 'fraudulent'. *First Monday*, 26(1).

Bronstein, C. (2020). Pornography, trans visibility, and the demise of Tumblr. *Transgender Studies Quarterly*, *7*(2), 240–254.

Browne, K. (2005). Snowball sampling: using social networks to research non-heterosexual women. *International Journal of Social Research Methodology*, *8*(1), 47–60.

Burgess, J., Cassidy, E., Duguay, S., & Light, B. (2016). Making digital cultures of gender and sexuality with social media. *Social Media+ Society*, *2*(4), 2056305116672487.

Carter, M. J., & Fuller, C. (2016). Symbols, meaning, and action: The past, present, and future of symbolic interactionism. *Current Sociology*, *64*(6), 931–961.

Cho, A. (2015). *Sensuous participation: Queer youth of color, affect, and social media*. (Doctoral dissertation).

Draw, S. (2022). RuPaul's Drag Race eliminee Maddy Morphosis talks dealing with the backlash to her casting. *Billboard Magazine*. 14 September 2022.

Duguay, S. (2016a). 'He has a way gayer Facebook than I do': Investigating sexual identity disclosure and context collapse on a social networking site. *New Media & Society*, *18*(6), 891–907.

Duguay, S. (2016b). Lesbian, gay, bisexual, trans, and queer visibility through selfies: Comparing platform mediators across Ruby Rose's Instagram and Vine presence. *Social Media+ Society*, *2*(2), 2056305116641975.

Ember, S. (2018). Condé Nast's 26-year-old man of the moment. *New York Times*. March 3, 2018.

Firmonasari, A. (2021). 'Si beau ma queen': The speech construction of queer identity perception in French social media. *Jurnal Kawistara*, *11*(3), 339–352.

Fischer, M., Haimson, O. L., Rios, C., Shaw, A., Thakor, M., Gieseking, J. J., & Cockayne, D. (2018). A conversation: Queer digital media resources and research. *First Monday*, *23*(7).

Goffman, E. (1967). *Interaction ritual: Essays on face to face behaviour*. Garden City, NY: Anchor.

Goffman, E. (1967). Where the action is. In E. Goffman, *Interaction ritual: Essays on face to face behaviour* (pp. 149–270). Garden City, NY: Anchor.

Griffith, K. (2022). Elon Musk mocks TWITTER and other tech giants for paying lip-service to LGBT rights by changing their logos to rainbows during Pride Month. *Daily Mail* online. 31 May 2022.

Han, C. S. (2009). Asian girls are prettier: Gendered presentations as stigma management among gay Asian men. *Symbolic Interaction*, *32*(2), 106–122.

Hausmann, C., Jonason, A., & Summers-Effler, E. (2011). Interaction ritual theory and structural symbolic interactionism. *Symbolic Interaction*, *34*(3), 319–329.

Hogan, B. (2010). The presentation of self in the age of social media: Distinguishing performances and exhibitions online. *Bulletin of Science, Technology & Society*, *30*(6), 377–386.

Hutson, D. J. (2010). Standing out/fitting in: Identity, appearance, and authenticity in gay and lesbian communities. *Symbolic Interaction, 33*(2), 213–233.

Javaid, A. (2020). The haunting of shame: Autoethnography and the multivalent stigma of being queer, Muslim, and single. *Symbolic interaction, 43*(1), 72–101.

Jenkins, E. M., Zaher, Z., Tikkanen, S. A., & Ford, J. L. (2019). Creative identity (re) Construction, creative community building, and creative resistance: A qualitative analysis of queer ingroup members' tweets after the Orlando Shooting. *Computers in Human Behavior, 101*, 14–21.

Johnson, P. M. (2020). *Coming out queer online: Identity, affect, and the digital closet*. Lexington Books.

Josselson, R (1996). *Ethics and process in the narrative study of lives*. United States: SAGE Publications.

Kataria, G. (2022). *LGBTQ digital cultures–A global perspective*. Springer.

Littlejohn, S. W. (1977). Symbolic interactionism as an approach to the study of human communication. *Quarterly Journal of Speech, 63*(1), 84–91.

Middleton, L. (2021) Are social media firms doing enough to protect LGBTQ+ users? *Gay Times*. Available at https://www.gaytimes.co.uk/life/are-social-media-firms-doing-enough-to-protect-lgbtq-users/ Access 23 September 2022.

Nash, C. J. (2016). *Queer methods and methodologies: Intersecting queer theories and social science research*. United Kingdom: Taylor & Francis.

Navar-Gill, A., & Stanfill, M. (2018). 'We shouldn't have to trend to make you listen': Queer Fan Hashtag Campaigns as Production Interventions. *Journal of Film and Video, 70*(3–4), 85–100.

Okech, A. (2022). #JusticeForSheila highlights the precarious lives of queer people in Kenya. The Conversation. 16 May 2022. Available at https://theconversation.com/justiceforsheila-highlights-the-precarious-lives-of-queer-people-in-kenya-183102 Access 01 October 2022.

Rodriguez, J. A. (2022). LGBTQ incorporated: YouTube and the management of diversity. *Journal of Homosexuality*, 1–22.

Roggero, G. (2010). Organized spontaneity: Class struggle, workers' autonomy, and soviets in Italy. *WorkingUSA, 13*(2), 201–212.

Scheff, T. J. (2005). Looking-Glass self: Goffman as symbolic interactionist. *Symbolic interaction, 28*(2), 147–166.

Sontag, S. (2018). *Notes on camp*. United Kingdom: Penguin Books.

Sousa, M. A., Lima, M. D. O., & Oliveira, P. A. (2020). Digital media and risks involved for the LGBT community. *European Journal of Public Health, 30*(Supplement_5), ckaa166–802.

Staples, L. (2022). Why do we care so much about Harry Styles' sexuality? *The Face*. Available on https://theface.com/society/why-do-we-care-about-harry-styles-sexuality-queerbaiting. Access 01 October 2022.

The Associated Press (2022). Florida students win yearbook flap over 'Don't Say Gay' bill. 11 May 2022.

Thiago, D. O., Marcelo, A. D., & Gomes, A. (2021). Fighting hate speech, silencing drag queens? Artificial intelligence in content moderation and risks to LGBTQ voices online. *Sexuality & Culture, 25*(2), 700–732.

Wang, Y. (2021). The twink next door, who also does porn: networked intimacy in gay porn performers' self-presentation on social media. *Porn Studies, 8*(2), 224–238.

Watts, B. (2020). The Mothman and other strange tales: Shaping queer Appalachia through folkloric discourse in online social media communities. University of Kentucky. *Theses and Dissertations--Linguistics.* 37.

Wilde, O. (2022). *The critical writings of Oscar Wilde: An annotated selection.* United States: Harvard University Press.

CONCLUSION

FROM GLOBALIZED QUEERNESS TO
POSSIBLE HOMECOMINGS

The earth, that is sufficient,
I do not want the constellations any nearer,
I know they are very well where they are,
I know they suffice for those who belong to them.
— Walt Whitman, 'Song of the Open Road'

The book's final chapter reviews evidence collected in the past chapters to settle the ideas on globalized queerness. The challenge in this research was to acknowledge that *queerness* as a concept has been detached from one's being queer and has been exploited in the unfettered media industries of our time. As far as queerness has existed as a varying notion of behavioural or cultural difference, which changes from community to community, *globalized queerness* emerges as a single factor influencing LGBTQ communities worldwide through a single repertoire of media texts and platforms usually headquartered in the West. Globalized queerness also contradicted a relatively simple, centralized process of queer media making much indebted to local queerness that has often gone underground for decades. Over the five years that it took me to finish this book, I placed questions that verified the extent of this process across numerous media acts, stretching from traditional artistic personae and the news to videos and trends on social media platforms. In all the questions posed here, I tried to pave the way for more discussions on whether globalized queerness still belongs in the same ideological spectrum of LGBTQ media content. I make the case for stressing new possibilities for content discovery, reproduction, and delivery, while recovering queer culture's subversive roots.

Since this research started, globalized queerness has been louder than ever, often entering the public sphere and capturing mainstream media debates. Rising Internet influencers have also been part of this prevailing scenario of taking queer expression to a new shape. More recently, TikTok trends have brought queerness not only to queers but to a whole range of social media actors. Broadway actor Dylan Mulvaney, for example, has transformed her transition in a series of TikTok videos that have catapulted the debate on trans prominence back to the binaries of acceptance or non-acceptance. By embodying all the stereotypical features of femineity, Jackie-O dresses and 1950s glamour, Mulvaney appears in 2023 as the ultimate trans influencer. A flamboyant personality, Mulvaney has met President Joe Biden and raised questions about her authenticity and agency on all sides of the spectrum. Mulvaney has divided opinions mainly because she jumps at this crossroads between online prominence, trans popularity, and media representation, in which nothing seems natural until it is. If Mulvaney's sudden popularity has inspired doubts on issues discussed in this book such as authenticity, sincerity, and algorithmic power, it certainly sits on the same dubious grounds of globalized queerness also explored here. In other words, far from blurry and unintentionally non-normative, recent queer culture happens to be more real and predictable, hence commercial, and exploited than in the past decades. This time, though, it is profiteered by and appropriated by queer actors themselves, no longer by Doris Day or Liza Minelli.

In the past chapters, I proposed a lengthy exploration of theoretical and methodological pathways that could apprehend the process of globalizing queerness in several media formats. By inviting debates on commodification, authenticity, cultural models, transculturation, cosmopolitanism, narrative studies, and facework, I suggested that a way forward for queer media studies lies in mingling with sociological thought focused on cross-cultural, cross-language experiences. In Chapter 1, I proposed the localization of queer studies to recover what has been lost to commodity queer. In Chapters 2 and 3, I discussed more traditional formats of queer publicity, namely digital news and pop culture. In the latter, I counterposed queer artists of two generations, seeing elements that lead current pop artistry into territories somewhat less queer than their predecessors. In Chapters 4 and 5, I prioritized the Internet as a changing environment and space for the trans community. The Internet is an essential forum for one's learning about queer life. Still, its ready-made model with algorithms and advertising expands only a few ways of being queer while offsetting knowledge of local factors and life issues. In all these discussions, I brought forward queer voices that have dealt with dilemmas regarding commodification and resistance.

Summary of the book and next steps

Chapter 1 discussed the impacts of media commodification on queer media. I proposed the framework of *genealogizing* queerness to track the commodification of queer media texts and their ramifications. As a Western invention, globalized queerness corresponds to a series of developments that have capitalized on queer life to sell products and homogenize ideas of queerness. This effort aims to channel queer decolonization but cut deeper by recognizing the bias against racial, ethnic, diasporic, and local cultures, together or separated. At the same time, local queerness has thrived independently while remaining unknown to mass audiences because of the same forces that have invested heavily in globalizing queerness. I proposed notions of sincerity and authenticity based on Trilling, De Beauvoir and Williams to question the possibility of authentic and sincere queerness as opposed to globalized stances as a product of mediatized stories. Globalizing queerness is eventually an interpolation of values that have not been inheritably *queer* but do stage a refusal of heteronormative images that suffice to the mediascape. Thus, the concept of local queer appears not only indebted to geographical specifications, as it becomes a keyword for the resistance against the wholesale capitalization of queer politics, its spontaneousness, and aesthetics.

Chapter 2 explored the universe of queer news in the world's most relevant media markets. The multiplication of digital news outlets dedicated to covering the LGBTQ world inspires questions on the quality of this coverage and where it comes from. By applying an LDA (Latent Dirichlet Allocation) based on News API, I grouped queer stories within topics and highlighted the main stances through which a vast audience learns about queer life. The so-called queer news has focused primarily on artists, cultural life, artists on tour, *come-outs*, and other forms of societal understanding of how fluid sexualities occur. By inquiring into the source of this news, its replication, and outreach, I could perceive many limitations in a much-anchored coverage in the English-speaking world. Despite the American origins of globalized queerness, circumventing queer epistemologies appear popular in countries such as Brazil and Russia. Lesser-known south-south coverage or non-Western artists mostly appear in reports when they are physically present in the West. Rarely, though, smaller productions or alternative viewings of queerness can receive reviews, but not without challenging the normativity of Western queer.

Chapter 3 provided a critical cultural model analysis by contrasting different generations of queer artists and their local or global interests. The goal was to think of cultural models that arose due to globalized queerness vis-à-vis the previous scenario of queer artistry. By applying a tailored method based on perusing artists' interviews and paratexts, this material was reviewed together with theories of cosmopolitanism, *mestizaje*, and transculturation. The chapter presented affinities and dissonances among artists' actives in scenes as diverse as in countries such as Hong Kong, Brazil, Italy, the United Kingdom and the United States. By triangulating their opinions, appearances, and existing literature, one sees changing expectations regarding queer self-identification to meet an intended globalized persona. Artists, otherwise, stressed local queerness ideas in consonance with early experiences in life, notions of class, and ethnicity. Once reaching the mainstream media or escaping local homophobia or transphobia, these artists' stories have proved a trade-off between local attachments and an interface with globalized queerness. At best, commercial success for queer artists has meant a hybrid between briefly visiting an idea of belonging and confirming the homogenous quests for being queer.

Chapter 4 focused on the growing popularity of trans influencers. I discussed how their texts have encapsulated local and global dilemmas. By surveying a sample of trans YouTubers based in Brazil, Taiwan, the UK, Spain, and Russia, this research acknowledged the criticality of online self-made videos and the trans sphere that develops under varying conditions and affordances. From pre-transition to de-transition, including issues with hormones, relationships, and violence, these videos have brought unprecedented trans knowledge to a broader audience. While focusing on their spoken text, computational methods revealed the top repeated words and the main topics in this conversation. This vocabulary forays into urgencies across countries and realities: From highlighting locally forged terms in countries such as Brazil and Russia to the social media controversies fed by Western vloggers. The most frequent topics as a group included their gender transition, health issues, and clashes within and outside the trans community. Regardless of the merit of these discussions, these topics point to synchronous conversations happening worldwide on a global platform, but which have often obfuscated other affordances and priorities of trans people on the local level.

Chapter 5 presented interview data from queer artists based on social media networks. This data informed the status of localness or the globalization in queer creative presence online. The chapter sought to apply a framework developed to investigate queer prominence in the volatile context of social media, often attributed to algorithmic-powered methods and bouts of digital labour. Goffman's theory of facework assisted in interpreting these findings to determine an agency in these voices and group them into social functions. Two sections split into an in-depth and a semi-structured interview profiled individuals with distinct levels of social media engagement and success. The in-depth conversation presented the trajectories of *Oliver* and *Giuseppe*, the former based in London, UK, and the latter in Bologna, Italy. Conversely, online fluent actors showed higher queer expectations regarding ideas of prominence. Older interviewees favoured a more political queerness, as the young cohort used it as their central identity. Based on Goffman's facework theory, these actors tended to reveal corrective or making-point stances based on where they were from, their age, and their ethnic background. Globalized queerness has affected many terms employed and their Internet affiliation, but not alliances that pre-dated the Internet.

The five chapters have revealed in common the growing rapprochement of media industries to queerness. Not least the role of queerness in expanding media projects, I also argued for the fast institutionalization of queer values according to media norms and standards. As shown in Chapter 2, the news language has not always been queer, but content queering up facts and events has meant a fresh kind of journalistic jargon. Still, the inclusion of personalities and celebrities who might as well buy that publicity, the use of clickbait titles, and the sheer adoption of queerness as a PR procedure can sabotage the genuineness of this new queer media expansion. It is the case of Harry Styles or Demi Lovato, but more importantly, it is the replication of an appearance that has led an allegedly heterosexual actor to consciously queer up his style while softening public displays of affection with heterosexual partners. Styles, for example, has set the tone for a way of behaving that can become true to any other influencer or aspiring celebrity wanting to gauge some visibility in both hetero and homo media environments by globalizing their queerness. This coupling of queerness with the control of specific behaviour, aesthetics, and appearance is not new. Yet, it has extended to YouTube videos, career-making pop stars, and Internet-based affiliations. It could be understood that at least on the mainstream level, queerness has replaced its subversive character in the name of seizing upon LGBT knowledge available in the media.

Moreover, to stay in the journalistic world, websites such as *Pink News* or *Them* have created queer standards that have ambiguously served to justify globalized queerness rather than contest it. It is the case of queer pop stardom that has produced stars who cannot always display support and commit to local queer communities. Celebrities such as Mahmood or Kim Petras, known for their LGBTQ fanbases, have been very shy activists, as Chapter 3 discussed the former's public quotes. Artists who have remained loyal to their queer brands, such as Christine and the Queens, have had less commercial appeal outside their country or language boundaries. There is also the story of Lil Nas X, the rapper that came out in unequivocally queer style, whose breakthrough was at the top of a horse dressed as a cowboy in a video clip. Nas X has upset any expectation of returning to local queerness since then. Instead, Nas X 'hijacked' Nike shoes in 2021, in an apparent publicity stunt. The performer's blood-filled snickers sold for more than $1,000 in hours. Nas X thus sold his brand as a system saboteur, a queer Robin Hood, but not for the sake of those who could not pay his price (Madani, 2021).

Looking elsewhere, even American-led queer culture has had its moments of diversifying the image of pop stars. The likes of Angel Olsen, for example, an American alternative act that has recently come out as queer and has displayed strong connections with the south. Sam Smith and Kim Petras, who have so far escaped the appeal for bodies that fit normative standards. Semler, a Christian non-binary act alongside Kehlani, 070 Shake, Christine and the Queens a.k.a. Redcar, and a new generation born in the 2000s that has injected more authenticity into queer self-projection. The problem with US-borne queerness is its necessary triangulation with digital media empires that remain tied to algorithms and their design. In this research, all Internet-based interviewees have voiced constraints due to social media architecture and governance. They referred to the terms they used, the kind of content they put out, and the formats seriously limiting what they could say and to whom. Queer causes have been frequently deemed unsustainable or too advanced for the moment, such as non-binarism, transmedicalism, or the agenda on sexual consent. That aside, the backlash against queer-inclusive policies and ways of being seen locally, fed by the algorithmic-boosted rabbit roles, threatens the inclusion of more progressive voices.

I wanted the last part of this book to be about queer public interventions, media practices, and repeated discourses that de-escalate globalized queerness and reverse the process of selling out lived experiences. I reflect on how not to commodify queers through excessive branding, clickbait, and the so-called creative industries. One could recover bottom-up innovation, speak local tongues, and build solidarity at the ground level instead of the automation of affinity via social media networks. As said, this book's chief impetus resides in criticizing queerness from the inside out, as well as depositing higher expectations toward *cultivating* queer culture that can be sustainably spread and used instead of boasted about. Below, I envision a process I call queer homecomings. I see this term as a vow to return to queer marginal and subversive belongings on the one hand. On the other, I see the re-establishment of a coalitional political ethos that does not necessarily abandon the current media outlets and platforms but re-enacts them to return to the local settings of queerness.

Re-enacting creative liberation: Defending local connections

While researching queer histories, I found several references criticizing the homogenization of queerness since long ago. One such example, among many others, lies in the brief encounter between Oscar Wilde and Andre Gide in 1895 Algiers. As Jonathan Dollimore (1988) recounts, Wilde aimed to remove Gide from the closet during a rapid exchange. As the latter tried to evade the former, to then regret and search for him, that revelatory moment propelled Gide later to come out and find his queer persona. But before getting to know Gide better, Wilde wanted 'to re-enact in Gide the creative liberation', in which he tried to 'undermine the law-full sense of self which kept Gide transfixed within the law' (ibid., 1988, Knox, 2011:105). In other words, queer interactions have entailed suspicion, denunciation, and expulsion from the standard order. It did invite criticism from within. The fact that Wilde, according to Dollimore, saw Gide's ethics as a 'protestant ethic with bourgeois moral rigour and repression' was a take against the localness that Gide displayed in that encounter in the face of the cosmopolitan, queer in exile, world traveller, Irish writer. Truly, Wilde, as the global queer, could not see any form of liberation by being a local catholic agent of the status quo, seen in Gide.

I argue that this constant sacrifice of local queerness at the expense of the global, supposedly liberational, and better, raises eyebrows to date. Domestic queerness has been tainted with accusations of 'pederasty' against colonial subjects, for example. It was the case of another Frenchman who came to be attacked: the forever gay outlaw,

Jean Genet. In *Disturbing Attachments*, Amin (2017) details accusations against Genet because of his involvement with a string of Algerian lovers in the context of the Franco-Algerian war (1954–1962). According to Amin, like Gide, Genet kept orientalist inclinations in his devotion to African and Middle Eastern men, knocking the latter off the pedestal as if he was romantic and not *the* outlaw queer of the early 20th century. After all, to admire Genet means returning to the ordinary world of European racism and colonialism. In Amin's words, 'Genet's queerness magnetized his attraction to the Palestinians and the Black Panthers', to which there were 'pederastic, carceral, colonial' of his queerness.

While I take Amin's argument of de-idealizing queerness as a common benefit for the advance of new voices and repertoire, I would restore Genet's presence as a queer luminary rather than a luminary that happens to be queer. In his lifetime, Genet worked for the benefit of all things local in Algeria and Palestine. However, his sexual context was not much different from anything in the world at the time. The critique is not only anachronic, but it fails to recognize the well-known thief before Genet was admired as an author. As a queer man, to place oneself in such homophobic contexts was not only a gesture towards liberation but also an attempt to re-insert oneself as queer in a profoundly homophobic society. To face off the threat of being seen with these men in public, as Genet did, and despite similarities, is not akin to neo-colonialism. The radical immersion in postcolonial activism of that time should not be confused with today's sexual tourism industry. In the same way, the undeniably queer political character should not be relativized.

I do not seek to deepen the complexity of colonial or postcolonial relationships, though. What concerns me is the localness of these historical queer encounters in northern Africa. These encounters, either Wilde's outing of Gide or Genet's incursions in the Middle East tells us that one needs a degree of bravery to go local and advance queer local presence. Gide and Genet lived under deep homophobic pressure, and displaying desire, speaking about it, and doing things to meet their desire were somehow true to their local queer self and how to read themselves in the world. By facing the liberated but rather opaque globalized queerness, I wanted to bring other examples to light because queer immersion in third-world politics is no longer with us today. Examples abound of queers who travel the world but do not face the poor; Grindr meetings are corollary to racism and body selection. Part of the blame should be directed at the engineering of global queerness and the cosmetics of an individualized model of freedom. In that sense, episodes of queer history should inform future thought and help to de-escalate the weight of commercialism and *TikTok* ways of life to amplify queer communication without reservations about the past.

Perhaps, the unanswered part of this question lies in the de-individuation of queerness that was so abundant in Genet's work. Both his work and life trajectory are about the life of the outlaws, the streets, the fight against fascism, and the liberation from framings born in the 19th-century patriarchy. In our time of artificial individualization of queer media, boosted by the advent of cookies and algorithmic suggestions, it is urgent to return to queer histories that can be as informative and inspiring. We need other pivotal moments for reconstructing a local queer self-identity and cross-cultural encounters that could dismantle an overarching, idealizing profile of a queer person. In this research, I found several trans YouTubers trying to blaze the solidarity trail in which episodes of violence, the blackout of mental health treatments, and the nuances of gender dysphoria continue to be obfuscated due to the prioritizing of the so-called 'happy stories'. According to them, only a tiny tip of the trans iceberg can appear due to how one is supposed to face transness from the inside and outside.

Projects such as *queerdigital.com* for the preservation of documents and social media pages such as Instagram-based *@lgbt_history*, which boasts over 700,000 followers and yielded books and talks, help to revitalize and inspire initiatives elsewhere. The main point here is the advent of the experience between queers of different parts of the world and the bridging of each one's context as a fundamental step to decolonize queerness and reduce the weight of the mainstream media in alienating other publics. The recent creation of a commercialized queer model does not encompass contexts in which present inequalities and privileges are rampant. Next, I discuss the importance of revisiting the notion of media positions regarding popular TV programmes as another takeaway of this research.

Contemporary media and the tiktokization of gender

From a scenario of sub-representation and gay shaming on 1980s TV, mainstream media has substantially increased the number of queer-themed productions. In 2022 alone, millions saw the profusion of news shows, series, and queer acts aired with different emphases. From the teen drama in *Euphoria* to the revival of the Lesbian conversational sitcom in *Orange Is the New Black*. On TV and social networks, LGBTQ

History Month has been featured every October as global media festivities started in June as the Stonewall riots were commemorated worldwide. Queer newsworthiness has highlighted not only celebrations but also pushback. In 2022, the monkeypox epidemic saw sectors of the media in the US and abroad liken it to a *gay* disease, with clear echoes of the AIDS crisis. Much backlash ensued, as right-wing media insisted on labelling the illness after gay men, who, supposedly, led the number of cases into an epidemic. The same year, Netflix tagged its series about the eponymous serial killer, *Dahmer*, as another LGBTQ show. Users were unhappy about the series being seen as a queer show: 'This is not the representation we want', many users repeated online (Navlakha, 2022). The streaming giant backtracked and removed the label.

But what is so concerning in such representations? Looking back at series such as *Queer Eye* and *Queer as a Folk*, queer series, films, and TV shows have conformed to what Alexander Doty (1993) had seen in *Queering Things Up*. The repetition of queerness as a theme park with its characters and rituals, inviting gay guests, and hinting at a curated fashion choice. This scenario forged a way of seeing us. Most people see queer presence on heteronormative channels and programmes according to their preferences. Even with more choices available today, this research has shown the tensions around commodifying the inner details of queer life, slang and failures. Streaming series have been more competent than TV productions in ensuring that queer issues are up to date and purporting to represent the truth. But as the *Dahmer* series showed, there is still a long road to mirroring queerness more as a question to the public than a well-cut choice made by third parties.

The actual scenario has not only shifted from the total queering of shows and series of all kinds but the attribution of *what kind* of queer you are. Shows such as *Euphoria* (2022), the HBO production, united queers and non-queers in its first episodes with nuanced characters. It panned out for multiple tastes, with male frontal nudes and empowering teenage girls to *own* their bodies. In 2021, the series *Sort Of*, also by HBO, innovated by featuring a non-binary character, Sabi, of Pakistani origin, who moves across gender roles and take ownership of their identity. While cable or streaming series bring gravity to global issues affecting queer people, platforms like TikTok are born in a queer-accepting world by default. By testing user reactions to queer come-outs, gender-affirming parties, and performative queer acts in public or private, the platform's algorithms surely are written to capture queer audiences in their specificities. More than anything, it is not a surprise that TikTok has the buy-in from the liberal US, including the LGBTQ community, which has seen instant celebrities such as Dylan Mulvaney as a fresh look into queerness and trans pride. Gays, lesbians, trans, and non-binaries are a massive slice of TikTok's audience and become objects of its sensational framing of whatever content one wants to display. It is the queer network *par excellence*.

Notwithstanding the automated manipulation of emotions and atomization of the user's agency on TikTok, we know little about its addictive design. For example, the queer sounds of TikTok can base a performance of gender as something that may or may not raise awareness of issues at stake (Messner, 2022). Continuous *shadow banning* of users limits their reaction to offensive content as the reception of such material is not ultimately blocked in their accounts (Rauchberger, 2022). As much as TikTok has given a platform to invisibilized or a younger generation of queer users, the performance required to be meaningful and engaging is not compatible with the grave tone of recognition and activism the community must pursue (Calabrò et al., 2022).

This recent unease about the *tiktokization* of social media should also concern queer communities as another stage of its commodification. As discussed in Chapter 1, queer culture has come a long way until it could be more accessible. Still, this is different from being transformed into a permanent stream of niches only aimed at surveillance, capitalization, and selectiveness. Contrariwise, TikTok fuels the myth of one *being* queer without culture, history, or past. It channels queerness through a minimal flashy clip, as one can suddenly be a human furry, a silent live streamer, or a gamer. Being queer demands content, empathy, and a following. Instead of favouring a place of belonging, the platform becomes the village and the metropolis. The social media logic slowly flattens out the possibility of speaking about concerns that do not fit the joke, the flair, or the meme intended. As a result, queer users that do not conform to such a standard of total surveillance will eventually *tiktokize* queer selves. The globalized side of queer TikTok lies in its impossibility of providing queers with safety, continuity, and a community in peoples' terms. The speed at which queerness becomes just another brand remains to be seen. Next, I enter another critical insight from this book's results, the globalization of queerness in the Global South.

We are everywhere! Or are we?

Over five years into this research, *queerness* has become more popular than ever in the Global South. Most evidence points to scenes in South

America, South Africa, Hong Kong, Japan, and a few spots in Africa and Southeast Asia. Despite new queer productions coming out of these countries, the spread of *queer* as a term in languages other than English or the global popularity of globalized queer celebrities has not yet happened on a grand scale. It is worth remembering that many media conglomerates worldwide remain in the hands of a few or suffer direct religious or political influence. One can confirm the diminutive space for queerness out of the West by revisiting how same-sex unions have been advancing worldwide. As far as gay marriage is legal and acceptable in the West and most of the Americas, there is no definitive legal blueprint for queerness elsewhere Global South, leave alone its globalization. In Latin America, since 2020, Bolivia, Costa Rica, and Cuba have been the last countries to approve same-sex unions. There has been some discussion in Asia, especially in Thailand, the Philippines, and India, but most countries either have constitutional bans or make it illegal. At its most tolerant, governments, such as Italy, Japan or Israel, offer no legal basis for same-sex unions. In Africa, except for South Africa, gay marriage has still been a taboo for most nations.

Different from Stonewall-time signs 'we are everywhere!' the gruesome reality of the hetero-exclusive world demands that we constantly name where homosexuals are not allowed to exist. Queerness remains a deviant fact at best and is punished with death in Afghanistan, Brunei, Iran, Mauritania, Nigeria, Qatar, Saudi Arabia, Somalia, the UAE, and Yemen. Vigilante-style punishments are still carried out worldwide, especially in Islamic countries, including Iraq, Libya, Syria, and Palestine. In the Chechen Republic of Russia, disappearances and other forms of torture are recorded. Uganda, South Africa, Kenya, Liberia, Gana, Cameroon, and Senegal are also known for the recurrence of anti-gay crimes, with the state turning a blind eye. As recently as 2019, Brunei has reserved homosexual citizens the death penalty by stoning. In December 2022, the FIFA World Cup happened in homophobic Qatar with endorsements by Western celebrities and artists. David Beckham, a gay icon of the early 2000s, has borrowed his image to a small Middle Eastern country.

Naming these nations is not only protesting the shameful human rights conditions in these places but remembering those who can still thrive under life-threatening conditions. In the wake of the US Supreme Court's reversal of abortion rights in 2022, one may only wonder where homosexual rights are genuinely secure and enshrined. Questions remain on where it is possible to return as a queer person, where local queerness is safe to be expressed, and which languages one can speak without fear. In brief, what possible homecomings are allowed in a media world interested only in globalized queerness? This book's central thesis lies in the potential of co-existing between oppression and creativity, trivialization and advancing queer causes. As Zanele Muholi, the award-winning South African visual artist, said, 'existence as insistence' (Mussai, 2018). Coming from homophobia and racism, they also brings their ancient exuberant culture. Which side should prosper? Their power stems from their locality, as local as they can be. As Muholi elaborated in their quest:

> The key question that I take to bed with me is: what is my responsibility as a living being—as a South African citizen reading continually about racism, xenophobia, and hate crimes in the mainstream media? This is what keeps me awake at night.
>
> ibid., 2018

Muholi's answer to the engendered prejudice and violence surrounding the issue of gender is not to abandon South Africa but to *depict* more queer people from Muholi's locality. As discussed in Chapter 3, Muholi's success happens while many other artists cannot return home safely both artistically and humanely. As Salley (2012) encapsulates her vision:

> Muholi's endeavor, thereby, embraces conflicts that pervade human history, tradition and everyday lived experience. In sum, the artworks provide ways of reimagining human existence and enable their viewer to imagine how people connect with, and belong to, their own communities and nations.

To talk of the globalization of queerness, especially in the Global South, is, on the other hand, to recognize personal missions of existing publicly. To counter-act all the side effects of globalized queerness, one must build upon traces, fragments, and individual acts of resistance. As in Chapter 4, the multiplication of trans voices via free streaming platforms, such as YouTube, podcasts, art projects, and academic-sponsored initiatives, gives another perspective of existing publicly through the media. Not least through the stardom of visual artists such as Muholi but the ever-growing queer-directed, queer-acted film production. Much of this production is not located in grand museum exhibitions or created with sums from private funding but is online, exhibited in small cinemas, or shared through crowdfunding.

Powerful film industries outside the West, such as India's Bollywood, are moving but still struggle to put forward truly committed productions. On another note, countries such as Brazil, Argentina, and Chile have proved that it is possible to place counterarguments against globalized queerness by going beyond the West-dictated LGBTQ agenda and demanding a fairer landscape for all. Small media production has grown to problematize class, race, poverty, and intersectional tensions arising from sexual or gender reparations sought in their contexts. Directors such as Marco Berger and films such as Favela Gay (Brazil, 2014) or Daughters of Fire (Argentina, 2018) have invited issues such as homo-hetero voyeurism, urban queer dilemmas, and the female body to the foreground. One can still find urban violence, right-wing politics, and religious barriers associated with queer struggle, as much as access to health care, right to property, minimum income, freedom of gender confirmation, gender-inclusive education, and crime statistics involving all communities. This ample agenda has seen in queer grassroots media production a genre of its own, in which coalition is the departure point.

Of course, one should not forget the hijacking of queerness by other agendas. Despite the anti-gay rhetoric championed by populist politicians such as former Brazil President Jair Bolsonaro, wealthy media companies have started to move in that respect. Groups such as *Globo* in Brazil, and *Televisa* in Mexico, to stay in Latin America, have for more than a decade sponsored LGBTQ-friendly productions. Until a few years ago, showing a gay kiss in a *telenovela* constituted the ultimate taboo. Still, today these media powerhouses invest in their queer celebrities or reality-show stars of their own making. Naturally, queer communities should be wary of such developments. Globo, for instance, is notorious for producing so-called queer films only to enable future white, straight stardom. *From Beginning to End* (2014) and *The Way He Looks* (2018) have set unrealistic stereotypes of gay men aimed at queerbaiting hetero audiences. These mainstream-sponsored initiatives have usually laid indifferent to the whole problem of racial and social exclusion as their productions have misconstrued the country's reality from below for years.

In sum, globalizing queerness in the Global South is not as distant as it seems. However, an enormous intersectional potential still meets audiences eager to see their own lives represented. Especially in countries with strict laws or religious mandates against homosexuality, queer media should seek to tell stories and expose divides. This sense of sharing and communicating queerness combats globalized queerness if it reflects first-hand accounts of the issues and the expectations of

LGBTQ people instead of board-approved exploitations of manufactured scripts. Next, I place my last reflections on how to antagonize globalized queerness by advancing the concept of *possible homecomings* as the return to queerness as a legitimate, locally-owned part of reality.

Possible homecomings

In this final section, I highlight some alternatives to globalized queerness. I fleshed out the above points about history, social media, and the resistance to the commodification of queer life in the West and the Global South. Past the acceptance phase of queers in the media, global *creative* industries have quickly positioned themselves to envelop queer individuals with languages and styles. Perhaps this book's main contribution is in tentatively visualizing alternatives to queer narratives that do not directly involve the same discourses employed to construct queerness these days. At the same time, one may not afford to isolate oneself from American-based queer commodities, the power of big tech grows overwhelming, and queer audiences live around these commodities. However, there *are* alternatives. Eventually, I preferred to suggest readings of contemporary media environments that can pinpoint existing pathways back to queer self-construal in the media rather than imagining an entirely new reality.

Likewise, the notion of *home* in queer theory has focused much on the institutional force that leads to the closet. Sedgwick (1990), for example, visited many of these mentions: It's Proust's room. It's Benedict Friedlander's 'Community of the Special' (1902). The home also appears in Foucault's *The History of Sexuality* (Foucault, 2019) as the place for the sexual doses or the *aphrodisia*. So cared about and revered by modest Christians, as he puts it, home as a place of 'order and memory'. A home is also a place feminists regarded with suspicion, expressly because of its close ties to motherhood, as Adrienne Rich wrote: 'Motherhood calls to mind the home (...), and we like to believe that a home is a private place.' (Rich, 2021:12). For modern queers the home can be as oppressive as it can get. It is where no one notices you. It is where you may find the world does not conform to you or otherwise, the only place where anyone tolerates you. It is where you post your TikTok or YouTube video from.

I chose *homecoming*, not as the antithesis of the globalized queer media world, which, as said, is harder to escape. I envision it as the next step after globalizing queerness. It will become an intermediary sphere of influence and communication among queers between their first life of acceptance and queer-ups. Indeed, it creates reflective and politicized stances that prevent the ultimate capitalization of their experience. The home remains a helpful example. To practice homecoming is an action toward concatenating local references that could preserve the place of queer history and politics. It allows for new aesthetics while focusing on the most active members of that community. This return does not mean abandoning queerness as a fluid and blurred spectrum of identity and behaviour. Still, it takes all queer knowledge and expertise and its participants into this big home, thus delivering value back to the commodity. Following a Marxian notion of commodity, it would morph from the status of queer media as an exchange value commodity, the one traded by other commodities (our time, attention), to one of social value, as others can benefit from it.

The home realm apprehended as a domestic space has stirred substantial research on the power of its metaphor. Bryant (2015) examined queer homes as a mix of narrative and material. Queer literature has shown the indication of returning home based on the former and home as a *shelter*, the latter. From the perspective of modern times, the queer home is also where someone happens to land. It is the virtual space for queer refugees, in which attachment comes from the comfort that is decentred from a heterosexual nuclear family (Fortier, 2020). Queer homemaking can still provide the basics for a life of struggle under racial and ethnic oppression on the outside, as in the case of Britain (Koegler, 2020). I take all these notions in, but to add a bit of dynamism to our vision of homecoming. It is not only inhabiting a previously owned queer home but building one home that dialogues with the outer world and promotes media products that cannot be otherwise commodified at the expense of one's missing home.

Let's take Twitter, for example. As demonstrated in Chapter 5, the much-blamed social network can be a central point of contact for queer people interested in arts, crafts, and illustration. Interviewees here demonstrated how much positivity one can derive if knowing how to choose the right people to communicate with or navigating the myriad of abuse. Looking at Twitter from Italy, where I wrote most of this book, I can see a vibrant context of queer home building among the so-called LGBTQ activists. It is a pulsating scene that gathers distinct generations. Many share links and beliefs that are both circumscribed in the Italian language, giving it an unequivocally national sense of community. At a second inspection, these activists also share multiple interests in the

English-speaking world and the so-called globalized side of queerness. What sets their tone apart is the dedication to Italian authors, queer history in Italy, and the cult of luminaries such as Pierpaolo Pasolini. They hold sway over a sense of shared identity.

Through this network, I discovered, for instance, the #*queerographies*. The hashtag pointed to a digital archive initiative focused on gender-themed, queer-oriented books written in Italy. It is a small initiative but remarkably relevant in a society where heteronormative structures are so well cemented, stemming from the robust foundations of Christianity. In effect, 'LGBT activism' in Italy has come a long way too. The difference here appears in the multimodality of these sources. Social media links give birth to other connections in the material world. These are books, exhibitions, events, and activist meetings. One of my interviewees, *Giuseppe*, had already confirmed to me this duality between imagining queerness from the outside and seeing it in the presence, in the company of friends, family members, and schoolmates, right in front of you in your community. His insistence in naming these extremely mediatized forms of queerness as 'too much, too much'. Everything we talked about regarding global social media networks signals this sense of miss more belonging in globalized queerness.

It is germane to this argument the recognition to avoid the impression that some homecomings are *impossible*. I have met many Italian activists that would rather be in Italy than elsewhere. Home for them was also where they were *picchiati* or beaten up on the streets with their boyfriends. The prevalence of stereotypes in Italian media, as anywhere else in the world, can embitter this struggle. However, sentiments about one's feelings of being at home can degrade quickly from nostalgia and protection to menace and combat with social agents, in which every queer person is on the frontlines. As discussed in the introduction, the localness of queerness has been immensely threatened and persecuted, but the idea of a place of acceptance and protection the global media has sold is also not true. The transmission of such knowledge that you ultimately have to leave home has more to do with the powerful media system that has spread queerness worldwide than the real thing.

In the end, one must resist the destabilizing force of globalized queerness in these and other forms of homecoming. The first kind of resistance should work on the immediate level of relationships. It explores the inner connections of queer selves to their early personae and goes full circle when one sees the world. It recovers languages and ways of saying being queer among family and friends. It reconnects authors, artists, and their queer forms of belonging. It re-attaches queerness to its original mould, including childhood memories, parental discussions, and family interactions. It re-integrates friends and close contacts into re-educating them to participate in queerness as spectators and as partners in diversity. On a second level, there is the material level of this possibility. It resets the importance given to global queer culture. It prevents sharing or publicizing global manifestations of queer that talk to realities lying miles away. It adopts an ethical principle not only based on the usual self-disclosure on social media, but it actively seeks one's interactions to local queer actors, sponsors, activists, and publicists. It adopts a socially conscious perception of where one's queerness starts and where the limits of it are. Whether boundaries are national, language-based, or culturally informed, these limits must not discriminate. They should inform how one can live fully and sustainably in a queer mediatized world.

This book ultimately reflected on possible homecomings as an ethical code for future generations of queer media users and spectators. From seeing a world taken by globalized queerness, ratings, celebrities, and profits that do not turn back to communities, one can also visualize a world of inter-communicating queer existence according to one's needs. The book chapters pointed to multiple issues arising from the lack of a unified ethos where queer scenes exist without being homogenous: the wholesale of queerness by brands and hidden agendas, the platformization of queer debates and politics or, lastly, the tiktokization of networking potentials. Local communities must increase pressure for new public policies that promote queer artists and media producers as part of their local culture and not as visiting acts. The disowning of queerness can only lead to the abandonment of an audience that buys into cheap franchise TV and loses any collective identity. The conjugation of a queer homecoming ethos plus better local recognition will indeed determine a queer media future for the generations to come.

Limitations of the book

This book has dealt with several limitations stemming from the period covered, the methods chosen, and the approach adopted in each chapter. Perhaps, the most challenging burden came with Covid-19 having stricken halfway into the book's research. While sectors of queer media industries have continued to produce series and launched TV shows, the Internet has become the epicentre of social life for nearly two years.

Lockdowns affected queer populations unprecedently due to the stop-in encounters and the highly suspicious environments for anything. This dislocation of social life to the Internet, at least until 2021, has derailed many web-based initiatives in queer media. It stopped interviews, interactions, and further conversations based on LGBTQ events, for example, largely dependent on nightlife. The lack of media coverage due to the ongoing reports on the virus, for instance, led to this research's survey into queer news being remade twice until there were minimum grounds of comparison between countries and life had been restored to an appropriate level.

Methodologically speaking, other limitations have arisen from the book's approach. Namely, its overarching look at several media platforms, the ambition of covering queer media and culture from an international but not comparative perspective, and the need to stabilize notions of global and local. The decision to make a book that could work as a survey rather than an in-depth analysis of each of a few queer environments has led to some blind spots regarding technology, for example. The software interface used in many apps and surveillance issues could have also been part of the discussion. Geolocation apps such as Grindr profit from being local and global at the same time, as far as the whole topic of proximity triggers other discussions that run absent from this book. Again, Covid-19 has yet to stop bolder efforts to engage in further discussions involving apps and geolocation as another demarcation for localness.

On the media arts side, the emphasis on the music industry meant less attention to film, theatre, and visual arts. While I tried to cover some of this artistic ground by working on profiles like that of Zanele Muholi, there was a lot to discuss on how visual arts appear, such as neglected in queer media studies. Photographers such as Sunil Gupta have conveyed a lot of the diasporical queer media that surged during the AIDS crisis. Visual arts in contemporary art have done a lot to include new queer audiences. As a result, the issue of the queer gaze is missed in this study as it could enlighten new pathways to a perception born from native eyes. The absence of trans artists interviewed for this book is also symptomatic of the poor literature available in the area. Cultural criticism has historically focused on trans public people as commentators, drag artists, or performers, as opposed to writers, journalists, philosophers, politicians, and, overall, thinkers. In the same way, Chapter 4 attempts to leverage the work of several trans producers on YouTube, yet without looking into other platforms and the rising podcasting industry that has also sheltered a lot of queer arts.

Chapter 5 investigated social media artistry and connected with several actors. By choosing mainstream platforms such as Instagram, Facebook, and Twitter, I could profit from their expectations of prominence in a global environment. By not including smaller social media platforms based on videos, such as Vimeo, or niches, such as Reddit, Discord, and even TikTok, this book's study was limited to fresh ways of contending as a queer person. The rise of queer TikTok appearances also holds some degree of novelty concerning affectivity, sensitivity, and overall expectation of virality that was eventually out of the discussion entirely. The same can be said about live streaming, which poses specific challenges to capturing social media presence in the long term. As elusive as these broadcasts can be, it leaves behind no trace except recordings that obfuscate the live context of their appeal. The point-making in these social environments is more complex than in the latter and demands a methodological approach that contemplates these nuances.

References

Amin, K. (2017). *Disturbing attachments: Genet, modern pederasty, and queer history*. United Kingdom: Duke University Press.

Bryant, J. (2015). The meaning of queer home: between metaphor and material. *Home Cultures*, *12*(3), 261–289.

Calabrò, D. G., Kant, R., Maharaj, S., & Kaur, J. (2022). Behind the mask: Intersectional (in) visibility of Indo-Fijian queer experiences. In M. T. Segal & V. Demos (Eds.) *Gender visibility and erasure*, Vol. 3, 33–50. Emerald Publishing Limited.

Dollimore, J. (1988). Different desires: Subjectivity and transgression in Wilde and Gide. *Genders*, (2), 24–41.

Doty, A. (1993). *Making things perfectly queer: Interpreting mass culture*. University of Minnesota Press.

Fortier, A. M. (2020). Making home: Queer migrations and motions of attachment. In A. M. Fortier, C. Castada, M. Sheller, & S. Ahmed (Eds.), *Uprootings/regroundings questions of home and migration* (pp. 115–135). United Kingdom: Taylor & Francis.

Foucault, M. (2019). *The history of sexuality: 2: The use of pleasure*. United Kingdom: Penguin Books Limited.

Knox, M. (2001). *Oscar Wilde in the 1990s: The critic as creator* (vol. 53). Camden House.

Koegler, C. (2020). Queer home-making and black Britain: Claiming, ageing, living. *Interventions*, *22*(7), 879–896.

Madani, D. (2021). Nike sues over Lil Nas X 'Satan Shoes' with human blood in soles. NBC News. 29 March 2021.

Messner, E. (2022). *The queer sounds of TikTok*. (Doctoral dissertation, Bowling Green State University).

Mussai, R. (2018). Zanele Muholi on Resistance. Aperture. 11 September 2018. Available at https://aperture.org/editorial/muholi-interview/ Access 11 April 2023.

Navlakha, M. (2022). Netflix removes LGBTQ tag from Dahmer. *Mashable*. 29 September 2022.

Rauchberg, J. S. (2022). # Shadowbanned: Queer, trans, and disabled creator responses to algorithmic oppression on TikTok. In P. Pain (Ed.), *LGBTQ digital cultures: A global perspective* (pp. 196–209). United States: Taylor & Francis.

Rich, A. (2021). *Of woman born: Motherhood as experience and institution*. United States: W. W. Norton.

Salley, R. J. (2012). Zanele Muholi's elements of survival. *African Arts*, 45(4), 58–69.

Sedgwick, E. K. (1990). *Epistemology of the closet*. United Kingdom: University of California Press.

INDEX

activism, 166–167
Africa, 119–121
age, 173–174
Ahmed, Sara, 4
Aids, 10, 13
Ajamu X, 122
algorithms, 173, 182
Almodóvar, Pedro, 107
Anysio, Chico, 100, *see* Brazil
aphrodisia, 20
Apple (singer), 81
Argentina, 176, 208
Arrizon, Alicia, 118
art
    photography, 79, 120
    Tate Modern, 79
    visual art, 79
artists, 91–93
Asia, 199
audiences, 17, 25, 106, 138
Australasia, 7
Austria, 40
authenticity, 38, 48–53

Babba, Homi K., 118
Bao, Hongwei, 13, 16
Barthes, Roland, 54
Beckham, David, 206
Berger, Marco, 208
Bersani, Leo, 46, 67
bicha, 112
Bixa Travesti, 81, 112, *see* Brazil
Bollywood, 10, 97
Bolsonaro, Jair, 110, 208, *see Brazil*
Brazil, 1–2, 81–82, 83, 100–101, 108–116, 144–145, 176
    periphery, 108–116
    Recife, 114
    São Paulo, 112

cabaret, 11
Cahun, Claude, 104
Calamity Jane, 1–2, 15
camp, 165, *see* Sontag, Susan
Cardoso, Zilda, 101
castrato, 52
Cazuza, 10, *see* Brazil
censorship, 185–187
Charles, RuPaul, 21
    biography, 49–50, 53, 94–95, 96
    RuPaul's Drag Race, 6, 7, 70, 79, 94–95, 166
Charlie XCX, 111
Chauncey, George, 8
Chicana studies, 16, 118
China, 12, 13, 54, 57, 82, 119–120
Christine and the Queens, 56, 92, 104, 200
Close, Roberta, 114
closet, 39
colonialism
    post-colonialism, 17, 42
commodification or commodity, 41, 44–48, 51, 210
community, 7, 10, 20–21, 37–43, 181, 183, 188, 190, 195, 205
Community of the Special, 209
Covid-19, 74, 106, 180

Da Silva, Antonio, 180
Day, Doris, 1, 2, 196
Degeneres, Ellen, 19, 100
de-commodification, 48, 54–59
de-gaying, 20

da Quebrada, Linn, 81,111–113, *see* Brazil
de Beauvoir, Simone, 52
De Laurentis, Teresa, 20
Dietrich, Marlene, 100
digital culture, 167, 172–173
Disney, 77
Dollimore, Jonathan, 201
Doty, Alexander, 5, 93
drag, 95, 115–116
Drummond, Orlando, 109, *see* Brazil

Eliot, George, 51
Eurovision, 19

facework, 171–172
film
    A Fantastic Woman, 154
    Berlinale, 112
    Paris is Burning, 42
    The Man Who Gave Birth, 95
    Wofoo to Wong Foo, Thanks for Everything! Julie Newmar, 21
    see also *Calamity Jane*; and Chapter 2
followers, 182
Foucault, Michel, 20, 28, 41, 209
France, 50, 81–82, 102–104, 121, 162
Friedlander, Benedict, 209
Friedrich, Su, 13

Gastrica, La Wanda, 115, *see* drag
gay
 etymology, 12
 gay village, 22, 41
 marriage, 206
Gaynor, Gloria, 48
Genet, Jean, 201–202
Gide, Andre, 201
genealogy, 38, 43, 53
GLAAD, 5, 162
global and local cultures, 7, 18, 22, 27, 38, 40, 41, 71–73, 85–86, 96, 105–106, 116, 144, 175–176
Global South, 3, 8, 10, 17, 20, 56, 98, 100, 145, 205–208
globalization, 178
 theories, 6
globalized queerness, 96, 125–126, 161, 176–178, 195, 207–208
Globo TV, 113, 208
Goffman, Erving, 170, 188–191
Grindr, 98, 183, 202

Halberstam, Jack, 15
Hammer, Barbara, 13
Harisu, 199
hashtags, 98, 166, 169, 211
Heche, Anne, 107
Hegazy, Sarah, 81
Hernandes, Clodovil, 101
Hirschfeld, Magnum, 8
Hollywood, 1, 10, 11, 13, 76
homecoming, 209–210
homophobia, 117, 206, 211
Hooks, Bell, 16

Isherwood, Christopher, 54
inequality, 44, 108, 114, 203
Italy, 22, 91, 104–107, 176, 210–211

Sanremo Music Festival, 125
Veneto, 178

Jackson, Michael, 80
Jagose, Annamarie, 20
Japan, 81
Jenner, Caitlyn, 134
Johnson, Marsha P., 79, 134
journalism, 68–69
 advocate.com, 68
 Aperture, 120
 BBC, 68
 Gay Times, 115
 Guardian, 95, 115
 New York Times, 70, 102–103, 164, 175
 New Yorker, 115
 Them.us, 68, 164
 Vanity Fair, 134
 Vogue Teen, 164

Kusama, Yayoi, 80–81

Lady Gaga, 105
Lafond, Jorge, 109–110, *see* Brazil
Latin America, 72, 105, 117–118
Latinx, 16
Law, Siufung, 119
lesbian
 Chicana lesbianism, 118
 film, 79
 Lesbian Jesus, 80
 Sapatão, 82, *see* Brazil
 YouTube, 149
LGBT rights, 20
liberation, 5
Lil Nas X, 96
Liniker, *see* da Quebrada, Linn
Little Britain, 18
local and global cultures, 7, 18, 22, 27, 51, 54–59, 165, 167
 see also global and local cultures
Louis, Edouard, 50

McConnell, Freddy, 95
McKellen, Ian, 79
Madame Bovary, 51
Madonna, 105
Mahmood, 22, 122–125
Malgioglio, Cristiano, 91, 104–107
Martel, Frederic, 11–12, 69
Marx, Karl, 210
Matogrosso, Ney, 110
meme, 162
Mercury, Freddy, 100, 107
Ménard, Phia, 81, 102–104
Mestizaje, 117–121
methods, 23–27, 54–59, 72–76, 99, 138–140, 163, 168–172
 discourse, 27, 56
 narrative analysis, 170
Michael, George, 96, 107
Morphosis, Maddy, 166, *see* Charles, RuPaul
Moreira, Roberta Gambine, *see* Close, Roberta
Muholi, Zanele, 120–122, 207
Mulvaney, Dylan, 135
Muslim, 22

naked photography, 179
nation, 38
Netflix, 97, 134
New York City, 8, 42, 116, 164
news, 67–87

O'Donnell, Rosie, 100
Onlyfans, 180
operaismo, 187, *see* Italy
Oxenberg, Jan, 13

Page, Elliot, 135
Paris is Burning, 42
Pasolini, Pierpaolo, 107

Picardi, Phillip, 164
pinkwashing, 40
popular culture, 3, 17, 21, 24, 48, 58–59, 93, 111
porn actor, 182
Portugal
  Fado Bicha, 47, *see bicha*
  Lisbon, 83
postcolonialism, 42
pride, 28, 78–79

queer
  activism, 166–167
  artistry, 81–82
  commodity, 41, 44–48, 72
  cosmopolitanism, 96–100
  digital culture, 167, 172–173
  etymology, 93, 173–174, 206
  photography, 121–122
  journalism, 68–69
  Latinidad, 118
  national treasure, 102–107
  phenomenology, 4
  prominence, 163–164, 168, 180, 190
Queer Lisboa, 83
queerbaiting, 77
queerness, 2, 3, 24, 175–176
Quiroga, Jose, 99

Rasmussen, Crystal, 115
refugees, 162
Rich, Adrienne, 209
Rossi, Vito, 11
Rowling, J. K., 142–143, 151
Ruixi, Han, 81

Saint Teresa of Avila, 52
Sedgwick, Eve Kosofski, 8, 14, 43, 73
selfies, 161
sincerity, 38, 48–53
Smith, Sam, 94, 96
social media platforms, 161–162, 168
  clickbait, 141
  Facebook, 162, 185
  Flickr, 184, 185
  Grindr, 98, 183, 202
  Instagram, 179, 181, 182, 185
  Methods, 26
  TikTok, 51, 135, 196, 203–205
  Twitter, 147, 165, 180, 210
  YouTube, 135–141, 162
  Vero, 186
Sontag, Susan, 12–13, 165
South Africa, 120, 207
Styles, Harry, 166
Sycamore, Mattilda Bernstein, 55
symbolic interactionism, *see* Goffman, Erving

Taïa, Abdellah, 50, 81
The Philippines, 40
Tom of Finland, 80
Tong, Liu Shiu, 8
trans
  dysphoria, 144
  experience, 16, 134
  hormones, 150
  models, 183
  topics, 135–137, 141, 147, 153–155
  tropes, 39
The Daily Wire, 135
transculturation, 122
transmedicalism, 152

transphobia, 134–135, 142
Trilling, Lionel, 50
TV series and shows, 5
  Cinderela, 114–115
  Big Brother, 106, 109, 113
  Dahmer, 204
  Euphoria, 204
  Eurovision, 19
  My So-called Life, 18
  Queer as Folk, 43, 70
  Queer Eye, 71, 77
  Sex in the City, 40
  telenovelas, 109
  The Death and Life of Marsha P. Johnson, 79, 134
  The Real World, 19
  see also Charles, RuPaul

United Kingdom, 84
  London, 179
United States, 84
  Americanization, 99

violence, 108, 163, 167
Vittar, Pablo, 56, 108–111
Vogue, 109

YouTube, 11

Wallace, Jeison, 114–115, *see* Brazil
Warren, Carol, 39
West
  Global North, 72
  Westernization, 42, 82–83, 162
  Western and non-Western, 116, 119
West, Kanye, 81
Wilde, Oscar, 51, 164–165, 201
Wurst, Conchita, 19, 40

www.ingramcontent.com/pod-product-compliance
Lightning Source LLC
Chambersburg PA
CBHW052107300426
44116CB00010B/1563